Wisdom from Franciscan Italy

The Primacy of Love

To Gudrun

God Bless Always

David

Wisdom from Franciscan Italy

The Primacy of Love

David Torkington

David Torkington

28th Jan 2012

O
BOOKS

Winchester, UK
Washington, USA

First published by O-Books, 2011
O Books is an imprint of John Hunt Publishing Ltd., The Bothy, Deershot Lodge, Park Lane, Ropley,
Hants, SO24 0BE, UK
office1@o-books.net
www.o-books.com

For distributor details and how to order please visit the 'Ordering' section on our website.

Text copyright: David Torkington 2010

ISBN: 978 1 84694 442 0

A CIP catalogue record for this book is available from the British Library.

Design: Stuart Davies

Printed in the UK by CPI Antony Rowe
Printed in the USA by Offset Paperback Mfrs, Inc

We operate a distinctive and ethical publishing philosophy in all
areas of its business, from its global network of authors to
production and worldwide distribution.

CONTENTS

I found the book echoes so much of our Franciscan spirit. The aspect that was particularly excellent was the succinct synopsis of the teaching of Scotus and the way he views theology in the light of the Primacy of Love. That is beautifully done. The setting is that of a journey towards a loving relationship paralleling the underlying story of Francis that re-echoes throughout its pages.

Fr Thomas More OFM cap Oxford emeritus Provincial of the Capuchin Order.

It was an unforgettable experience to read this book and to re-visit Franciscan Italy under the spiritual guidance of Peter Calvay, that fascinating and profound character I had first met many years ago in David Torkington's trilogy on prayer. With his deep insight Peter has led me with a steady hand through those places where Francis planted the seeds of that mysticism which, after eight centuries, is still capable of drawing those who thirst for simplicity, joy and peace.

Fr Mario Conte OFM Conv. Editor of Messenger of Saint Anthony, Padua

This is the best book on Franciscan Spirituality that I have ever read. Its teaching on the Primacy of Love is revolutionary and will make all Christians realise how far they have strayed from their origins. It should be mandatory reading for all who call themselves Christians.

Emilia Tyler past president of the Third Order of St Francis (Florentine Province).

The author is to be congratulated. This is a fine book that will be a valuable addition to the large Franciscan library. It portrays well and accurately, the principal elements of Franciscan spirituality. I find the style simple and easy to read. It flows. It presents very well the essence of Franciscan prayer.

Fr Quentin Jackson OFM PhD emeritus professor and former Provincial of the English province

To my wife Bobbie
Without her help, encouragement and advice this book
could not have been written

Author Note

Cover painting by Fiona Graham-MacKay
www.fionagraham-mackay.net

The model for the Franciscan friar is Sebastian Graham
The background is the hermitage of Le Carceri near Assisi

For those wishing to study the ancient Franciscan sources for
themselves, there is no better collection than *St Francis of Assisi:
Omnibus of Sources* published by St Anthony Messenger Press
(USA). I am indebted to them for giving me permission to quote
from this work throughout my book.
(www.AmericanCatholic.org)

Chapter 1

A Friend in Need

On the morning of our departure for Franciscan Italy I found myself in a state of emotional turmoil. To be more precise it was about five o'clock in the morning. I had already been awake for about an hour going over and over the traumatic events of the previous week. During a walking tour in the Lake District, I had fallen in love for the first time since the death of my wife Jennifer in childbirth over fifteen years before. It was a whirlwind holiday romance that took us both by surprise. On the final evening we declared our love for one another. When I asked her to marry me, she said yes, and I was in my seventh heaven. But two days later, she wrote to say that despite our mutual love she could never be my wife. She said she had been so swept off her feet that she had chosen to forget she was already engaged; her father had spent a small fortune on the wedding, which had been arranged for the following month. She admitted that she did love me far more than the man to whom she was engaged, but there was nothing she could do about it, so the quicker we could forget the holiday romance, the better. She made it clear that she would not write to me again and that any letters she received from me would be returned unopened.

I was so devastated that I'd hardly had a proper night's sleep for over a week. I was in no mood to begin a pilgrimage to Franciscan Italy, but I'd already committed myself and my air ticket had been bought for me. The pilgrimage had been arranged by Father Rayner, the director of Walsingham House, the retreat center where I had just spent the night. The pilgrimage was a special treat for his brother Peter, to celebrate the eight hundredth anniversary of the birth of St Francis. It was over fifteen years since Peter's last visit to Assisi where he had been inspired to become a secular Franciscan. Peter – or Peter Calvay as he came to be called – had ended up building a small hermitage for himself in the Outer Hebrides, where he lived in comparative solitude. I had gone to visit him years ago for help and advice shortly after my wife died. Since then, I had regularly turned to him for spiritual advice. Although I was originally from New York I had decided to stay and pursue my academic career on this side of the Atlantic. The fact that I was an Anglican (or as I was called in the States, an Episcopalian) and Peter was a Roman Catholic made no difference to our relationship. In fact it was with his encouragement that, like him, I became a secular Franciscan, but attached to the Anglican Friars, whose way of life so impressed me.

Peter had told me that a young doctor called Bobbie, who lived next door, would meet me at breakfast and fill me in about the travel arrangements. She too was a secular Franciscan and she would be coming with us. I thought it might be the ideal oppor- tunity to ask her to prescribe something to help me sleep; otherwise I would never get through the days ahead.

When Bobbie came in for breakfast I had already begun to eat. She was perhaps eight or nine years younger than me, bursting with the vital life and energy that had drained out of me in the past few days. She was how I should have been, but the man that stood up to greet her was more a zombie than a human being.

'James Robertson,' I said, as I rose to offer her my hand. She was indeed full of life – lithe, willowy and naturally friendly. If I hadn't still been in deep mourning for the woman I loved, I would have described her as beautiful, but I could see beauty only in that person whom I would never see again. In later years when my heart had healed, I often thought that in other circum- stances Bobbie would have perfectly fitted my dream of the wife and soul mate I sought, but at that time there was only one woman totally absorbing my attention.

'You're looking very tired,' Bobbie said, as we both sat down for coffee. She wasn't prying, but she looked genuinely concerned and her empathy was so obvious and my need was so great that I couldn't help myself: I started telling her why I looked so exhausted. I had had no one to speak to since Elizabeth had deserted me, so I told her everything. After all, she was not only a doctor but, as the cook had told me, a psychiatrist too, so I felt sure she would understand and respect my privacy. I told her the whole story – not just about the prospective wife I'd lost in Elizabeth but about the wife I'd lost in my first partner Jennifer and about my son whom I had lost with her in childbirth. I told her about Peter too and how he'd helped me in my personal spiritual quest.

When I asked Bobbie to explain how a woman could be so cruel to me, she said that she was not the best person to ask as she had been cruel too to the man who wanted to marry her. He was good, decent and honorable, and genuinely loved her, but she felt that the deep pull that drew her away from him meant that they would never be fully happy together.

Yet despite this, she said quite emphatically, 'I've always been convinced that my vocation is to marry and have children.' Then after a pause she added, 'I don't mean I want to marry just anyone for the sake of getting married; I mean someone I can respect, someone who has the same ideas and ideals. Without these, life would be meaningless for me.'

I noticed no accent in her voice so I was surprised to hear that Bobbie had grown up and completed her studies in South Africa. Although she did have English ancestors it soon became obvious to me that the retention of an unalloyed English accent symbolized her abhorrence of the apartheid regime, which she deplored. The family had long since lost touch with their English relatives so she wrote to Fr Rayner, Peter Calvay's younger brother. She had met him whilst he was giving a series of lectures in South Africa some years before. When she asked him to look for accommodation for her, he found a flat next door that was convenient for her new job in Epping.

In his very first lecture he spoke with such precision about spiritual experiences that had exerted a determining influence on her life that she went to see him privately several times. These meetings turned out to be momentous for both of them. He explained in far more detail the meaning and significance of her spiritual experiences and confirmed the authentic nature of her spiritual journey. He then gave her detailed instructions on how she should proceed and encouraged her to write to him if she felt that he could be of any further assistance.

She, in her turn, explained to him something that he had never understood about himself, something that had mystified him throughout his life – and had mystified everybody else for that matter. In short, from the very outset she had diagnosed that he was dyslexic. Strange, she said, how a man who was endowed with such spiritual insight that he was able to help so many others had been totally ignorant about his own predicament.

He couldn't thank her enough for making sense of his whole life. In a flash Bobbie's diagnosis had enabled him to see with hindsight what he had been unable to see before. It all happened so quickly and he was so surprised and relieved that he told Bobbie the story of his life, which in other circumstances she would never have heard.

Although it had been Fr Rayner's plan to take his brother to Italy for the eight hundredth anniversary of the birth of St Francis, it was thanks to Bobbie that the pilgrimage turned out to be so successful. Shortly after her arrival in England she had met Emelia, who had come to the center to make a retreat. After Emelia sought her advice on a medical matter, the two became firm friends. Bobbie told her something of her own spiritual journey from the Presbyterianism into which she was born, to the Catholicism to which she had converted with her sister in her teens, so her new friend reciprocated.

Emelia was an Italian, born in Milan, who had married an English diplomat not long after the Second World War. She had run her own fashion shop in New Bond Street, importing designer clothes, mainly from her home city. When her children grew up and started to think about their future, she started to think about hers too. Although she was in her own words 'just a Sunday morning Catholic', she hungered for a deeper spirituality. This led to a long search through almost every 'ism' under the sun until she ended up at the place where she had first started and, as T.S. Eliot promised, she came to know that place for the first time.

She reached a decision with her husband Michael, who was an Anglican. She would sell up and he would resign from the Foreign Office and they would buy an old farmhouse in Tuscany where they would set up a house of prayer. This house of prayer was called Casa al Gallo. It was situated on high ground at a little hamlet called Castagnoli in Chianti, just twenty minutes from Siena and about fifty minutes from Florence by car. Emelia had become the president of the Third Order of Franciscans in Florence, the first group to be founded in the lifetime of St Francis.

During a brief stay at Casa al Gallo, Bobbie had decided to become a secular Franciscan too. Thanks to Emelia, the pilgrims – Peter, his brother Fr Rayner, Bobbie and now me – would fly to Pisa and then take the train to Florence, where Emelia would meet us and take us back to base camp at Castagnoli in Chianti.

On our way to Heathrow to meet up with Peter and Fr Rayner (or David, as we called him on the pilgrimage) Bobbie told me that the two brothers had only recently returned from their father's funeral. I didn't really know David, because I'd only met him once and that was briefly at his mother's funeral . When both of the brothers arrived I could see that Peter was not his true self, at least to begin with, nor did the David that I now saw in the flesh match up to the man that Bobbie had described to me, and the picture that had begun to form in my imagination. But if anyone was obliged to make allowances for their bereavement, it was me. I had indeed just lost someone who I thought would be the love of the rest of my life, but Peter and David had just lost their father whom they had known and loved for a lifetime, having already lost their beloved mother; I knew from Peter just how much his parents meant to them both.

I was lucky to get a seat on the plane as Peter had only invited me at the last moment when he had heard of my 'bereavement'. The others had booked earlier, so they all sat together at the front whilst I was on my own at the back. When we were airborne Bobbie came and handed me a book entitled *The Second Christ*, written by David. He had led several pilgrimages to Franciscan Italy in the past and he would always send the pilgrims his own brief summary of the life of St Francis beforehand. It was a good idea and I accepted it from Bobbie with a smile, although I really felt I knew the story well enough; after all, I had been a secular Franciscan for over three years and I had read more than one book about the saint I admired more than any other. And frankly I was still feeling sorry for myself. However, it was written by the man whom I had heard so much about from Bobbie that very morning and I needed something to occupy my mind.

At first it appeared to be no more than a fairly competent summary that did not dwell too much on the fanciful aspects of Francis' story or some of the more incredible miracles to which early hagiographers were particularly addicted. However, reading it in the light of all that I had learned from Peter about the spiritual life, it suddenly came alive, enabling me to understand the secret of St Francis in a way that I had never understood it before. But first let me reproduce it for you just as it was given to me.

Chapter 2

The Second Christ

by Father Rayner

St Francis was born towards the end of 1181 or at the beginning of 1182. The date may mean little, so let me put it in the context of English history. Henry II was on the throne of England with his equally famous or infamous wife, Eleanor of Aquitaine. He is remembered by most of us from our school days for three things. Firstly, he was the first of the Plantagenets. Secondly, he was the first to set up law courts or assizes for all. Thirdly, he was the first to have an acrimonious row with the Church that culminated in the murder of Thomas Becket, the Archbishop of Canterbury, who was savagely cut to pieces in his own cathedral by the king's three knights.

I'm sure Francis didn't know anything of all this, but he would most certainly have known about Henry II's son, Richard I, known throughout Christendom as *Coeur de Lion*, the greatest warrior king of his day – and 'his day' was from 1188 when Francis was about seven, to 1199, when he was seventeen going on eighteen. We know for certain that when Francis was growing up his head was full of the legends of the great knightly warriors of the past like King Arthur, Lancelot and Roland. He also hero-worshipped the great Crusaders, who were at the time fighting Saladin in the East to win back the Holy Land, under the flamboyant leadership of Richard I of England, Coeur de Lion.

Most of us who were brought up on films about the fabled Ivanhoe and Robin Hood, both 'contemporaries' of St Francis, cast Richard I as 'Mr Goody' and his brother John I as 'Mr Baddy'. Well, Mr Baddy died in 1216, the year after he had signed Magna Carta in 1215. This was the year when St Francis met St Dominic at the Fourth Lateran Council in Rome in 1215. The friars arrived in England shortly before St Francis died in 1226, so fans of Friar Tuck will be sorry to hear that he couldn't possibly have been a Franciscan. You can still see the kitchen of the first friary to be built in Canterbury; it straddles the river and has a trapdoor through which 'brother cook' could fish for the friars' supper. Francis spent his whole life trying to do with peace and kindness what Robin Hood had tried to do with violence and the sword. He really does deserve a better film to commemorate him than *Brother Sun and Sister Moon* by Franco Zeffirelli. The fact that such a brilliant director, whose other works I can hardly fault, can so misunderstand the patron saint of his homeland is one of the reasons why I have written this little essay.

Like Zeffirelli, all too many biographers of Francis have tried to remake him in their own image and likeness. Incorrigible romantics are beguiled by his love of nature; they see a man who walked amongst the birds and talked to them, who spoke to Brother Lamb and tamed Brother Wolf, and they see little else. For others he is the first great hippy, the dropout, the New Age hero, the toast of every alternative spirituality under the sun. For yet others he is the archetypal humanist, the social worker or, as he was for Lenin, the one to inaugurate the first classless society, something communism dreamt about but never reproduced. The stoics amongst us like to revel in his fearsome acts of fasting, the stigmata that lacerated his body and the extreme asceticism that they think made him the man that he became. I want to try and introduce you to the real Francis and to the profound spirituality that made him such a unique saint. Most important of all, I want these facts to enable me to trace for you the mystical influences that led him from being just another typical young man of his time, with more money than he knew what to do with, to one of the greatest mystics who has ever lived.

St Francis was in fact baptized John, in honor of John the Baptist. His father was away trading in France at the time of his birth and when he returned he wanted to celebrate a particularly successful trip by calling his firstborn son after the country where he had just made his money. Although Francis was never called John by others, his baptismal name perfectly embodied the man he was about to become. He was soon to emerge as a second John the Baptist, calling people to repentance in preparation for the second coming of Christ. Christ did come again at the beginning of the thirteenth century, mystically embodied in the flesh and blood of Francis himself. That's why people in medieval times called him 'the Second Christ'. However, only the first Christ was sanctified from birth; all later embodiments of him were forged in some mysterious way out of a profound interrelationship of human endeavor and divine grace.

Current fashions have always determined the way the lives of the saints were viewed and then written down. When it was fashionable to show that saints invariably come from blue blood, pious genealogists suddenly discovered that Francis' father Pietro Bernadone had noble origins and his mother Pica came from similar stock. When it was fashionable to emphasize the power of God's grace, the would-be saint had first to be presented as a wicked sinner. When it was considered disrespectful to suggest that saints could be anything other than paragons of virtue from the very beginning, they had to be shown imbibing righteousness with their mother's milk and even refraining from it during Lent. When Francis came to be called 'the Second Christ', the artists of the day had to show that he was born in a stable, and a spurious stable had to be built. It can still be seen in Assisi to this day.

He was actually born into a family with no pretensions about their past but with the usual pretensions about the future that always color the dreams of the 'nouveau riche'. They dreamed about fulfilling their own unfulfilled ambitions through the success of their children. These dreams seem to have been invested in their firstborn, who was spoilt with all the money that Pietro Bernadone undoubtedly made as a merchant. He specialized in importing the finest fabrics produced by the weavers in the Low Countries and sold his stock in the leading markets, such as those of Provence where he had been trading when Francis was born. This upbringing didn't make Francis into the *enfant terrible* that some would like to make of him but, as the son of one of the richest men in Assisi, it did make him profligate with the money he helped to make in his father's shop. His father was proud of his son's business skills and that he seemed a chip off the old block. He was proud too that he was very popular with his peers, and he looked on with admiration to see the sons of the local aristocracy vying for his friendship and favor along with the other 'lager louts' of his day. Father and son had dreams, and the money that they made together made these dreams rise on the horizon and seem almost within their grasp. The age was already dawning, indeed it had already come, when a man of substance could rise up beyond his origins to take his place with the minor aristocracy and have some say in the running of the world, unlike his forebears who had lived as little more than minions for more than a millennium.

An opportunity to further these dreams came to Pietro Bernadone and his fellow citizens in 1198, when Francis would have been 'sixteen going on seventeen'. At the time, Italy was ravaged by wars between the Emperor and his followers, called the Ghibellines, and the Pope and his followers, called the Guelfs. For years the fortunes of both parties waxed and waned, but in this particular year, when the powerful Innocent III presided over the papacy, the balance of power tilted towards the Guelfs. The feudal lord who had been appointed to rule over Assisi by the German Emperor Henry VI was suddenly isolated and in danger of losing his authority. In order to retain his power and position the lord of Assisi, Count Urslingen, Duke of Spoleto, left the town with the main contingent of his retinue to pay homage to his new master Innocent III. The German overlords were hated in Italy, so the moment Urslingen left Assisi the population rose and sacked and destroyed the Count's castle, all but leveling it to the ground. In a matter of only weeks the remnants were used to build a wall around Assisi to make sure the tyrant would never return. Francis would most certainly have joined his father and his fellow citizens to build the town walls, some of which are still standing today.

He would undoubtedly also have been involved in the 'pogroms' that were to follow. Whenever there is occupation by a foreign power you will always find toadies who will collaborate, just as you will find the resistance. Once the walls were built, all the aristocracy who had collaborated were slaughtered or sent into exile. Now Assisi was proclaimed a 'free town', 'a commune'. Although we can hardly believe that Francis wasn't personally involved in these traumatic upheavals that changed the face and the destiny of his hometown, we know for a fact that he was personally involved in the serious repercussions that followed four years later. The remaining collaborators fled to Perugia, hardly a dozen miles away, where they found it easy to rouse the town against its old enemy. Inevitably both sides took to the field in 1202. At the age of about twenty-one Francis followed the call to arms and fought at the battle of Collestrada near the bridge of San Giovanni. The Perugians were victorious and Francis was captured, made a prisoner and incarcerated for about a year, from the autumn of 1202 to the autumn of the following year. Although his parents must have been beside themselves with worry, at least his father must have felt a certain pride that his beloved son, in whom his dreams hoped to find fulfillment, was imprisoned not with the commoners but with the aristocracy. If he could be associated with them in the prisons of Perugia, why not in the palaces of Assisi when he returned to raise his family's fortunes with his own?

All augured well when Francis returned and tried to resume the old pleasure-seeking lifestyle to which he had become accustomed, but he was laid low by a mysterious illness which was probably contracted in prison. Nobody has ever been able to diagnose it with certainty. Francis would never be quite the same again, nor would he ever again have perfect health for the rest of his life. When he was back on his feet he went for the walks in the beautiful countryside that had always moved him before, but now it moved him no more. Soon he returned to the profligate life he had enjoyed with his cronies, but somehow it didn't engage him as before. Truth to tell, his heart wasn't in it any more. It was somewhere else, but he didn't know where.

He tried everything else, but everything else seemed to leave him flat. However, when Assisi was caught up in a frenzy of excitement Francis was caught up in it too, at least for a while. A much-respected nobleman and knight called Gentile was recruiting warriors to join him in fighting with the papal forces against Markwald, the leader of the Ghibellines in southern Italy. There is no evidence that Francis' father was anything other than delighted to array his son with all the paraphernalia that was expected of a would-be knight, including two horses, one for himself and one for his squire. The night before Francis left for the south, he had a dream in which all that he hoped for seemed to be promised. His father's emporium was no longer a draper's shop but a palace adorned with the finest arms and armor that he could possibly hope for, and it was all destined for him. Further to this, there was a promise of a beautiful maiden, whom any knight would be proud to champion, waiting for him in a secluded chamber. The dream made it clear that he was to be her champion and that her favor would be his when he returned triumphant.

It should not be surprising, then, that when he set out for Apulia to join the Norman champion Gautier de Brienne, he set out full of hope and expectation. But after only a day's ride he arrived at Spoleto to have yet another dream. This time he heard the words 'Where are you going?' When he replied, the same voice said, 'Tell me, Francis, who can best benefit you? The lord or the servant?' When he gave the obvious answer, the voice replied, 'Then why do you desert the lord for the servant, the prince for the vassal? Go home, where it shall be told to you what to do. The dream that you first had must be understood in a different way.'

He didn't seem to have any shame in returning home so soon, with his tail between his legs, nor did anyone seem to laugh at him, let alone suggest that he was a coward. Despite what anyone might think, he was still a rich merchant's son and nobody wants to look a gift horse in the mouth, especially as he quickly reverted to his old way of life. But it was out of habit rather than conviction and what else should he do anyway, at least until he was told what he was to do?

His friends made much of him, because there is sufficient evidence to show that he was a likeable young man and, when a likeable young man has more money than he knows what to do with, why not like him? Why not single him out, as they did at one of their parties, crowning him as 'king of the revels'? It was on the way home from this event, as he lingered behind the rest, that something happened to make him realize what he should have been doing. He was caught up in a 'mystical premonition'. He'd had similar experiences before while gazing at the beauty of the surrounding countryside before his imprisonment in Perugia, but nothing had held his inner gaze quite as fully as this. It was a sort of weak ecstasy that made him want to pause to savor what he was experiencing. His pals ragged him mercilessly when they turned back to see what had happened to him. 'He's fallen in love!' one of them said. 'He's fallen in love with love!' said another. And this other had come closer to the truth than he knew. Francis admitted that he had indeed fallen in love – with a lady whose beauty they could never imagine.

Although this wasn't the first time that he had had such experiences, it was the first time he reacted to them in a specifically religious way. He began to visit churches and places of solitude where he could pray. First he went with a friend, and then on his own. He was tempted to believe that all his efforts were a waste of time. Then one day everything changed. Whenever he had met lepers in the past he would always give them whatever help he could, but, as he couldn't face them in person, he had sent others to give them alms. That day everything changed. He was out riding in the valley of Spoleto when he came face to face with a leper whom he couldn't avoid. This time he didn't spur his horse and gallop away but leapt from his saddle, not just to give him alms but to kiss him on the mouth. Then he did the same for the patients in the local leprosarium, whilst begging their forgiveness for his cowardly behavior towards them in the past. His attitude to the poor was changing too. Long before he became aware of a specifically religious calling, he had always been generous to them whenever he came across them. However, there was a further change in his behavior, because now he positively sought them out. On one occasion, whilst on pilgrimage in Rome, he gave all his money away and exchanged clothes with a beggar just to experience what it felt like to be truly poor.

He knew that his new behavior towards lepers and the poor was not the action of Francesco Bernadone but the action of the Holy Spirit, who, despite his temptation to believe the contrary, had after all been working within him in his solitary prayer. The process of turning Francis into the man he admired more than any other had already begun, but until then he had hardly noticed it. Prayer was not, after all, the waste of time that he had been tempted to believe. He needed more of it, so he returned to prayer with ever-greater commitment. He began to wonder whether or not his new God-given calling to outcasts was God's way of telling him what was wanted of him, or was it more? He simply didn't know, so he began to pray more earnestly than ever before so that he would be ready and open to hear God when he chose to tell him what was wanted of him.

It was towards the end of 1205, when Francis was praying before an old Byzantine crucifix in the tumbledown Church of San Damiano just outside the city walls, that something unexpected happened. He heard words spoken to him that at last made it clear what he must do.

'Francis, rebuild my church which, as you can see, is falling down.'

So that there could be no misunderstanding, the words were spoken three times. Francis took the words literally, put on a mason's apron and, with trowel and mortar, started rebuilding the Church of San Damiano. He was of course just a cloth merchant's son, but months spent building the walls around Assisi had taught him what to do. Later he would realize that the church that he was called to rebuild was the Catholic Church itself which, as Pope Innocent III himself admitted, was indeed falling down for failing to be faithful to its founder. But at the time Francis was not ready for such an enormous task. He needed several years working and praying in solitude to prepare him for the real task for which he was called. However, no mere beginner can spend twenty-four hours a day praying and living in solitude whilst retaining their sanity, so the manual work helped to put balance into his spiritual life, which would have floundered without it.

Full of 'first fervor', Francis rushed home, selected the best cloth he could find from his father's shop, loaded it onto his horse and sold the lot, including the horse, at the market town of Foligno ten miles away. However, knowing that Francis' father wouldn't approve, the priest in charge of San Damiano wouldn't touch the money. Nevertheless he gave the young man shelter and allowed him to continue repairing his church. The inevitable happened. His father turned up, enraged that his son had made a laughing stock of him and his family, not to mention taking part of his precious stock. But Francis had scampered away and hidden himself in a cave nearby, where he was fed by a friend for a month or more before he came to his senses. Yet again it was in prayer that he was changed. He came to see that he had played the coward and then, through the same prayer, he received the strength to act like a man. So, grubby and disheveled, he began to make his way home to confront his father, only to be pelted with stones and mud by the same street urchins who had once idolized him from afar. Further humiliated by the son who had already shamed him, Pietro Bernadone rescued him, only to lock him up as a prisoner in his own home. The moment Pietro had to go away on another of his business trips, Pica, Francis' mother, was moved to pity and released him. When his father returned it was to confront him at San Damiano with a warrant from the civil authorities. This time Francis didn't run away but calmly informed his father that, as he had now consecrated himself to God, he could be tried only by an ecclesiastical court.

The scene was set for the final confrontation between father and son before Lord Guido, the Bishop of Assisi. He decreed that Francis had done wrong to take his father's goods without permission and told him to give them back. Whereupon, in a gesture that was to fire the imaginations of hundreds of biographers and inspire the works of many an artist, Francis returned everything, including all that he wore, until he stood naked before the court. Then he proclaimed that he disowned his own father on earth for his Father in heaven, to whom he committed himself for the future. The bishop clothed his nakedness with a gardener's smock, on which Francis painted a cross.

He set off for Gubbio, where he was given new clothes by an old friend. On his way there, he was thrown into a snowdrift by robbers, not just because they discovered he had nothing on him worth taking but because his claim to be 'a herald of the great King' made them write him off as a lunatic or a religious fanatic who needed cooling off for a while. He didn't receive much better treatment at the Benedictine abbey where he had to do hard labor to earn the pig food that barely kept him alive. He no doubt suffered at the time, but he had his reward later and from the very monks who had treated him so badly. When he became famous for his sanctity the guilty monks gave him the little church of St Mary of the Angels, which became then, as it is now, the mother church of his Order, although it's not much bigger than an oversized garage.

When he finally arrived at Gubbio, the clothing that his friend gave him symbolized the life to which he now committed himself for the next two to three years. It was the long robe of a hermit tied round with a leather belt, with sandals on his feet and a staff in his hands. He was still only a journeyman hermit so he journeyed all the way back to Assisi to complete the rebuilding of San Damiano, then to San Pietro and finally to St Mary of the Angels, hidden away in deep woods about a mile outside Assisi. It's no longer in a deep wood today but inside a vast basilica that also marks the spot where Francis died in 1226.

It was in the Church of St Mary of the Angels that a momentous event occurred in the life of St Francis. It took place in 1208 on the Feast of St Matthias, which was in those days celebrated on February 24th. When the priest was reading the Gospel, St Francis' heart leapt within him. He became totally convinced that at last God had spoken to him. This time he spoke through the words of the scriptures.

As you go, proclaim that the kingdom of God is close at hand. Cure the sick, raise the dead, cleanse lepers, and cast out devils. You received without charge, give without charge. Provide yourself with no gold or silver, not even a few coppers for your purse, no haversack for your journey or spare tunic or footwear or staff, for the workman deserves his keep. Whatever town or village you go into, ask for someone trustworthy and stay with him until you leave. As you enter his house salute it, and if the house deserves it, let your peace descend upon it; if it does not, let your peace come back to you.

(Matthew 10:7–13) The Jerusalem Bible

As soon as the priest had explained the reading, Francis threw away the garb of a hermit and dressed himself in a single grey robe with a rope around his waist instead of a belt. He threw away his staff and kicked off his sandals, ready to set out as ordered to proclaim the Good News that the Kingdom of God was close at hand. In those early days the cheapest cloth was undyed wool – or grey – and that's why the first Franciscans came to be called 'Grey Friars' and why so many of the streets in our major towns and cities are to this day still called 'Greyfriars', in memory of those early mendicants who once made their homes there. When cloth came to be dyed in the production process, they chose brown, because that was the cheapest dye available.

Before he set out, Francis asked the priest to explain the reading in a little more detail. He told Francis that this is precisely what Jesus had told his disciples to do and how they should set out on their missionary journeys, proclaiming that the Kingdom of God's love was close at hand. Even though it was close at hand, it would enter into the hearts and minds only of those who freely chose to receive it. Love cannot be forced on anyone so they must freely turn and open themselves to allow it in, or to use the biblical word, they must 'repent'. When in his first sermon St Peter had proclaimed that Jesus had risen from the dead and was ready to fill everyone with the same Love that had raised Jesus from the dead, the crowd asked what they were to do. They were told to repent. In future this would be the essence of the preaching of St Francis and his followers. But, as Francis never tired of insisting, they must first call people to repent by the sheer goodness of the lives they lived before they ever opened their mouths. Nobody listens to hypocrites.

With the words of the Gospel ringing in his ears, Francis set off for Assisi to do as he had been commanded. The last time he had gone into his hometown it was to be ridiculed and pelted with mud by the street urchins. Even his old cronies had disowned him then, for he was a beggar and no longer able to finance their 'rave ups' around the town. They had seen him disowned by his own father and mocked by his own brother Angelo, who had offered to buy the sweat that poured off him as he struggled to heave heavy stones into place and strained every muscle to rebuild San Damiano. Three years later, however, everything was different; nobody laughed any more. Now everybody seemed to listen as Francis preached, not just in the marketplace but by invitation in the Church of San Giorgio where he had first gone to school (and where he was first buried before the great Basilica of San Francesco was built as his mausoleum). In no time at all disciples flocked to follow him. They were important men too, who were well respected by everyone. Soon he was asked to preach in the Cathedral of San Rufino, where he inspired a certain teenage noblewoman called Clare to leave home to join him.

In eighteen years' time Francis would be dead. Why, oh why couldn't he have started his preaching earlier to make use of every possible moment to finish the rebuilding that would be far from finished when he died? Why did he have to spend almost three years of wasted time in solitude? Why couldn't God have spoken to him earlier? The answer is quite simple – because he couldn't have heard.

Francis was no different from anyone else at the beginning of his calling. He was a beginner with the best of intentions, no doubt about it, but a beginner nonetheless. I believe in everything from instant coffee to instant resurrection – instant conversion, instant healing, instant miracles and instant phenomena of every shape and form if there's evidence – but instant sanctity? No – there's no such thing. It takes time precisely because people can't hear properly until they have been purified of all the selfishness, all the prejudice and all the arrogance that at first only enables them to hear what suits them. That's why, behind all the enthusiasm and all the fervor of a spiritual beginner, there is a person so lost in 'them and theirs' they couldn't do the right thing even if they could hear what it was. That was Francis at the beginning of his journey. He might have had the best of intentions, but he was nevertheless going through what's called 'first fervor', when common sense often goes out the window. This does not mean that the time he spent in prayer was a waste of time; it certainly wasn't. What it does mean is that it was only the beginning of his journey. His prayer did bear fruit with immediate effect, but transformation into the man whom medieval people called 'the Second Christ' would take much longer.

It was in his solitary prayer that Francis received the spiritual strength not just to help the poor when he came across them but to seek them out. It was here that he was given the power to do what would have been impossible before: not just to give charity to lepers from afar but to do so face to face, and to kiss them with a love that he knew was beyond the power of the old self who had shrunk from them in the past. It was here too that he finally received the strength to confront his own father when he had fled from his anger before. Francis had already prayed incessantly for God to speak to him so that he would know what to do, but first God would have to teach him how to listen and how to silence the unruly desires and longings that drew his attention elsewhere. This would take time – years rather than months. Meanwhile the adolescent had to blunder on, undoubtedly with the best of intentions but without the wisdom and the prudence that would come later.

That's why, although we may well admire him for his good intentions when he sold his father's cloth and his horse to buy bricks and mortar, it was nevertheless his *father's* cloth and his *father's* horse, which he took without asking. Any court would call that theft. That's why he was rightly ordered to give them back to his father in open court by Lord Guido, Bishop of Assisi. Everyone may understandably be moved by the scene where he gave everything back to his father to the last stitch, but why should his father always be depicted as the 'baddy'? Until Francis 'got religion', his father had indulged him in every way possible. If he wanted to be the 'king of the revels', Dad would provide; if he wanted to wear the latest fashions from Provence, again Dad would provide; and if he wanted to be dressed and equipped as the noble knight he never was, yet again Dad would provide. There's nothing to show that his father had been anything other that the provider of all Francis had wanted to further his daydreams, until he got religion.

The trouble with yesterday's converts is that they all expect everyone else to be converted to their way of thinking by the following day at the latest, and are irritated when they're not. There was no need for Francis' petulance, no need for the histri-onics in the court; he was after all in the wrong and, truth to tell, he wouldn't have behaved like that later. He behaved like that then, because he was going through his first fervor, still full of himself and the way he thought the Gospel should be interpreted and acted upon. He was wrong because he couldn't hear. When he set off on his way to Gubbio, singing like an effete charismatic from Zeffirelli's masterly misconception, it was no wonder that the robbers threw him in a snowdrift to cool off. Who wouldn't be tempted to do the same?

The deep life-changing prayer began in the months ahead while he worked away on other tumbledown churches after he had finished San Damiano. The strength he had already received in prayer had convinced him that it was there, and there alone, that the sinner that he knew he was would eventually be trans-formed, though he had no idea how, any more than he knew what for.

Although there's nothing in the sources to suggest that St

Francis was ever a serial sinner, it would be naive to suggest that this passionate and exuberant young man was totally blameless. Even when he was an established saint in the eyes of his contemporaries he used to say, 'I may yet have children.' When temptations became all but unbearable in the hermitage at Sarteano, he left the warmth of his bed to build a snow wife and children for himself in the bitter cold, until his passions were as cool as the snow with which he built them. On another occasion, when there was no snow to hand, he had to make do with throwing himself on rosebushes to assuage the sexual temptations that all but seduced him. If these are some of the battles that he fought and won when he was all but a spiritual master, imagine how many were fought and lost when he was just a beginner, not to mention those when he hadn't even begun.

It is often forgotten that he fought in bloody hand-to-hand combat at the battle of Collestrada. Few soldiers return from the front guiltless. They feel guilty either because they killed another human being, or because they didn't and, playing the coward, were responsible for the death of a comrade in arms. Few return without being forced to see another side of themselves that they'd never seen before. In medieval times it was commonplace for nobles, racked with guilt and fearing for retribution hereafter, to build hospitals, abbeys, monasteries and convents in reparation for their sins and for the war crimes that kept them awake at night. There's no reason to suggest that this wasn't an important element in the hard labor that occupied Francis for almost three years. We know for sure that deep down he was still burdened with guilt for past sins that remained with him for some time to come. He had to wait for six months or more after hearing that decisive Gospel reading, before he was assured that all was forgiven. That assurance was finally given to him while he was deep in prayer at Poggio Bustone, high up above the Rieti Valley.

There was another reason for his solitary labor that he was not aware of at the time, but it was undoubtedly known to the One who called him. From earliest times, would-be hermits had gone out of their minds as a result of living for prolonged periods of time in the solitary confinement that they unwisely imposed on themselves. Later, the great Franciscan reformer St Bernadine of Siena admitted that there were some who had been driven to insanity by the imprudent way they had abandoned themselves to solitude in the hermitages. It was precisely for this reason that the Desert Fathers had always insisted that a monk had to perform seven hours of manual work each day to balance time for work with time for prayer. This leads on to the main reason why Francis needed to spend those hidden years in the 'desert' like John the Baptist and like so many other saints in the making who preceded him and who would follow him. Beginners are always so intoxicated by first fervor that their own 'spiritual' desires and aspirations prevent them from hearing the voice of God, though they think they know it better than anyone else. That's why adolescent fervor has to evaporate and they have to be led into the 'Dark Night of the Soul', where they come to see, as never before, all the sin and selfishness that enthralls them. It was this that had been creating the inner turmoil that had prevented them from hearing the voice that can only be heard by the pure in heart. Then, it is only by accepting the purification that ensues whilst waiting patiently on God that the true mettle of a serious spiritual traveler is laid bare. If they can now journey on relentlessly in the full knowledge of their utter need of God, a new departure in their journey can take place, one that depends totally on him.

It is only then, with the clamor of self-seeking and personal ambition silenced, that they can hear the word of God as they had been unable to hear it before. God is love and, when he speaks, it is in and through love that his word reaches out to all who are ready to receive it. It is this mystical love that St Bonaventure described as 'a shaft of light that flashes out from the divine darkness', suddenly enabling them to see the truth that they had never seen before. For the first time, they begin to see the truth about themselves that they didn't want to see before. Then they begin to see the truth about God, rather than falling in love with a 'God'whom they have created in their own image and likeness. This mystical 'shaft of light' fills them with wisdom and understanding, enabling them to interpret the truth, and then fills them with the strength to *do* the truth that they could never have done before. This is why Francis was able to hear and understand the Gospel reading on the Feast of St Matthias and to receive the inner spiritual strength to act upon it.

It was only now that he made an impact – the same people who had openly mocked him listened to him as never before. They could see that the charismatic 'hippy' was no more. Instead it was a new man who stood before them, a more balanced and mature man who in some way embodied the goodness of the man in whose name he spoke.

The first two to join him were highly respected citizens of Assisi. One was Bernard of Quintavalle, an extremely wealthy man; the other was Peter Cattani, a secular lawyer who had been made a canon at the Cathedral of San Rufino. When they asked St Francis what they were to do, he took them both to the Church of San Nicolo where all three prayed, before opening the Gospels three times to read:

If you wish to be perfect, go and sell what you own and give the money to the poor, and you will have treasure in heaven. (Matthew 19:21)
If anyone wants to be a follower of mine, let him renounce himself and take up his cross and follow me. (Matthew 16:24)
And he instructed them to take nothing for the journey. (Mark 6:8)

Francis was filled with joy and said, 'Brothers, this is our life and our rule and for all who wish to follow us.' After they had given away all their possessions to the poor, they took up residence in a little hut near St Mary of the Angels where they were joined by Giles, a man who had begun life as a farmer and who would end it as a famous hermit to whom many would turn for spiritual help and guidance long after St Francis had died. In order to obey the word of God they set off two by two to proclaim the Gospel. When asked who they were, they replied that they were penitents from Assisi and they preached repentance to all who would hear them. Francis and Giles went to the Marches of Ancona and Bernard and Peter to Florence. When on their return their numbers increased, they moved to a few small buildings at a place called Rivo Torto, so called because they lay alongside a brook that twisted and turned like a snake. Then, when their numbers had increased to twelve, St Francis wrote his first rule based entirely on the Gospels and, with Bernard of Quintavalle elected as their leader, they set off for Rome to seek approval for their way of life from Pope Innocent III.

Innocent had no illusions about the state of the Church and the need for fundamental reform, but he had so far been unimpressed by the myriad firebrands who had set themselves up to reform the Church with their apocalyptic followers. Even though he'd encouraged some of them to begin with, he usually ended in suppressing or condemning them for their offbeat interpretation of the Gospels and their uncanny habit of antagonizing clergy, whom they loved to damn to hell in their fiery sermons. Francis was different from these self-appointed prophets of doom for three reasons. Firstly, his simple honest-to-God goodness was quite transparent, unlike most of the self-styled reformers who had preceded him. Secondly, he never at any time pointed the finger at anyone else for failing to live up to the ideals he sought for himself. Nor would he even think of preaching in the diocese or the parish of any bishop or priest against their will. By instinct rather than by calculation Francis knew that only the humble can speak to the proud and hope to be heard. And thirdly, his rule of life was the teaching of the Gospel, the whole Gospel, and nothing but the Gospel, without the bizarre misinterpretations of the prophets of doom.

Nevertheless it was finally this so-called rule of life – little more than a string of Gospel texts – which made Innocent III think twice, because he feared that nobody could possibly live by it. If it hadn't been for the words of Cardinal John of St Paul, a former Cistercian monk who had already befriended Francis, and for the Pope's famous dream, things might well have turned out quite differently. The words of the Cardinal were simply these: 'To say his rule of life is too difficult to live by is tantamount to saying that the Gospel is too difficult to live by.' And that would of course be a criticism not only of the *Poverello* from Assisi but also of the man whose teaching he, like the rest of the Church, was trying to follow. If these words made Innocent pause for further thought, the dream that he subsequently had decided the matter. In this dream the rather grubby little man who, the day before, had presented his rule to him now prevented the walls of the Lateran Palace from falling down. In those days the Lateran Palace was what the Vatican is today, so despite appearances the Pope came to see that the man he had initially mistaken for a swineherd was in fact sent by God to do for the Church what all the prophets of doom put together had failed to do.

To this day there is nothing left in writing of that first rule of St Francis which he and his brothers followed for more than a dozen years. Nor did Pope Innocent III give Francis anything other than his word to ratify it and the permission to preach repentance to a world that had all but fallen back into paganism. But that was not a problem for Francis – if a gentleman's word is his bond, what of a pope's? 'Go with my blessing and try to live by it,' he had said to Francis. He was using the well-proven wisdom of Gamaliel: If it is of God it will surely succeed, but if it is of man it will surely fail (see Acts 5:38–39). If all went well

Francis was told to return, for Innocent had work for him to do.

Francis and his little band rejoiced all the way home with unalloyed joy, but Pope Innocent's hopes for the new foundation were not unalloyed; one question still troubled him as it had already troubled Guido, the Bishop of Assisi, before him. For Francis had also asked permission to live in absolute poverty – how can anyone follow Christ in absolute poverty, owning nothing whatsoever, either personally or in common? And was it correct to say that this was the poverty lived by Christ himself and his followers? There is certainly evidence to suggest that the first followers after the resurrection pooled their resources and lived a life in common, but no evidence to suggest that this became a universal norm in the early Church, and that is a very long way from living without any personal possessions whatsoever. These are questions that have exercised the minds of Franciscan scholars for centuries.

One thing is for certain: this is precisely what Francis wanted for himself and for his first followers, so the moment a peasant drove his donkey into the little shed that was home to the brothers at Rivo Torto and claimed it as his own, Francis left without argument. The brothers moved to the small piece of land that came to be known as the Portiuncula, which surrounded the little church of St Mary of the Angels. It is a very difficult word to translate into English. It is actually an Umbrian word, spelt as Porzioncula or Porziuncola, taken from the local dialect with which Francis would have been familiar. It means, literally, a small insignificant place or a piece of land of little value. Just the sort of place that Francis would have loved and valued as he did, imbuing the word for himself and all Franciscans with the sort of frisson that the word 'home' gives to most of us, no matter how high or how lowly our origins might be.

Although the Benedictine monks of Monte Subasio wanted to give Portiuncula to Francis, his own personal commitment to absolute poverty impelled him to refuse it. He only finally consented to accept it on the condition that it would remain in the possession of the monks. It was therefore only loaned to him and to his followers for the annual rent of a basket of fish, which is still paid by the friars to this day. The Portiuncula has its own feast day on August 2nd on which the 'rent' has been paid to the monks for over 800 years. Francis surrounded the little piece of land with a rectangular hedge to give the brothers some privacy from the outside world and then built a series of huts, so that each brother would have some privacy. They were built simply by plastering mud onto wickerwork walls with rainproof roofs. Later examples of these huts can still be seen inside the friary at La Verna or at the hermitage of Monteluco high up above Spoleto. The only other building was a simple shed where the first friars could meet together outside the church. And that was all that comprised what was, for Francis, the blueprint that he wanted to be used for all other friaries. He wanted its very simplicity to speak to the world of the holy poverty that was so dear to him and yet so misunderstood by so many others.

A moving passage from *The Mirror of Perfection*, a work that owes its authorship to Brother Leo more than to any other, perfectly sums up how Francis felt about future friaries and how they should be built by his brothers:

Let them go and make a trench all around the land and let them set up a good hedge as a wall, as a sign of holy poverty and humility. Then let them make poor houses out of wattle and daub, and some little cells in which the friars may pray and work, for greater seemliness and to avoid sloth. Let them also make small churches for they ought not to make great churches, neither to preach to the people nor for any other reason, since their humility is greater and their example better when they go to other churches to preach. And if at any time prelates and clergy come to their dwellings, the poor little houses, the little cells and the tiny churches will speak to them and they will be more edified by them than by words.

Innocent III was more than skeptical about Francis' commitment to total poverty and his insistence that it was the clear teaching of the Gospels for him and for his followers. But Francis was adamant. After all, he had heard the words of Christ for himself on the Feast of St Matthias and they couldn't be clearer: 'Provide yourself with no gold nor silver, not even a few coppers for your purses, no haversack for your journey, no spare tunic or footwear or staff, for the workman deserves his keep.'

The Bishop of Assisi was skeptical too and so for that matter were many of his later followers. The bishop was grudgingly won over when Francis explained that once you own something you have to be prepared to fight for it when someone threatens to take it away from you, either on the field of battle, or in the courts of law. The bishop was at the time involved in numerous legal battles over his possessions so he was able to see and even sympathize with the logic of Francis' argument, even though he himself had no intention of embracing what Francis called 'Lady Poverty'. The citizens of Assisi had even less sympathy when the self-same neighbors whom they had seen handing out their money to all and sundry came knocking at their doors with begging bowls in their hands. However, even they began to have second thoughts when the friars soon became a source of cheap labor, because all they would ask as recompense was just enough food and drink to keep body and soul together for a single day. Not a bad deal, especially when many of them turned out to be skilled craftsmen. Francis made it quite clear that they would only become beggars – or mendicants, as they came to be called – if there was no work and they would otherwise perish for lack of food.

Francis wasn't trying to suggest that the poverty that he had chosen to embrace for himself and his followers was for all. Nor that it is essential for anyone who wants to live the teaching of the Gospel, or even for all who choose to preach or teach the Gospel to others. Jesus did not make the same demands when he later told his disciples to go and preach the 'Good News' after the resurrection. However, Francis freely chose to base his way of life on the poverty that Jesus imposed on those first disciples whom he sent out to preach during his public ministry. And who is to say that the preaching of those first friars was not effective? Was it not as effective as any other preachers before or since, if not more effective?

Just as Francis needed time to grown spiritually, so did the new recruits for whom he now had to act as spiritual mentor, so that they would be able to do at the dawn of the thirteenth century what the first apostles had done at the dawn of the first. However, just as St Francis had made something of a fool of himself when he was going through his first fervor, some of his new recruits did the same, as is only to be expected. Many suffered the same indignities as those that Francis had to endure – and even worse – until gradually prayer, solitude and asceticism did for them what they had done for Francis. When a person first 'gets religion', it is only to be expected that their enthusiasm and their religious fervor can become a little irksome to those who do not share their newfound convictions, or to those who are years ahead of them on the journey that they have just begun. Swift progress into the mystic way demands a compact and disciplined way of life where daily time for personal prayer, solitude and asceticism is mandatory. This does not necessarily involve leaving the 'world' for the 'religious life'. Angela of Foligno managed to reach the heights of the mystical life as a wife and as a mother, as did many others who joined the Third Order of St Francis. This was founded only a short time after the rule of the First Order had been sanctioned. If anyone is prepared to follow the example of Francis of Assisi and embrace the unique way of life that he copied from the Gospels, they can be sure to travel with the utmost possible speed. That's why his first followers quickly climbed the foothills to the heights of spiritual maturity and that's why within only ten years there were between 3,000 and 5,000 brothers who had given up everything to follow in his footsteps.

Ever since Charlemagne's enthronement in Rome as the Holy Roman Emperor in 800 AD, Europe had gradually become a safer place in which to live. It became increasingly easy to travel and to trade as the centuries rolled by. It was a slow process, but by the time Francis was a young man his father was only one of many merchants who had made a fortune in the sort of trading that would have been impossible before, when sacking and pillaging was the most common way of getting rich. In the Middle Ages the best sackers and pillagers tended to become the worst landowners, as they enslaved most of their minions and taxed the rest into permanent penury, offering only safety from other sackers and pillagers for their pains. Gradually in Europe the 'survival of the fittest' dictated the arrival of a new world order with the strongest at the top and the weakest at the bottom. This new world order came to be called feudalism.

In theory the Emperor was at the top, followed by kings, dukes, counts, earls, barons, sheriffs and knights, all of whom paid homage to their king for the lands that he allowed them to keep in exchange for their obeisance and for military service. In Italy the nobility from the knights upward came to be called the *Majores* while the minions were called the *Minores*. That's why, on their return from Rome when they were residing for the second time at Rivo Torto, Francis decided to call his band of brothers *Minores* – *Fratres Minores* – or, in English, 'Friars Minor'. He wanted to make this quite clear because, by the time he was born, many of the merchant classes were becoming so wealthy that they were beginning to climb their way into the upper classes – into the Majores.

Francis had already seen this happen in his own town when most of the Majores had been thrown out and Assisi had been proclaimed a commune. Before his conversion he had certainly had pretensions. Fed by stories of the daring deeds of the Knights of the Round Table, he was inspired to follow them and would have certainly been knighted had he fought with honor and won glory in battle under the leadership of Walter of Brienne. But once his eyes were opened, he felt nothing but disgust for the dreams that had once deceived him. He felt contempt too for his own class who were consumed with lust, not so much for the glory that had bedazzled him but for the money that would enable them to climb into the upper ranks of society, where they were laughed at for their uncouth ways and boorish manners. At least the old order, which had now been banished from Assisi, had practiced the code of chivalry that had once inspired Francis, and the courtly manners that were so noticeably absent from the new pretenders. They had known how to treat the noble ladies whose favor they sought and whose keepsakes they wore with pride whenever they fought, as they spurred their horses into combat at the tournaments or on the field of battle.

Francis did not abandon the ideals that had inspired him as a young man, but he transposed and transformed them from the secular world to the spiritual. He would still be a knight, as would his followers. They would be like the knights who sat together at a round table, to show that no one was superior to the others. If one of his brothers was raised up for a time, it would only be to serve the others as a guardian, a warden or a minister for a brief period of time before returning to his place at the round table, where equality reigned supreme. Francis didn't want to be just any knight, but a knight chosen to perform a particular task by his lord. In short he wanted to be a herald, a knight singled out for his courtesy and his courtly manners to announce the arrival of the king at court, at the tournament or on the battlefield. He would have a lady too, whom he would honor and serve with all the dedication that was expected of him.

When on an impulse he had told the friends who were

mocking him that he had fallen for a lady far more beautiful than they could ever have imagined, he probably knew no more about this mysterious lady than they did at the time. They were the words of a young man who had fallen in love with love, but her true identity was soon to become clearer to him. The rise of the new moneyed classes to which he had belonged worshipped the new god of mammon and he too had been all but seduced. But now he wanted to divorce himself from that world, so that he could wed what he came to call 'Lady Poverty'. It was not just because poverty was despised by his peers, but because it had been embraced by the only person in whose footsteps Francis now wished to follow with all his heart.

In abandoning his heavenly home and birthright, the man he would call 'Brother Jesus' had entered into a world of spiritual and material poverty as a helpless baby in a wooden crib and had chosen to leave that world as a helpless man on a wooden cross. It was in imitation of him that Francis wanted to embrace total physical and spiritual poverty. He knew that it would enable him to be completely open and receptive to the same love that had progressively possessed Brother Jesus. The radical outer poverty that was to be the hallmark of his new Order was but the expression of a profound inner poverty. In the words of the Franciscan poet and mystic Jacopone da Todi, this Franciscan poverty consists in 'possessing nothing, desiring to posses nothing and yet possessing all things in the spirit of liberty'. Without the inner poverty all the outer show would be nothing other than show, and the 'show off' would be nothing other than a hypocrite.

Embracing Lady Poverty, whom Brother Jesus had wed before him, enabled Francis to be filled with and guided by the Holy Spirit, who he insisted was the real Minister General of his Order. If he had had his way, this deeply rooted conviction would have been written into his final rule. Needless to say, the canon lawyers would have none of it.

Francis chose a very specific way of life in which to embrace Lady Poverty and it was quite unique. It was quite simply the way of life lived by Jesus and his followers before the resurrection. For him it had three inseparable characteristics. It is an eremitical or solitary life, a community life, and an apostolic life. All these three ingredients are so inseparably bound together that no authentic Franciscan life can exist if one of them is permanently lacking. The monks who had preceded the mendicants based their way of life on that of the first Christian community in Jerusalem when everything was owned in common. The Benedictine monks, for instance, whose form of monasticism predominated in Europe before the Franciscan rule was approved, positively excluded this way of life by adopting a vow of stability, which tied them to their monasteries. This is not a criticism of this form of monastic life, because it was never founded to evangelize the world through apostolic work in the world, but primarily through contemplative prayer and the work that the monks performed that was inspired by that prayer. The many disparate lay preachers and 'prophets' who had preceded Francis based their way of life on the apostolic life as lived by the first apostles after the resurrection. Nowhere in the writings of Francis does he use the phrase 'the apostolic life' to describe the life to which he and his followers wanted to commit themselves. It is always the Gospel way of life, more specifically the way of life imposed on those first disciples sent out by Jesus before the resurrection to preach the Good News.

For the first time in history Francis chose to base his way of life on the life as lived by Jesus and his disciples before the resurrection. Jesus himself lived in a traveling community with his disciples, and he preached to others as part of that community and sent his disciples from that community to preach to others too. Nevertheless he needed to keep turning aside into solitude to receive what he was to give to others, and he taught his followers to do likewise by both word and example. This is why Francis taught his disciples to follow this example by repeatedly turning to God in both communal and solitary prayer to receive the same love that had transformed Brother Jesus. Only then would they be able to share it with others. This continual repentance would open them ever more fully to the love of God or the Holy Spirit, who would bond them into a loving, caring brotherhood that would speak to others far louder than mere words.

When you go to Franciscan Italy you will see communities of friars living amongst the people they serve in the villages, in the towns and in the cities, but look up high above the valleys and you will see the remote and solitary hermitages on the hillsides. It is to such places that the friars regularly returned to receive in profound prayer the same Holy Spirit who progressively permeated and transformed the human body and soul of Brother Jesus before them. Then they would return to make pools of contemplative stillness in the friaries, from where they would go out to breathe the breath of supernatural life into a world that is dead without it.

From the very beginning St Francis had continually sought out solitude. Whether he was working on rebuilding tumbledown churches, mentoring the first friars at Rivo Torto or building the first Franciscan friary at the Portiuncula, he would repeatedly steal away to his beloved 'prisons', Le Carceri – lonely caves cut into the side of Monte Subasio where he could be utterly alone with his Lady Poverty. Sometimes she would show him only the darkness of his own nothingness; sometimes she would show him the light of God's goodness, for this is the only way that saints are made out of sinners.

Thanks to Bernard of Quintavalle we have a clear insight into the sort of prayer that sustained him in his solitude. Although Bernard had been impressed by Francis, he didn't want to make a final decision to join him until he had tested his spiritual mettle, so he invited Francis to stay overnight. When they settled down for the night Bernard pretended to sleep and waited to see what his guest would do. Once he thought his host had fallen asleep, Francis knelt by his bed and prayed through most of the night, and he prayed the same prayer time and time again. The prayer that he used would later become the motto of the Order. It was simply *'Deus Meus et Omnia'* ('My God and my All').

This gives us a profound insight into Francis' spiritual development at the precise moment when he was about to found his Order (April 1208). The days of first fervor were now over; he no longer meditated on the life of Brother Jesus as he had before. He no longer wept uncontrollably as he meditated on his passion and death. He had now already passed from meditation to contemplation. 'Contemplation' is the word used to describe the experience of God's love when it first begins to make itself felt. At first the experience of this love is painful, because it always lays bare the sin and the selfishness that has to be purified away before it can possess the mystic in the making. When a person is in extreme pain or joy they need only a few words to express their feelings. In contemplation these few words were first called the 'prayer of the heart' by the Desert Fathers.

In the darkness that a beginner experiences when his or her sinfulness is laid bare, this prayer often comprises a desperate cry for help that lasts for very many months. However, Francis was not a complete beginner in the mystic way as his prayer clearly indicates. The prayer of the heart that he chose to use now no longer comprised the prayer of desperation and the cry for help, but an exclamation of sheer joy. For now he was experiencing a sublime spiritual joy at the realization that the God who was now his all was beginning to make his presence felt within him. *'Deus Meus et Omnia!'* he cried out. 'My God and my All!' If St Francis had still been crying out to God from the depth of the dark purification that afflicts a beginner in the 'Dark Night of the Soul', Bernard of Quintavalle would have probably cut and run – and who would have blamed him? He would hardly have been inspired the following day to give all his money away to the poor, don an old sack for a tunic and run off barefoot to a cow shed to pledge his life to Lady Poverty. In short, St Francis was already sufficiently advanced in the spiritual life to inspire people to change their lives, if not by becoming beggars in mud huts, at least by becoming better people in their own homes.

Before leaving this revealing little episode there is a further conclusion that can be drawn from the contents of St Francis' prayer of the heart. Notice it was not directed to Jesus Christ, who had spoken to him in San Damiano and for whom he had wept in the days when he would meditate for hours on his painful passion and death. It was directed to God alone. Those who are ignorant of the mystic way are often quick to condemn it for seeming to forget the most important truth of our faith, the Incarnation. Where is Jesus Christ in the strange new world, they ask? Where is he indeed, the poor spiritual traveler begins to wonder, when his presence and all the fervor that once surrounded meditating on his humanity seems to have evaporated? The question seems even more pressing when the saint most venerated for bringing back the sacred humanity of Jesus into Christian spirituality seems himself to have lost sight of the Incarnation. The answer is simply this: at this point of his spiritual odyssey Francis, along with those who have traveled along the same way before him, has not abandoned Jesus Christ. Far from it; he is now not just traveling *with* him as before, but *in* him.

As Jesus promised at the Last Supper, his love for his followers is now such that he is in them and they are in him; and in, with and through him they are more fully open to the Father and to the Father's love than ever before. Once this love has purified the mind and the soul, the body and the whole human personality is purified too. When this happens, what was once predominantly experienced in the mind or in the soul alone is experienced in every part of the body, as what is called the 'Transforming Union' or the 'Mystical Marriage' takes place.

When this started to happen to Francis he began to experience Jesus being brought to birth again within him by the same Holy Spirit who had first brought Jesus to birth in Mary's womb. This was not just a new conviction that had been implanted into his head, but a deeply felt experience that enveloped and suffused every fiber of his being. The man he now came to call Brother Jesus was as close to him as he was to himself, and in him he came to experience the vortex of life and love that endlessly flows between the Father and the Son, which is the Holy Spirit.

It was now through mystical experience rather than through intellectual reasoning that Francis came to see and understand the sublime mystical vision that is at the heart of authentic Franciscan spirituality. The one St Francis called Brother Jesus, who had humbled and emptied himself of his supernatural birthright and entered into him, was the very Word of God who had reigned with the Father from eternity, in whom everyone and everything had been created from the beginning. This led St Francis to realize that if everyone and everything had been created in Brother Jesus then all the world must be a friary. The Greek philosopher Plato said that the world was a prison. Shakespeare said that all the world was a stage and the men and women merely players. And a president of the United States said that all the world was a marketplace and the men and women merely buyers and sellers. But for Francis of Assisi all the world was a friary, and everyone and everything within it were therefore brothers and sisters to one another. It is not just Brother Francis and Sister Clare, then, but Brother Sun and Sister Moon, Brother Wolf and Sister Lamb, Brother Fire and Sister Water, for the whole of creation is a brotherhood and sisterhood with a common Father in whose embrace all were created from the beginning.

When St Francis was a young man, even before he had felt called by God, he had reveled in the natural beauty of the flora and fauna of the idyllic countryside that still leaves visitors to

Umbria spellbound to this day. He was something of a natural mystic long before he was called to the mystic way. But once he had been drawn into the mystical purification that was to prepare him to become 'a Second Christ', everything changed. The senses that had gloried in the natural paradise that surrounded him became as dead as they were alive before, as the mysterious presence that drew him into the mystic way became more and more absorbing, to the detriment of all else. The desire for God, and God alone, possessed every part of his consciousness, though that desire seemed to remain forever unfulfilled. It was as if every fiber of his sensual self became numb and frozen over, awaiting a spring that never seemed to come.

For those few who, like St Francis, have the patience, the courage and the faith to persevere, spring does finally break through when winter has cleansed not just the mind and the spirit but the body too and the heart that throbs within it. When the Transforming Union takes place, it is as if their very bodies, which felt as if they were frozen and impervious to all feeling before, have thawed out and become sensitive once more. It does actually feel like the thaw after winter as the fire of the Holy Spirit defrosts what seemed to be frozen, bringing the man or woman who had thought themselves sensually and emotionally dead back to life. Now they are fully human as they have never been before. As this happened to Francis, his love for the natural wonderland around him suddenly returned, and now that the emotions and the senses of his old self had been purified from the selfishness that had distorted them before, a new man emerged. It was now for the first time that Francis was not only able to see and express his unique vision for the brotherhood and sisterhood of all creation but also to tangibly feel it. He actually felt he was a brother to all, just as all began to feel a brother and a sister to him. Now even the lowliest and most timid of creatures came to him. They felt safe and even listened to him, as they had with Adam in the first paradise once lost, but now regained by Francis.

Francis now loved all things and all people, not for what he got out of them, not even for the pleasure they gave him, but for themselves. When a person is loved for themselves and for the good that is seen in them, no matter how deeply it may be hidden from view, they are made to feel accepted; they are made to feel at home and loved, no matter how unworthy they may be. And when the person who loves them is a Francis of Assisi, who speaks of the sort of life for which they have long since yearned, they just want to throw away every vestige of their old life to follow him and the new life that he promises. That's why, as his faithful confrere Brother Masseo said, 'The whole world is now running after you.' They came in their thousands – men and women, and children too.

How could anyone resist such a man? The future St Clare had been spellbound listening to his sermons in the Cathedral of San Rufino during the Lent of 1212. Francis was well prepared for these sermons – his first major series in his hometown – for he had spent the previous Lent fasting and praying on a little island on Lake Trasimeno and the following winter in a remote hermitage at Sarteano near Chiusi. St Clare was the daughter of Favorino de Scifi, who came from the most prominent family in Assisi and bore the title of Count of Sasso-Rosso, the name of the peak that rises above the town. Her two cousins, Sylvester and Rufino, had only recently joined the new band of brothers. Sylvester was a priest who finally spent most of his time living as a hermit at Le Carceri. Rufino was one of 'the three Companions', with Leo and Angelo, who strove to remain faithful to the primitive way of life after the death of Francis. They were the main source for the work that came to be called *The Legend of the Three Companions*, which gloried in the primitive way of life that they had shared with Francis when others wanted to forget it. When they died, their particular closeness to St Francis was recognized when they received the honor of being buried close to him in the Basilica of San Francesco.

Despite her noble and aristocratic birth, Clare left home the day after she heard Francis preach on the Palm Sunday of 1212. Her hair was cut off by Francis in St Mary of the Angels; then her fashionable clothes were exchanged for sackcloth and her shoes for bare feet. After spending a little time with the Benedictine Sisters of Isola Romanesco nearby, she and her sisters moved to San Damiano, which had been given to them by the Camaldoly monks of Monte Subasio. Many other women were inspired to join Clare, including her own sister Anne; and after her father died she was joined by her mother Ortolana and her other sister Beatrice.

What is known in the mystic way as the Transforming Union takes place the very moment purification comes to an end. It is instantaneous. The very moment a person is sufficiently purified of the selfishness that keeps the pure unadulterated love of God out, that love comes flooding in instantly – not just into the mind or the higher part of the head where it has already been partially experienced before, but into every part of the personality. The receiver swoons with the sheer delight of experiencing what Jesus Christ experienced throughout his life. Before, mystical experiences had come and gone, but now in the Transforming Union the experience of being possessed by the love of God is all but permanent. That's why it is often called the Mystical Marriage. Now marriage is not the end but the beginning of a love that grows deeper and deeper as, with years of mutual self-giving, the lovers are irrevocably bonded together. It would be all but impossible to pinpoint the exact moment when this happened to Francis. However, the sources enable us to see quite clearly the immediate effects of this profound transformation within him. Whenever a person experiences the delight of being totally possessed by the Holy Spirit, they just want to revel in that experience. Understandably they are tempted to do nothing else but relish what they have received, to the exclusion of all else.

This is precisely what happened to Francis. Only a few years before, God had spoken to him in the little church of St Mary of the Angels, commanding him to become an itinerant preacher, but now he experienced a desire to stay at home to bathe in the glory of what he had received. Did this mean that he should forsake that calling? He didn't trust himself to decide, so he sent Brother Masseo to Sister Clare at San Damiano and to her cousin Brother Sylvester at Le Carceri to pray to God for enlightenment. The reply from both of them was in complete accord: 'God did not call you for yourself but for others.' The moment he heard their reply from Brother Masseo he took to the road again, taking Masseo with him and also Brother Angelo, a young knight he had recruited into the brotherhood at Rieti. But now it was a different Francis who took the road to Rome by way of Montefalco.

The Desert Fathers had their own way of describing the pinnacle of the mystic way on earth. It was seen as a return to 'Paradise Lost'. What was lost by Adam could be regained by those who had been purified of the sin and the selfishness that had expelled him from paradise. That is why the great father and founder of Egyptian monasticism, St Antony, was finally at one, not just with himself but with the whole of creation, symbolized by his familiarity with the wild animals with whom he lived in complete harmony and without any fear. St Francis had now arrived at that very place himself and his arrival was symbolized by what is perhaps the most iconic picture that we have of him, preaching to the birds on the roadside between the villages of Cannara and Bevagna on his way to Rome. The many paintings of this idyllic scene depict the time when a new departure had just begun in the spiritual life of Francis: the birth of his unique vision.

In the first book of the Old Testament the author of Genesis presented the world that God created as a temple. The firmament comprised the vast dome in which the whole of creation resided. Each day that God had spoken, his Word had been embodied in as many animals, plants and inanimate wonders as he chose, to give him praise and glory just by being and doing what he created them for. In the first chapter of St John's Gospel we are given the world-shaking news that God's Word, in whom and through whom all things were created in the beginning, is now, 'in the fullness of time', made flesh in the person of Jesus Christ. He is now not only the new temple in which all creation resides but also the supreme King of that creation, who has come to rule over it and, as its supreme priest, lead it in an unending offering of love, praise and thanksgiving to the Father who sent him.

Everything seemed so simple to the man who had just been suffused by the 'Wisdom of God'. If all things were created in Brother Jesus then all things are brothers and sisters to each other. Indeed the whole world must then be a friary, and the highways and the byways of that world must be the cloisters of this friary. So from now on, whenever Francis walks through these cloisters with his brothers, he orchestrates the whole of creation around him to give praise and thanks with him to their common Father through Jesus their eldest brother, beginning with the birds of Cannara and Bevagna.

As the story of Francis further unfolds, it is full of his love for his brothers and sisters, the birds, the animals, the trees and the plants and even inanimate things, which listen to him and obey him without question when some of his own brethren do not. When he tells the swallows to remain silent at Alviano so that his listeners can hear what he is saying, they obey him. When he asks the falcon to wake him in the night for prayer, it does so, and when he orders the man-eating wolf to stop attacking the villagers of Gubbio, it obeys. But most of all, his story is full of his love for Brother Jesus, who emptied himself of everything to enter into the world that was created through him and in him, just so that he could enter into us. For St Francis, this was the ultimate expression of the poverty that Brother Jesus chose to embrace. It was not just that he abandoned a home of absolute bliss to make his home amongst us, but that he finally humbled himself to enter into our common food and drink – bread and wine – to make his home within us, as he had promised at the Last Supper, and to lead us into the ultimate mystical union.

The vortex of supernatural life and love that endlessly revolves between the Father and the Son is the Holy Spirit, whom Francis wanted to be the inner dynamism that animated and ruled the brotherhood that he founded. From now on, these are the predominant themes that begin to characterize the preaching and teaching of Francis and the letters and the writings that he completed towards the end of his life.

In the long purification that Francis had recently undergone, inner sensual feelings only seemed to be dead because they were being systematically purified of the self-interest that had poisoned them before. Once the profound spiritual detoxification was over they returned to life, imbued with the sublime spiritual love that could now express itself through the senses. The human warmth, the compassion and the care for others that had been restricted before now overwhelmed all who met him. Sudden and emotional expressions of sheer joy and delight or moments of deep sadness and uncontrollable tears would now regularly overcome him, as he was transformed ever more fully with each passing day into 'the Second Christ', as he was soon to be called by his contemporaries.

The expression 'Mystical Marriage', used to describe the final stage of the mystic way, is preferable to the expression 'Transforming Union' because marriage is not the end but the beginning of a new phase of love, which is meant to go on deepening and developing throughout the rest of life. This is precisely what happened to Francis. His newfound love had no end: he not only wanted to give his all for the man who had given his all for him, but now a deep desire began to rise up within him to give his very life. For the first three centuries after the death of Christ martyrdom was seen as the perfection of the Christian life. Then asceticism came to be seen as the preparation for it, so that a believer would be ready and prepared for what came to be called 'the final sacrament of love'. It was for the early Christians the sign of the perfect disciple, the sign of perfect imitation and the sign of perfect identity with the Risen One. As his love for Brother Jesus grew and grew, Francis wanted to express that love by embracing this unique 'sacrament'.

Therefore shortly after arriving in Rome in 1212 Francis sought permission to go on the Crusade to the Holy Land with John of Brienne, brother of Walter whom Francis had wanted to serve as a knight eight years before. The desire to become a knight was not dead in him, but now he wished to become a spiritual knight who would fight with the sword of the spirit to convert the Muslims to the Christian faith. Then he wanted to visit the holy places to see for himself where Brother Jesus had been born, where he lived and died, and then to die for him and receive the 'sacrament of martyrdom'. Although storms in the Adriatic forced him to return to Italy, he set out the following year for Morocco with Bernard of Quintavalle, this time with martyrdom foremost in his mind. Again ill health forced him to return home and, fortunately for us, he now received Thomas of Celano into the Order. It was he who wrote the first life of Francis shortly after his death and then a second life, ten or more years later.

It is thanks to Thomas that we have the only detailed description of Francis:

> He was of middle height, inclining to shortness; his head was of moderate size and round, his face somewhat long and prominent, his forehead smooth and small: his eyes were black of moderate size and with a candid look. His hair was dark, his eyebrows straight, his nose symmetrical, thin and

straight, his ears upright but small, his temples smooth. His words were kindly but fiery and penetrating. His voice was powerful, sweet toned, clear and sonorous. His teeth were set close together, white and even. His lips were thin and fine, his beard black and rather scanty. His neck was slender, his shoulders straight, his arms short, his hands attenuated with long fingers and nails. His legs were slight, his feet small, his skin fine and his flesh very spare.

The description is not particularly flattering, but it was not the outside of the cup that mattered but the inside, which was so open and empty that he received the love of God until it overflowed onto all who met him. None of Francis' sermons survive, but Thomas assures us that they were delivered with passion and with what he described as 'ardent gestures and movements' that often had dramatic effects on his audience. There is a contemporary account of his preaching that has survived thanks to Thomas of Spalato, who heard him preach at Bologna in 1212:

> His tunic was dirty, his person unprepossessing and his face was far from handsome. But God gave such power to his words that many factions amongst the nobility, amongst whom the fierce anger of ancient feuds had been raging with much bloodshed, were brought to reconciliation. The reverence and devotion of his listeners was such that men and women rushed upon him anxious to touch the hem of his garment and to carry away bits of his clothing.

The more his fame spread, the more people worshipped the very ground he walked on. Celano, who must have seen for himself, writes that 'if he entered any city the clergy would be joyful, the bells would be rung and the men and women would be exalted and they would rejoice together, and children would clap their hands and often took branches off trees and went in procession to meet him singing psalms'.

He had an extraordinary way of reading people's hearts and minds, and there were many stories about cures and miracles too that were told after his 'visitations'.

In the years that followed his second attempt to go to the Holy Land, Francis spent much of his time involved in organizing the sudden growth of his fledgling Order. He gave his time relentlessly, dealing with the many disputes that were now beginning to surface concerning the interpretation of his rule and how it was to be observed. However, throughout all this, the desire to go to the Holy Land and to seek martyrdom was never extinguished. This desire burst into an unquenchable flame when he received news that six of his brothers had been martyred while preaching to the Muslims in Morocco. Taking Peter Cattani, Brother Illuminato and several others, he set out without delay, leaving someone else in charge. He arrived at Acre early in 1220. His stay was short but eventful. With Brother Illuminato as his companion he managed to speak before Melek-el-Kamel, the Sultan of Egypt, after the siege of Damietta. St Francis so impressed him that the crown of martyrdom had to be postponed, but not for long. The last five or more years of his life were one long continual martyrdom.

There are many different accounts of what went on between Francis and the Sultan, but as St Bonaventure derived his information from Brother Illuminato, who died as early as 1273, his account is probably the most reliable. When the Sultan asked where they had come from, Francis told him they had been sent to him by God to preach the Gospel to his people. Not surprisingly the Sultan was impressed with Francis and invited him to stay with him for a time. It was during his stay that Francis offered to walk into fire with the Sultan's own priests to prove whose faith was the more authentic, but his priests didn't seem too keen on the idea, nor did the Sultan when Francis offered to go it alone. What if he succeeded? The Sultan couldn't possibly become a Christian, no matter what miracles Francis performed, for he knew very well that to embrace the religion of his enemies was to sign his own death warrant. Francis refused the gifts that were offered to him, although it is generally believed that safe passage to visit the Holy Land was one that he accepted. But his time was running out.

A certain Brother Stephen of Narni arrived to say that there was trouble at home and so, with Peter Cattani and Elias of Cortona who had preceded them to the Holy Land, they made for Assisi. Innocent III had died a year after the Fourth Lateran Council in 1216, to be succeeded by Honorius III, so Francis went for help to Cardinal Hugolino, who had been appointed by him as the Cardinal Protector of the Order. The wrangles over the rule were many and lasted for almost three years. Inevitably, a rule written by Francis at Rivo Torto for no more than twelve men would have to be rewritten when, unexpectedly, almost 4,000 or more had poured into the Order by the time he had returned. However, that was not the problem. The problem lay in the sort of rule many now wanted. A new generation of friars, many of whom were priests and highly educated, wanted to water down the rule that Francis believed had been given to him by God himself.

It was for this reason that Francis decided that it was time to update the rule sanctioned verbally by Innocent III ten years before. As it had already been added to, over the years, to include various directives for religious orders that were promulgated at the Fourth Lateran Council and other directives agreed upon at general chapters of the Order, St Francis decided that it was time to incorporate all these additions in a new rule. Then at last it could receive the written approval of Pope Honorius III. This would also enable him to balance the predominantly legal additions with exhortations to live by the spirit of the first rule, despite the interpretations of those who wished to dilute it. For this purpose he employed the services of a highly erudite friar, educated at the University of Paris, who had recently been received into the Order by Brother Elias in the Holy Land, where he had been the provincial superior. His name was Caesar of Speyer and it was with his help that what came to be called the *Regula Non Bullata* was written by Francis and presented to the General Chapter in 1221. This rule, which still exists to this day, is an enduring testimony to the mind of Francis at the time, but it was nevertheless rejected by the ruling party as too strict. Disappointed, St Francis went to Fonte Columbo, where he was in the process of dictating a new version to Brother Leo when they had visitors – Brother Elias suddenly turned up with all the Italian 'Ministers Provincial'. Brother Leo tells us what happened in *The Mirror of Perfection*. The ministers had come to tell Francis that, from what they had heard, his new rule would be too strict and that they would not be bound by it. In his own words Brother Leo, who witnessed everything, tells us what happened next:

Then Francis lifted up his voice and cried out, 'Lord, answer for me' and then everyone heard the voice of Christ.

'Francis, there is nothing in this rule of yours that is not mine and I want it to be obeyed literally without interpretation, without interpretation, without interpretation! And whosoever will not obey it may leave the order.'

And then Francis turned to the brothers and said, 'Have you heard that? Or shall it be said once more to you?'

But the ministers went away terrified.

Bonaventure tells us that when this new rule was finally finished it was still too strict for the ministers, and soon after Brother Elias received it he conveniently claimed to have lost it. When Francis finished rewriting it this time he took it straight to Rome and to Cardinal Hugolino. After it had been heavily edited by the curial canonists at the insistence of Pope Honorius and Cardinal Hugolino, it was promulgated in a papal bull known as *Solet Annuere* in 1223. This came to be called the *Regula Bullata* because it had papal approval, as opposed to the *Regula Non Bullata*, which didn't. After all the work had been done, Francis stayed in Rome to catch his breath and rest for a time in one of the Cardinal's palaces.

He was not happy with the editing nor with the additions, but what could he do? So he spent what little time was left to him trying to put over what was so dear and so important to him, by his own personal example and by a series of personal letters and writings, the most important of which was his Testament. This is entirely his own work and shot through and through with the spirit that animated his whole life. To those who wished to do so, like Brother Leo, he gave special permission to live by the spirit of the rule, stripped of the interpretations and what he called the 'glosses' of those who did not understand it as he intended. He had wanted to add a clause to this effect in the final rule, enabling others to do likewise, even to the point of disobeying superiors, but for the canonists it was a non-starter.

The faction within the Order who wished to dilute the rule may well have had human prudence on their side, but when did human prudence produce saints like Francis of Assisi? The literal following of the rule – which was totally biblical and which he believed was given to him by God himself – most certainly produced one of the greatest saints that Christendom has ever known.

When St Francis had returned from the Holy Land the trouble causers had been removed from office and Peter Cattani put in charge of the Order. When he died the following year, Elias of Cortona took his place. Elias was an extremely able man but sadly dominated by the human wisdom with which he tried to rule rather than serve the Order. That's why he conveniently lost the first draft of the new rule that Francis wrote and opposed almost everything else that Francis wrote before he died.

Once the final rule was 'set in stone' and the Order was legally in the hands of Elias and bound to his interpretation, Francis was free of all responsibility whether he liked it or not. Henceforth he supplemented and exemplified his writings by the example of his own life. He wanted to live the Gospel as perfectly as possible. However, his health, which had never been good, grew worse with each passing day. He soon sensed that the end was not far away. For the last time he stayed briefly in Rome with Cardinal Hugolino, who had been for several years the 'go between' between him and those who could not accept the rule as he had chosen to write it. He took his leave from another too, whom he would never see in Rome again. She was a devoted follower of Francis, ten years younger than him, whom he had known well since his visit to Rome in 1212, just after he had preached to the birds near Bevagna. He said he knew the faces of only two women: Sister Clare and the Lady Jacoba de Settesoli whom he called 'Brother Jacoba'. She was an elegant aristocrat descended on her father's side from Norman nobility. She had been married at an early age to Gratiano Frangipani, a Roman nobleman. He was a direct descendant of Anicius Petrus who came to be called the 'Breaker of Bread' or, in Latin, *Frangens Panem,* for saving the poor of Rome from starvation in the eighth century. Her husband died shortly after she had given birth to two sons.

On leaving Rome in 1223 Francis made for the Rieti Valley and the hermitage of Fonte Columbo where he had written the rule. It was here that he had an idea which was to stain the memories and the imaginations of everyone with the mystery of the Incarnation. As Christmas drew near the following year, he approached John Vellita, who owned land in the vicinity of Greccio, and asked him for permission to use a cave on his property to re-enact the birth of Brother Jesus at Bethlehem. This involved bringing an ass and an ox into the cave and setting up a manger with a statue of the Christ-child lying in the straw. Francis was deacon at the Mass and spoke with such love and tenderness that many believed that the statue came alive as he cradled it in his arms. Whether this was true or not, one thing was for sure: Francis had brought back to life the humanity of Jesus Christ in the minds and in the imaginations of his contemporaries. His achievement was graphically symbolized by this event that took place in Greccio in the Christmas of 1224 and by its aftermath. Henceforth the practice of making cribs at Christmas spread all over the world and all down the centuries to the present day, to remind all of the world-shaking truth that is at the heart of Franciscan spirituality.

After Christmas the health of Francis seemed to get worse. The ascetic regime that he had imposed on himself hadn't helped. He had subjected 'Brother Body' to innumerable fasts and, when he did eat, it was his custom to spread ashes on his food so that he wouldn't enjoy it. He also slept little; when he did, he would use a stone or a piece of wood as a pillow. The hemorrhages from his stomach worsened and so did an eye infection that he had contracted in Egypt. It was time to prepare for the end, though there were two more years of daily martyrdom before it came. Francis set out for La Verna, the mountain which had been given to him by Count Orlando dei Cattani as a place of retreat ten years before. It was here that he began to pray as never before for the two things that he believed would enable him to attain perfect identity with Brother Jesus before he died.

Firstly, he prayed that he would be given the privilege to experience the suffering that Christ had had to endure on the cross. Secondly, that he would be given the privilege of experiencing the love that drove Christ to give his all for others. When he ordered Brother Leo to open the Gospel three times to find out God's will for him, and three times it was opened at the account of the passion of Jesus, he knew that his prayer would be answered. It was on the morning of September 14th 1224 that that prayer was answered in a way that he could never have expected. As he was once again praying for perfect union with Brother Jesus, he felt a flame of love burning within him with ever-increasing intensity. Then he looked up to see an angel that he was given to understand was a 'seraph', but although it had six wings – two above its head, two to cover its body, and two with which to fly – it had a human body: the body of a crucified man. As he gazed upon the vision with fear and trembling, Francis was simultaneously filled with joy. Then he was given to understand that it was not through physical martyrdom, which he had long since desired, that he would be transformed into Brother Jesus, but by the inner fire of love that had animated the whole of his life on earth.

When the vision finally disappeared, he experienced that love as never before, while at the same time his body was transformed into the likeness of the crucified man, enfolded by the wings of the seraph. The sources are all in agreement that he was left not just with wounds but with nails in those wounds. The heads of the nails were in his palms and on the top of his feet, while the sharp ends curled round underneath in such a way that it was possible to put a finger through the ring that they made. Although he tried to hide them from his brothers the blood was such that it soaked his clothing, particularly the blood from the wound in his side. Despite this, Francis was in a continual state of joy, which he expressed in a hymn that he composed, praising the God who had granted him all for which he had prayed.

In contrast, his closest friend and follower Brother Leo was depressed and dejected. Shortly before Francis had received the stigmata, he had rebuked Leo for 'spying' on him whilst he was at prayer in the middle of the night. It was something of a misunderstanding and Leo had been forgiven, but the memory of the rebuke came back to haunt him when, after receiving the stigmata, Francis seemed distant. The truth of the matter was that he had been swept up into a sublime spiritual stratosphere where he became all but oblivious of his brethren for a time, including Brother Leo. There was nothing personal; it was just that he had become so absorbed in the supernatural love that enveloped him that it had made him neglect his dear friend. He was not purposely giving him the cold shoulder for his innocent mistake, but nevertheless that's how Brother Leo took it.

Once he was told about it, Francis called Leo to him and reassured and consoled him by writing a special blessing just for him on the other side of the hymn of praise that he had just composed. Then he signed it with his own special signature that took the form of a 'Tau'. The Tau looked like a stylized cross in the form of the letter 'T' and it was usually colored red in remembrance of the blood that Christ had shed on his real cross. Innocent III had used it as a badge of the reform that he wanted to introduce into the Church and as a sign that the bearer had been designated as an instrument of that reform. That's why Francis used to paint it upon his door and his walls and sign his letters with it, and now it was used to sign his special gift to console Brother Leo. It is still used by many Franciscans to this day as a sign of their calling. It changed Brother Leo's darkness into light and he carried it with him at all times, next to his heart, until his dying day.

Francis traveled all the way back to Assisi on a donkey, for he couldn't walk. Nor could he see or hear much, because he was filled with such sublime joy that most of the time he was lost in ecstasy. But on his return he was filled with a new lease of life that enabled him to set off on brief missionary journeys in the surrounding countryside. It was the last flare of a flame that was about to peter out. Soon the first part of his prayer was about to be answered, as serious sickness enabled him to experience something of the sufferings that Brother Jesus had to endure on the cross. Yet it was when he was at his lowest ebb, living in a mud hut outside San Damiano and pestered by a plague of mice, that he wrote his beautiful poem in praise of Brother Sun. It was the first great poetic work to be written in the Italian language.

Most high, all powerful, all good Lord!
    All praise is yours, all glory, all honor, and all blessing.
To you, alone, Most High, do they belong.
    No mortal lips are worthy to pronounce your name.
Be praised, my Lord, through all your creatures,
    especially through my lord Brother Sun,
    who brings the day and you give light through him.
    And he is beautiful and radiant in all his splendor!
    Of you, Most High, he bears the likeness.
Be praised, my Lord, through Sister Moon and the stars;
    in the heavens you have made them bright, precious and
    beautiful.
Be praised, my Lord, through Brothers Wind and Air,
    and clouds and storms, and all the weather,
    through which you give your creatures sustenance.
Be praised, my Lord, through Sister Water;
    she is very useful, and humble, and precious, and pure.
Be praised, my Lord, through Brother Fire,
    through whom you brighten the night.
    He is beautiful and cheerful, and powerful and strong.
Be praised, my Lord, through our sister Mother Earth,
    who feeds us and rules us,
    and produces various fruits with colored flowers and
    herbs.
Be praised, my Lord, through those who forgive for love of
    you;
    through those who endure sickness and trial.
Happy those who endure in peace,
    for by you, Most High, they will be crowned.
Be praised, my Lord, through our Sister Bodily Death,
    from whose embrace no living person can escape.
    Woe to those who die in mortal sin!

Happy those she finds doing your most holy will.
The second death can do no harm to them.
Praise and bless my Lord, and give thanks,
and serve him with great humility.

The problem with his eyes became much worse and so painful that Brother Elias sent him to the Papal Court, now in residence at Rieti, to be treated by surgeons, who applied red-hot irons to his temples close by at Fonte Columbo where he and Brother Leo had worked on his rules. After blessing Brother Fire, Francis felt no pain at all from the irons, but his eyes pained him as before; so he was sent to Siena, a town famous for its eye specialists at that time, but they did no good. His doctors had all pleaded with him to treat his body with more respect. He now listened to their words of advice and took them to heart. He even asked pardon for the way he had treated his body throughout his life, but it was too late. It has to be said that he had always preached moderation to others, most of whom had listened, except, that is, for himself and Sister Clare at San Damiano. Saints are there to be admired and to inspire us, but their example should not always be followed infallibly as they were certainly not infallible. What is always infallible, however, is their best of intentions. When a person sees and experiences love being lavished on them, as Francis did, they feel impelled to express their thanks and their gratitude in ways that are not for the faint-hearted.

When his health worsened and he began to hemorrhage, it was thought that he was dying, so he begged to be taken home to Assisi. When he arrived at the hermitage of Le Celle near Cortona he began to suffer from dropsy too and his legs and feet swelled up. Then his stomach couldn't retain any food and he began to have severe pains in his spleen and in his liver. Fearing that the Perugians might kidnap Francis and bury him in their town to attract the pilgrims with their precious money, Brother Elias ordered him to be carried home by way of Gubbio, and sent a detachment of soldiers to guard him. Once back in his beloved Assisi he was taken to the Bishop's Palace, still under guard for fear of the Perugians. When Francis heard that, as usual, the bishop was at loggerheads with the mayor, he had an extra verse added to his 'Canticle to Brother Sun' in praise of peace and pardon, and ordered his brothers to sing it before them both. It was the last act of reconciliation that Francis performed before he died.

The moment his doctor told him that he would soon be dead, Francis opened his arms and cried, 'Welcome, Sister Death!' Then he added yet another verse to his poem, in praise of her. From now on he wouldn't let Brother Leo or Brother Angelo leave him. He wanted them by him at all times to sing about Sister Death whenever he wanted. Nor would he allow them to stop, despite the protestation of Brother Elias who feared people might doubt the sanctity of a man who made merry on his deathbed. If he wasn't to be revered as a saint then what was the use of the vast basilica Elias was planning to build as his tomb? No saint, no money. It was whilst he was still in the Bishop's Palace that Francis wrote his final Testament. It is a deeply moving document that reveals the real St Francis as he looks back on his life from his deathbed. Then it looks forward to try and ensure that those who come after him will remain faithful to the spirit of the Gospel that he lived by – and lived by to the end.

Suddenly his illness took a turn for the worse and he was plunged into terrible agony. Although he accepted what he had in fact prayed for, he was forced to admit that the sufferings were far worse than the martyrdom that he had once sought with such simplicity. The dropsy that had bloated his lower body seemed to fade away, leaving him looking more like a skeleton than anything else. Thinking he was dying, he placed his hand on Brother Elias and blessed him and confrere through him, the countless generations of brothers who would follow him in centuries to come. It wasn't the end but it wasn't far off, so he begged to be taken to the Portiuncula so that he might die in the poverty to which he had been accustomed all his life, surrounded by the brothers who loved it as he did.

The long procession that accompanied him came to a halt when it was halfway to its destination and Francis was raised up by two of his brothers to gaze upon his beloved Assisi for the last time. He could hardly see the bare Rocca with the remains of the German castle perched on its peak against the backcloth of the great Monte Subasio, with the hermitage of Le Carceri buried into her side. The walls he'd helped to build in his teens still framed an idyllic view of the town with its medieval houses huddled around the towers of the Cathedral of San Rufino where he was baptized. To the far right, outside the walls, was San Damiano, which he had rebuilt with his own hands after he had heard Jesus speak to him from the cross. Clare and her community were living there now, eager to hear any word about his well-being and his whereabouts and storming the gates of heaven on his behalf.

When he was settled into a small hut a few feet away from the little chapel of St Mary of the Angels, he insisted that he should be placed naked on the ground. When he was given clothes to wear, but warned under holy obedience that they were not his to give away, he was overcome with a frisson of joy that reverberated through his emaciated body. Now he was indeed at home again, away from the Bishop's Palace and back in a squalid little hut surrounded by all that would please his Lady Poverty. For those of us who have never traveled further than the foothills of the spiritual life, it is all but impossible to appreciate that for those who have reached the heights, their greatest joy is to express the otherworldly love that envelops them. Pleasure in suffering, which might elsewhere be seen as some perverse masochistic fetish, is, for one who is bursting and brimming over with spiritual joy, the only way to express their gratitude for the inexpressible love that they experience. Their joy is to suffer, at least for some of the time!

When he was placed into his simple bed Francis forgave all who asked his forgiveness and blessed all absent brothers who could not be there. Then he had a special blessing for Brother Bernard who had been the first to give all his money away and embrace Lady Poverty with him, and he commanded that all the brothers in the Order should honor Bernard as if he were Francis himself. His thoughts were then with Clare and her community at San Damiano and he sent her a message promising that they would see his body before the burial. He was in the middle of writing a letter urging Brother Jacoba to come quickly if she was to see him alive, when to his surprise and joy she arrived with her retinue and her two sons, having been alerted by news of his mortal illness. She had brought all that was necessary for his funeral, including a cushion for his head in the coffin (the pillow he had never permitted himself when alive), a veil for his face and a haircloth shroud. She also provided all the candles necessary for the funeral and for the wake and, confident that she would find him still alive, she brought some of the sugared almonds that he had loved as a rare treat when he had visited her in Rome. Although no woman was allowed in the Portiuncula, an exception was made for Brother Jacoba who knelt at the bed of Francis, bathing his body with her tears in such a way that her behavior was later likened by the friars to Mary Magdalene at the feet of Christ. At Jacoba's presence he seemed to rally for a while and she had thoughts of returning to Rome, but he knew the end wasn't far off and begged her to remain.

As the end drew near, the strains of his 'Canticle to Brother Sun' could be heard coming from his poor abode with the verses that he had added in praise of Sister Death. On Friday October 2nd he re-enacted a scene from the Last Supper. Taking bread, he broke it and shared it with the brothers who surrounded him. The following day at his request the Passion of St John was read to him. Then when he knew that Sister Death was about to arrive, he asked the doctor to announce her arrival and opened his arms to welcome her – and welcome her with joy, because it was she who was going to lead him to the gates of Eternal Life.

As he had ordered, Francis was stripped and laid down on the ground as naked as Brother Jesus had been when he was born into poverty and as naked as he had been when he died on the cross. Then, according to his wishes, dust and ashes were sprinkled over him as, in no more than a whisper, he intoned Psalm 41: '*Voce mea ad Dominum clamavi.*' ('With my voice I cry out to the Lord.') When his brothers bent over him at the end of the psalm it was to see that his prayer had been answered; Sister Death had indeed led him to the gates of Eternal Life. The silence that followed was broken only by his favorite birds – a flock of larks which descended on the roof of his hut. They sang like larks ascending, half in sadness, half in joy, as their brother ascended to the place whence they had all ultimately been conceived and into the Brother in whom they had all been created.

Once a body is relieved of the suffering that precedes death, it often seems that it is bathed with a bygone beauty, as the muscles that were recently so tense and taut, trying to bear the pains of the final agony, relax and are at rest. By all accounts this was true of Francis, but there was something further. His whole body, once weather-worn and swarthy, seemed to take on the hue of pure white marble. In stark contrast to the black nails that remained embedded in the flesh, it seemed to be as white as snow and all but translucent. Later, Brother Leo was to liken his body at that moment to the body of Christ when it was taken down from the cross and placed in Mary's arms.

The contemporary descriptions remind me of that artistic masterpiece painted by Cimabue that stands in the apse of the Church of La Santa Croce in Florence. The crucified Christ is depicted on the cross the very moment after his death. Despite the nails that keep the body fixed, spread-eagled to the post and crossbeam, it is nevertheless soft and supple now that the ravages of death have passed. But further to this, the delicate work of the master craftsman has made the body look transparent, as if one is gazing upon it at the very moment when it is beginning to fade away into another dimension. It is the closest that I have ever seen to a depiction of the beginnings of the glorification that began the moment Christ died.

The next day a massive procession of friars and townsfolk followed the body of Francis to its place of temporary burial in the Church of San Giorgio where St Clare had first heard him speak. This was of course not before the cortège had stopped at San Damiano, so that St Clare and her community could say their last farewells. Like Brother Jacoba, Clare bathed his body with her tears and reverently kissed the marks made by the stigmata.

During the days that followed his burial, it was as if a heavy black pall was spread over the little Umbrian town. But gradually the pall lifted, lightened and evaporated to be replaced by a distinctive aura that to this day seems to surround and pervade Assisi. It is an aura of peace, the peace 'that surpasses the understanding'. It speaks, even to the most skeptical visitor, of the one characteristic above all others that impressed all who met the man who once lived there, the supreme ambassador of peace. On July 16th 1228 Pope Gregory IX, the one-time Cardinal Hugolino, friend of Francis and protector of the Order, canonized this 'ambassador of peace'; and two years later, on May 25th 1230, his body was taken for burial to the newly completed Basilica of San Francesco.

With the agony and the ecstasy of the last years that Francis spent on earth there was a certain holy truce that bound all his 'family' together as one. The stigmata, the only case that the church has ever officially recognized, seemed to have stamped the divine approval on his teaching in such a way that what had been questioned before was now hardly questioned at all, at least for the time being. However, as so often happens once the funeral is over, family squabbles began to assert themselves.

Soon separate factions were voicing different interpretations of the teaching and way of life of Francis, raising questions about how these should be understood in an ever-expanding religious order. The massive proliferation of writings that was produced within a generation of his death was witness to the myriad differences that threatened to destroy the Order.

The Omnibus of Franciscan Sources is about three inches thick and a little short of 2,000 pages long – and these are just the most prominent of the early sources. They are a minefield for any serious historian who wants to discover the real Francis, stripped of the many spurious interpretations that he would have deplored. The task is daunting. However, with his letters and other brief writings, all agree that the Testament is entirely his own work and shines like the sun through the clouds of so many other ambivalent works written by those with their own agendas. As the years turned into centuries these interpretations became legion, not only within the Franciscan family and the Christian churchesbut in other religions too. The simple transparent goodness of the Poverello of Assisi claimed the hearts of so many who saw in him a man they admired and wished to claim as their own. Sadly, the temptation to re-create Francis in their own image and likeness has proved irresistible for all too many.

In the immediate aftermath of his funeral there can be no doubt that the spirit of the primitive observance lived on amongst the three companions – Brother Leo, Brother Angelo and Brother Rufino – and those who looked to them for leadership. In the Second Order that same spirit lived on in St Clare and in her devoted sisters at San Damiano, and in the Third Order it found a unique embodiment in Brother Jacoba, who did not return to Rome but stayed on in Assisi where she lived out the rest of her life. Her home became the meeting place for the many faithful followers of Francis and her presence was a continual support to all who turned to her for whatever help she was able to provide. It would seem that she outlived St Clare, who died in 1253, and

Brother Leo who died in 1274.

Although, in the centuries that followed, the authentic spirit of Francis was regularly diluted beyond all recognition, this was happily not the whole story. Virtually every generation of Franciscans has produced its own reforms and its own reformers, eager to replicate in their own lives the primitive way of life that had first inspired Francis. The histories of these movements are deeply inspiring, but it is a history that will have to be explored elsewhere. On this pilgrimage we will restrict ourselves to studying the profound spirituality that was personified in the man the Medievals called 'the Second Christ'.

Chapter 3

A Change of Plans

The train to Florence was so packed that we couldn't all sit together. Peter and David were in one compartment and Bobbie and I were in another.

'What did you think of it?' said Bobbie as I handed the booklet back to her.

'Very good,' I replied. 'It was accurate and concise and does something that nobody else I've read has attempted.'

'What's that?' asked Bobbie.

'By analyzing the events of his life it manages to uncover the personal spiritual development of Francis – that was new. By the way, have you any idea of the itinerary?'

'No, not really,' said Bobbie. 'All I know is that we leave for Assisi immediately after my profession.'

'Your profession! Do you mean you're going to become a nun?'

'Oh no!' exclaimed Bobbie, bursting into hysterics. 'No, not a nun, but like you I'm going to be received into the Third Order. I came out here three months ago to stay with Emelia. She's the president of the Florentine branch, the first province to be formed in the lifetime of Francis. It is into her hands that I will make my profession tomorrow.'

I had no idea about all this, but why should I? My mind had been on other things, and in the few days that I had spent at Walsingham House there had been so much to do and so much else to talk about.

In a recent BBC opinion poll Tuscany had been voted the best place to live in Europe, and as Emelia drove the four of us to Castagnoli I was not surprised to hear it. I was simply spellbound by all that I saw. The scenery was stunning and so was the position of Emelia's farmhouse home, 2,000 feet up in the hills and twenty minutes from Siena.

After supper that evening Peter made an announcement. There would be a change to our plans. We wouldn't be going to Assisi the following day. After the profession we would be free. Those who so wished might like to visit Siena and in the evening we would be told details of the change of plans. This suited me fine. I didn't know that there were any plans in the first place – everything had happened so quickly – and the thought of being able to visit Siena delighted me.

The residential part of the farmhouse sprawled over the byres and barns below. All the rooms, including the kitchen and the bedrooms, opened off a large sitting room with stunning views over the Tuscan countryside that fell away from what, thanks to Emelia, had become a house of prayer. A flight of stone steps led up to a chapel within a large tower that presided over the old farmhouse. Several visitors came to the profession from Siena, where Bobbie had first been introduced to the local members of the Florentine Province three months before. Naturally David presided at the Mass and said a few words before the profession took place. Frankly he looked exhausted and kept his words to a minimum. But what he did say was personal and deeply moving because they came from the heart, albeit from the heart of an exhausted man.

He thanked Bobbie for all she had done for him. As a psychiatrist she had diagnosed his dyslexia and explained his life to him – a life he had never understood before. But there was something else that she was able to do for him, thanks to her diploma in theology. It was to remind him 'in the most sensitive way possible' of the words of St Thomas Aquinas: *Nemo dat quod non habet*. In other words, you can't give what you don't have. If you don't have anything to give because you are too tired then go and rest. This was not just Bobbie's advice for him but the advice of one of the most ascetic of all Franciscan saints, St Peter of Alcantara, the Spanish reformer. After the ceremony, when all the visitors had departed, Emelia, Bobbie and I set off to explore Siena while Peter and David stayed behind for a long overdue rest.

It was love at first sight. I had of course been enormously impressed with Florence, but we hadn't had enough time to visit the Duomo or any of the other churches (save one), or any of the museums, nor the incomparable Uffizi. Michelangelo's *David* would have to wait for another time. I was delighted that the only church we did visit was La Santa Croce, to see Cimabue's master-piece: the stunning crucifix that hangs in the apse dominating the church. It has to be seen to be believed. We all gazed in silence at the sublime and deeply spiritual masterwork that David had described so movingly in *The Second Christ*. The only other stop in the city was at Ponte Vecchio to do the 'tourist thing', but we didn't stop for long. The many jewelers' shops on the bridge didn't really interest a group of Franciscan pilgrims, though I did notice that the female of the species would have liked to linger longer. Emelia made one last stop outside the city, high up on the hillside on the south bank of the River Arno, so that we could see the magnificent panorama of the capital of the Renaissance from the Piazza Michelangelo.

Nevertheless it was the smaller but perfectly formed Siena that I fell for, with its awe-inspiring Piazza del Campo surrounded by the Palazzo Pubblico, with its towering Torre del Mangia and various Palazzi Signorili, gazing down on the site where the Palio takes place every July and August. I was deeply moved when I visited the birthplace of St Catherine of Siena and the room into which she retired for three years of solitary prayer, like Francis before her. Without this preparation neither of them would have had anything to give when they finally emerged. When they did come out, both were tempted to return to spend the rest of their lives enjoying the eremitical way of life. It was only when it was made clear to them that they weren't called just to enjoy the pleasures of mystical contemplation for themselves but to serve the needs of others, that they abandoned their solitude for the world that was awaiting them. But neither saint ever forgot to keep returning to the place where they had received what they were called to give to others, knowing that if they didn't, they would have nothing to give – as Bobbie had just reminded us, *Nemo dat quod non habet.*

Emelia took us to see the very spot where the great Franciscan reformer St Bernadine of Siena used to preach. He too had spent years in solitude before he exploded onto the city with his dynamic sermons that drew tens of thousands to listen to him for hours on end. For him a 'short' sermon would last three hours, but this deterred nobody. Not even the great Duomo could contain all who wanted to listen to him, so a large pulpit was built in the shadow of the Torre del Mangia. It had its own pole on which a flag was hoisted shortly before he was due to speak, so that his listeners could position themselves directly before the prevailing wind to catch his every word.

David did not appear with his brother for supper. Apparently he had been brought his meal on a tray in his room and was not to be disturbed, so we weren't surprised when he didn't turn up for the meeting after supper when Peter was to address us. Peter had worn his Third Order habit for Bobbie's profession, as had the other members of the Third Order from the Florentine Province, but I never saw him wear it again throughout the rest of the pilgrimage. So when he sat down to address us in the sitting room he was wearing an old pair of black corduroys and a large navy-blue Guernsey. It was surprisingly cold in the evening, but after all we were over 2,000 feet above sea level.

'I don't need to tell you that my brother is exhausted,' said Peter, looking at the floor in front of him, so we couldn't see the emotions betrayed in his eyes. 'You see, in recent years demand has turned him into little more than a retreat-giving machine, mainly because he couldn't say no. Well, he has, quite frankly, come to the end of his tether and I have convinced him that he simply can't go on, or he will have a breakdown and then he will be no good to anyone. Naturally he feels that he is letting you all down because he was going to lead the pilgrimage, but I have insisted that that is now quite out of the question. So I have managed to convince him that I can take his place. Of course I don't know Franciscan Italy as well as he does, but Emelia does, and of course Italian is her first language. She has therefore agreed to take David's place as our guide, while I'll try to take his place explaining Franciscan spirituality.

'I have had a talk with Emelia and she has made a few phone calls – so this is what we are going to do. Tomorrow morning we will leave first thing for Assisi. In the afternoon we will leave Assisi for Montefalco, where we will stay for several days at the guesthouse attached to the Friary of San Fortunato. Each day, we will visit Assisi and return to base in the early afternoon for rest, reflection and personal prayer. Then we will meet each evening after supper to talk over our experiences and I will try to put everything in context and answer any questions that have arisen during the day.

'On the final day we will go to La Verna. It's quite a long trip so I have allocated the following day as a rest day. After that we will split up and spend three days of solitude in different hermitages to digest all that we have received and for personal prayer. The format of the pilgrimage is not original. It was used by Madame de Gaye, the provincial of the Parisian Third Order who brought me here on pilgrimage over fifteen years ago. It was she who received me into the Third Order in Paris shortly before I left for my new home in the Outer Hebrides. However, nothing is set in stone; if the weather or opportunity dictates otherwise, we can change our plans at a moment's notice.'

Peter smiled and looked up for the first time. He had spoken in an almost funereal tone of voice, but who was to blame him?

He had a lot on his mind and a lot to rearrange at such short notice.

'Any questions?' he said, as he looked at all of us for the first time with that unforgettable smile which his friends knew so well.

'Where is David going?' asked Bobbie.

Although Peter had never met Bobbie before, he read her concern perfectly.

'He phoned up a friend of his, Father Anthony, who is using his sabbatical to spend a year in solitude at Fonte Columbo. Michael has kindly offered to drive him there. You see, Michael has done this pilgrimage many times before, so he wasn't coming with us anyway. He and Emelia have just returned from a long stay in England visiting their children, so he is weeks behind with his garden work, which keeps them almost self-sufficient in fruit and vegetables.'

Emelia and Michael went to the kitchen to clean up after supper. Bobbie went to see David, and Peter went up the stone steps to the chapel. I did make a rather perfunctory attempt to help with the washing up but Emelia ushered me out. I didn't protest too much – it had been a hectic day and I was tired out so I went straight to bed. But I didn't fall asleep immediately. Something Peter had said jogged my memory and raised unanswered questions in my mind. Several years after my first meeting with Peter in the Outer Hebrides, it was believed that he had been 'lost at sea'. The funeral was even held without his body. Then, as both his brothers were away in Africa and nobody was able to reach them, I had spent the best part of a week sorting everything out. Before I'd finished, Peter suddenly turned up safe and sound after an extraordinary adventure that I have written about elsewhere. It was while reading one of his journals about his early spiritual life that I had come across the Madame de Gaye to whom he had just referred.

What kept me awake, however, was not the thought of her but

of her beautiful daughter Françoise, with whom Peter had fallen in love just after he had committed himself to the life of a hermit! I have written about this extraordinary love affair elsewhere, so I won't repeat it. That night I wasn't just wondering about the past but about the present. Where was Françoise now? Had they kept in touch over the years? Was she herself still living in the Third Order hermitage near Foligno where they had last met fifteen years ago? It was these unanswered questions that kept me awake. They put a stop, for the first time, to the endless pining for Elizabeth that had been ruining my sleep for days, so when I did finally drop off it was to have the best night's sleep since she had abandoned me.

Chapter 4

Spirituals and Fraticelli

David was fast asleep when we left at first light, but Bobbie was satisfied that he was fit enough to travel and she had made him promise to ring her if he needed help. We would have been in need of medical attention ourselves had Emelia not executed a brilliant emergency stop to prevent our car crashing into the postman – and all for a single letter. Emelia handed it to Peter with a look that said, How on earth did they know where to find you? He read it quickly, smiled and put it in his inside pocket.

The countryside was stunning, especially at that time in the morning when the air was intoxicating. It was so clean and pure that it was simply a joy to breathe. We made such good progress that we reached Lake Trasimeno by about ten o'clock.

'We should be arriving at Assisi in about forty minutes,' said Emelia who was driving the car with Peter beside her.

Trasimeno is not as large or as beautiful as Lake Garda in the north which is surrounded by the Alps, but that morning, as the summer heat was already rising, I for one would have loved to plunge into her clear blue waters.

Suddenly Peter began speaking to Emelia in Italian. His Italian seemed quite fluent – after all, he had studied modern languages at the Sorbonne before he retired into solitude. The pilgrimage was punctuated by these tête-à-têtes in Italian between Peter and Emelia, partly because Peter wanted to bring his Italian up to speed and partly, as we discovered, to discuss changes in the itinerary and get Emelia's approval before announcing them to Bobbie and me. On this occasion it was to announce a change in the itinerary. I thought Peter had been seduced by the limpid waters of the lake, which sparkled in the morning sunlight. Its serenity seemed to be accentuated by what looked like a toy ferryboat, making little rivulets on its way to a tumbledown pier hardly 200 meters in front of us.

'Look,' said Peter, 'I've just had an idea and Emelia agrees with me. We're going to stop here and take a trip on the ferry to visit the largest island on the lake, Isola Maggiore, where Francis spent the whole of Lent in 1211 fasting and praying in preparation for Easter. The island was uninhabited in the time of Francis but a large friary was built there a hundred years after he died, though it was abandoned at the end of the nineteenth century.'

Although I was delighted to visit the island, especially as it was such a beautiful day, I couldn't help wondering why we should start our pilgrimage there when Assisi was hardly more than half an hour away. We could easily have visited the lake on our way back, but I had reckoned without Peter and without his uncanny sense of care and compassion, which enabled him to realize that I needed to clear my heart and mind before I could give my undivided attention to the pilgrimage ahead. The jaunt was improvised not to enjoy a sumptuous picnic on an enchanted island but to give me the opportunity to talk. Of course I had already spoken to Bobbie and she had been an immense help, but I needed to talk to Peter too. He was still my spiritual director and I knew only he could give me the help that I needed to let me move on in life without Elizabeth.

'I was so sorry to hear about your bereavement,' said Peter after the picnic, as if Elizabeth had died – which in a sense she had, at least to me. 'How did it all happen?'

Although I'd already given a blow-by-blow account of what I considered to be a terrible betrayal to Bobbie, I went over everything again. Peter was genuinely compassionate, because he had suffered a similar bereavement too.

'I know it's of little comfort when someone says "I know how you feel", when you know they couldn't possibly, but I really do,' he said.

It was not just the tone of Peter's voice that made me believe him but the truth about his own love found, and love lost, that I had read about in his personal papers. Then he told me about his love for Madame de Gaye's daughter Françoise. When he had finished he spoke to me decisively and with authority.

'Before this pilgrimage is over, you will meet the person you are to marry. I feel quite sure about it.'

Peter's words carried such conviction and authority that I couldn't possibly doubt them, but I had no idea who he was thinking about.

As it was too late to go to Assisi, yet another change of plans set us off in another direction. This time it was Emelia who suggested a brief diversion to the ancient hermitage of Le Celle, close to the town of Cortona less than ten miles to the north. The guidebooks will tell you that it only takes forty minutes to walk to Le Celle from Cortona. Don't believe them. It is a beautiful walk that's worth the effort, but we could see that it would be too much for Peter. He wore an iron caliper on his right leg due to a polio attack when he was only six.

The hermitage is hidden behind a fold in the hillside that hides its rather dramatic contours until the last minute when its sheer size, at least for a hermitage, takes you by surprise. It is an amazing sight to see it spilling down the precipitous slopes of Monte Sant'Edigio until it has to stop suddenly to save itself falling into a crevasse that carries the waters of the Vignone below. At first sight it looks more like a monastic prison than a Franciscan hermitage, especially if you are familiar with the other hermitages that Francis used to frequent, but Le Celle has a history that explains its unusual size, as I was to hear later.

Taking the old stone bridge across the Vignone, we entered the ancient sanctuary to see the cell once used by Francis, with nothing but a stone bed for him to lie on and a wooden pillow to rest his head. The friar who showed us round told us that Francis had first come here after his sojourn on Isola Maggiore. His preaching deeply moved the inhabitants of Cortona, most particularly one of its most important and richest citizens called Guido, who promptly gave all his possessions away and with Francis founded a new home in the crevices that carved a network of small caves into the side of Monte Sant'Edigio. There was a little church nearby dedicated to St Michael the Archangel. The ancient little churches that you often find near caves used as hermitages by Francis usually indicate that the caves had been inhabited by other hermits long before him. He was merely making use of them for himself and his followers. Eventually the adjacent buildings had to be added to accommodate those who wished to steep themselves in the same contemplative stillness where Francis received what he gave to others.

The caves used by Francis, and the original hermitage built by Guido for those who joined him, are hidden at the back of the Convento delle Celle, as it is called today, so we were unable to see them. Our guide told us that another Franciscan who was received into the Order at Cortona, about the same time as Guido, had also been touched by the preaching of Francis. It was the infamous Brother Elias. After he had been removed from office as General of the Order, he moved to Le Celle, but it was too stark and spartan for him so he moved into Cortona. Here he built San Francesco with a friary to which he lured some of Guido's companions who had found the simple eremitical life too burdensome to bear.

Our guide told us that from about 1285, long after Guido had died, a heretical sect called the Fraticelli took over Le Celle until 1318 when they were expelled. Then the hermitage became vacant until 1537 when the Cappuccini moved in, and they have been there ever since. I wanted to ask who these people were, but as everybody else seemed to know I didn't feel like making a fool of myself, so I decided to keep my powder dry and ask Peter later. I was disappointed that our guide didn't take us to see the caves and the first hermitage built by Guido, but they were hidden behind the door marked 'Enclosure'. Instead our guide led us into the church and left us to do what generations of hermits had done before us. It was indeed a privilege to pray in a place that was sanctified not only by Francis' first visit to Le Celle but most of all by his final visit when he was suffering so much, only a short time before his death. It was this final visit that came into my mind, as I realized that it was in that solitary cell, the one we had just seen, that his stigmatized body would have been laid on his way from Siena to Assisi. It was not a body bathed in glory but racked with pain.

I was so lost in my own macabre meditation that I didn't notice an old and saintly-looking friar until he was a few meters away, as he shuffled towards us down the centre aisle of the church. He briefly glanced at the four of us as he made his way to the back. Only Peter failed to notice him because he was lost in prayer, but the aged friar must have noticed him because he came back to have a second look. Then he made his way along the pew in front of us until he was directly in front of Peter. He looked at him for the third time and said, 'Peter, Peter, is that you?'

Peter opened his eyes and peered in front of him for a moment or two as if he had just returned from another world; then he looked into the old man's eyes until recognition brought him to his senses.

'Antonio!' he exclaimed. 'Is that you?'

The two men embraced each other like long-lost brothers.

'Why didn't you tell me you were coming?' asked the old man.

'But I did!' said Peter. 'I wrote to you only a week ago to say that I would be coming to see you.'

'Of course,' said Antonio. 'You would have written to Monte Casale, but Padre Bernardino arranged for me to be moved here, because he felt I was getting too old to look after myself in my hermitage.'

Then Peter excused himself and asked us to wait a few minutes as the two of them disappeared into the enclosure.

Bobbie and I exchanged glances and we both nodded to each other, smiling simultaneously. This was indeed the famous physicist turned hermit who had been such a help to Peter when he had stayed at Monte Casale over fifteen years ago. What a thrill to meet the man I had read about in Peter's writings and whose profound teaching on mystical theology had been such a help to me too! So much had already happened that day. I had so much to digest, but despite everything, within a few minutes my mind went back to my meeting with Peter on Isola Maggiore and the decisive way he had assured me that I would meet the woman I was to marry. Whatever did he mean? Whoever did he mean? Surely he couldn't have been thinking of Bobbie. But why not? I thought. I just didn't know what to think nor did I have any time for it anyway as I saw Peter coming back into the church with Antonio. We all left the church so that Peter could introduce us properly. And what a privilege it was too! He was a delightful and genuinely holy man. I felt sure that if Francis had lived to the same age he would have been exactly the sort of kindly, caring human being that I had just met in Antonio.

Peter told us his whole story on the way to Montefalco. Unbeknown to Peter I knew it all from his personal papers, but the others didn't, so they were fascinated to hear how Peter, like me, had had a breakdown when his beloved wife died in child-birth.

It was getting late so we drove straight to the Friary of San Fortunato outside the town of Montefalco. We only had enough time to be shown to our rooms and to have a wash and brush-up before dinner.

After dinner we all met together in the common room to reflect on the first day of our pilgrimage. When nobody else seemed to have any questions, I asked Peter who the Fraticelli and the Cappuccini were – the groups mentioned by our guide while showing us around Le Celle. Peter put his head in his hands for a full minute before removing them to reveal a broad grin. It was not his usual smile but more of a grimace.

'I was dreading that question,' he said, as his grimace faded into a genuine smile. 'You see,' he went on, 'the question that you ask seems so simple and yet the answers are so complicated. All I can do this evening is to give a very brief overall view of the reforms that took place after the death of Francis, for this is the only context that will enable me to give you the answer to your question.'

We all gave Peter our undivided attention, in such a way that it was clear that Emelia and Bobbie were no wiser than me.

'There were already different factions in the new Order even when Francis was alive,' Peter began, 'but after his death they came out into the open, and two main schools of thought became apparent. They eventually came to be called the "Spirituals" and the "Conventuals", though inevitably within each there were many shades of opinion. The Spirituals looked to Brother Leo and his companions as their inspiration and they wanted to base their way of life on the way that Francis had lived with his close companions. They were particularly devoted to every word of his last Testament, which was for them the prism through which they viewed and interpreted his rule. Absolute poverty, as Francis had understood it, was the hallmark of their way of life but only as the outer expression of a deep inner poverty. It was this inner poverty that would open them, through profound contemplative prayer, to the same Holy Spirit whom Francis had wanted to be named as Minister General of his Order in his final rule. That's why the Spirituals loved to live in hermitages where they could spend protracted periods of time receiving what they felt called to give to others.

'The Conventuals insisted that they were no less devoted to Francis as their founder and to his teaching, which they revered, but they argued that what was an admirable way of life for Francis and his first followers could not possibly be maintained a dozen or more years later. When as many as 5,000 new recruits joined the fledgling Order even before he died, Francis' primitive ideas and ideals had to be adapted accordingly or anarchy would reign supreme. Even Francis saw this, they argued. That's why he made Brother Elias the Minister General after Peter Cattani had died. He saw and admired in Elias the organizational and administrative skills that he himself lacked. When more and more learned men and priests joined the Order, it was only to be expected that the Church authorities would see it as the instrument to bring about the reform in the Church that Innocent III had deemed so necessary at the Fourth Lateran Council in 1215.

'In order to do this successfully, successive popes dispensed the friars from certain interpretations of the rule that would hinder this reform. And in order to maintain the requisite learning, they needed to study. They also needed teachers, books and libraries and so they needed larger houses or convents – that's where the word "conventual" comes from.

'For three centuries these two distinct schools of thought persisted under the umbrella of one and the same Order. Of course there were squabbles and there was in-fighting, not only between the two main schools but also within each of them, as everyone fought to claim legitimacy for their particular interpretation of the rule. For a time, unity was maintained under the influence of wise Ministers General, like the scholar and mystic Bonaventure, whom some have called the second founder of the Order. Although he was in sympathy with those who wanted to adapt the Order to better serve the needs of the world, he was also deeply committed to the aspirations of the Spirituals, sometimes called the *Zelanti*. He spent time with them in their hermitages, where he practiced the profound contemplative prayer that he wrote about in his mystical masterpiece *Itinerarium Mentis in Deum*, "The Journey of the Mind into God", written in his cell at the hermitage of La Verna.

'Nevertheless the Conventuals gradually seemed to gain the upper hand when many of the Spirituals were discredited, when they were caught up in the fanciful teachings of Joachim of Fiore towards the end of the thirteenth century. He left his Cistercian monastery to found a more austere branch of the Order at Fiore. It was here that he wrote his controversial writings which he submitted to Rome, but he died in 1202 before any judgment was passed on them.

'The essence of his teaching was this: he divided history up into three periods. The first was "The Age of the Father", which encompassed the Old Testament. It was characterized by fear and servile obedience and was ruled by married people. The second period was "The Age of the Son", characterized by faith and filial obedience, and ruled by the clergy. The final period was called "The Age of the Holy Spirit", and it would be characterized by love and liberty and would be led by monks in the immediate future. It would herald what was called the "Everlasting Gospel", which would usher in an age of universal love. The final age, he insisted, would be inaugurated by the "Angel of the Sixth Seal", whom the Spirituals identified with Francis, and would be led by barefooted monks whom they identified with themselves. Some of the Spirituals took Joachim's teaching too literally and too far, taking them outside the Church; they elected their own superiors and had their own bishops who ordained priests to serve them, and they encouraged women to preach the good news of the Everlasting Gospel. They came to be called the *Fraticelli*. This was the cult which occupied Le Celle from 1285 until 1318 when they were thrown out by the Inquisition, which tortured many of them to make them recant. Those who wouldn't were burnt alive. However, there were small groups of Fraticelli all over Europe, and many of them survived and flourished for a hundred years and more, thanks to their radical ideas about poverty. When they held that the Church should be poor like Francis, they received the support and patronage of many of the landed classes, from the Emperor downwards, and that included several kings who coveted the Papal States and the riches invested in the Church.

'Not all the Spirituals became Fraticelli but most of them became tarred with the same brush, so they had to keep their heads down whilst they watched the Conventuals thrive. Eventually, inspired by the Spirituals and their attempts to follow as closely as possible the life that Francis had lived with his first followers, Paul de Trinci from Foligno received permission to live with a few like-minded friars at Brogliano, high up in the hills above his hometown. From slow beginnings this new reform finally took off when men of learning and great spiritual stature joined their ranks, including St Bernadine of Siena, St John of Capistrano, St James of the Marches and Blessed Albert of Sarteano. In time they came to be known not as Spirituals but as "Observants".

'The same sort of controversies that divided the Conventuals from the Spirituals in the thirteenth century divided the Conventuals and the Observants in the fourteenth and the fifteenth centuries, until they became separate orders in 1517. After this date the Observants came to be called "Friars Minor" or "Friars Minor of the Strict Observance".

'However, a certain Observant lay brother called Matteo da Bascia thought that even the Friars Minor of the Strict Observance were getting too lax. It was his inspiration that resulted in the foundation of another Franciscan order in 1225. Although he left to inspire the new foundation, he returned to die as an Observant, leaving others to complete the work he had inspired. They came to be called the "Capuchins". It was they who took over the deserted hermitage at Le Celle where they have remained to this day.

'Does that answer your question?' asked Peter.

He smiled with pleasure when we all simultaneously nodded

with approval.

'So that's why the friars we saw today wear a different habit to David?' inquired Bobbie.

'Yes, that's right,' said Peter. 'You see, as a sign that he wanted to return to live exactly as Francis had lived, Matteo chose to wear a pyramid-shaped hood attached to a single tunic, and those who followed him chose to wear a short beard too for the same reason. The hood David wears is detachable from the tunic, like the habits worn by the Conventual Friars, but their habits are grey. They all call themselves Friars Minor and place the letters "OFM" after their names, which stands for "Order of Friars Minor". To distinguish themselves from the other two, the Conventuals write "OFM conv" after their names and the Capuchins write "OFM cap", whereas the descendants of the Observants simply write "OFM".

'Well, that will have to do for now. Tomorrow we start our pilgrimage proper with our first visit to Assisi. Last night I read David's brief *The Second Christ* and I'm pleased to hear that you have all read it. It's an excellent summary that I, for one, could not better. What I will have to say to you is by way of a commentary on his work. I will try to show you, with Emilia's help, the places closely associated with Francis' own personal spiritual journey and his unique vision. Then I will try to expand on its crucial significance, not just for the Order that he founded and for the Church he was called to "rebuild" but for the whole of Christian spirituality. It was through him that it experienced a "new spring", which replicated the spiritual teaching and ethos that prevailed at the dawn of Christianity. In short I will try to do as an amateur what my brother would have done as a professional, if his health hadn't let him down.'

We thanked Peter for all that he had said and went to bed early, dreaming about our visit to Assisi the following day, though I woke up in the middle of the night dreaming about something else.

Chapter 5

Lady Poverty and Prayer

I was bursting with anticipation as we approached Assisi. My excitement heightened as I saw St Mary of the Angels to the right with the fabulous vistas of the old town in front of us. But I was disappointed when we didn't stop in Assisi but swept through the narrow streets and out the other side to begin the ascent of Monte Subasio. Then to my surprise and delight we stopped outside Le Carceri. I had seen pictures of it many times before, but none of them could conjure the aura that surrounded the most atmospheric place to which I had ever been.

There was no need for the sign requesting visitors to remain silent in respect for one of the most holy and hallowed hermitages in Franciscan Italy. In a matter of minutes everyone is encompassed by a sense of otherworldliness that makes even the most skeptical person question the frenetic life which they once described as the 'real' world, and which they are suddenly tempted to abandon forever. I was not surprised when Peter told us that it was here that he had finally decided to give himself up to the eremitical life in the name of Francis, for the saint's heart and soul can be savored here in his beloved caves more than anywhere else.

As at Le Celle, there was a little church here for the hermits who had consecrated the place long before it was reconsecrated by the presence of Francis, Sylvester, Rufino and the other solitaries who followed them. There is no sense of the struggles that led them on to experience the 'peace that surpasses the understanding' but only a sense of the peace itself, which seems to have penetrated and permeated the walls. They still seem to exude the profound tranquility that these Franciscan mystics finally attained.

The outer buildings were mainly added at the time of Bernadine of Siena. Thanks to him, there was a sudden upsurge of would-be Franciscans, which made him extend the primitive hermitages so that the newcomers could be formed by solitary prayer and contemplation.

After we had explored every nook and cranny of this enchanting spiritual oasis, we were shown into a tiny parlor by a simple lay brother bribed by Emelia's inimitable charm. There was just enough room for us to sit around an ancient table on which the good brother had placed a jug of cool scented water and four glasses. Peter opened a small briefcase and took out a sheaf of notes and a couple of books. He was obviously taking his new role seriously.

'You were no doubt surprised and disappointed that we drove past so many of the famous Franciscan shrines without stopping,' he began, 'but I wanted to bring you here first, because it was here, more than anywhere else, that Francis was formed and fashioned into the image and likeness of the man he had committed himself to follow. During the years that he spent rebuilding San Damiano, San Pietro and Santa Maria degli Angeli, Francis freely and willingly embraced Lady Poverty in a way that all could see – by the way he lived, worked and begged for food. However, what could not be seen was the Lady Poverty whose presence resided in his very heart and soul. It was here at Le Carceri that he was alone with her, and through her that he was totally open to receive what Jesus had received before him. Although Jesus did not use the expression "Lady Poverty", the reality behind the medieval symbolism that so appealed to Francis was at the heart of Christ's spiritual relationship with his Father.

'The Greek fathers used the word *Kenosis* to describe the state into which Jesus chose to enter when he emptied himself of all things, as St Paul put it, to enter into our human weakness. It was the realization that the one in whom and through whom the whole of creation came into being had freely divested himself of everything that inspired Francis to embrace absolute poverty. It was not just that Christ had once emptied himself in the past but that he continues to empty himself in the present, by daily entering into our common food to remain with us to the end of time:

> Every day he humbles himself as he did when he came down from his heavenly throne into the Virgin's womb; every day he comes to us and lets us see his abjection when he descends from the bosom of the Father into the hands of the priest at the altar. In this way our Lord remains continually with his followers, as he promised, "Behold I am with you always even unto the consummation of the world."
>
> (Admonition 1)

'Francis' material poverty was there for all to see, but the spiritual poverty into which he entered at Le Carceri was hidden from view. Here he was stripped of everything, so that the same Spirit who progressively filled the emptiness of Brother Jesus progressively filled him too. Finally he came to experience something of the *Pleroma* – the cornucopia of love that filled Jesus when he rose from the dead on the first Easter Day.

'In his mystical masterpiece *Itinerarium Mentis in Deum*, St Bonaventure describes the journey into God that Francis embarked upon in this hermitage. So far, Francis had searched and found God in his footprints in the world that he had created in Brother Jesus. Then he discovered more than mere footprints in Brother Jesus himself, who inspired him to embrace Lady Poverty. It was his early attraction to the world of chivalry that inspired Francis to personalize and feminize his desire to imitate the self-emptying of Jesus by calling the object of that desire "Lady Poverty".

'Like all beginners, St Francis was taken by surprise when

suddenly the prayer of first fervor was taken away from him, in order to prepare him to experience God not through his footprints in the world outside but as he is in himself in the world within. Now he was being called to a new form of prayer that begins in darkness, where he had to learn to fix his gaze on God alone. The way forward in this new phase of prayer, later called the "Dark Night of the Soul" by St John of the Cross, was summed up perfectly by St Bonaventure in his *Itinerarium Mentis in Deum* three centuries before:

> If this new phase is to be genuine and perfect then all labor on the part of the soul's reasoning faculty must cease, and the soul's deep longing must be centered on God and transformed as it were into him. So mysterious and sublime is this experience that none save those who have experienced it know anything about it, and nobody receives it save those who desire it and this desire only comes to the person whose whole being is inflamed by the Holy Spirit.
>
> (*Itinerarium*, chapter 7)

'St Bonaventure was about nine years of age when Francis died, so he had no doubt learned about mystical prayer from the oral tradition of those other Franciscan mystics who had learned it from Francis himself. After all, he wrote his mystical masterpiece in the hermitage at La Verna in 1259 where friars who had known Francis still lived and prayed. We know for a fact that one of them was Brother Leo who had witnessed the incredible events that happened before, during and after Francis had received the stigmata on September 14th 1224. We know this because Bonaventure tells us himself that it was from listening to Brother Leo's account of these happenings that he was inspired to write his masterwork. So when we hear him encouraging his readers to journey on in the darkness, it is not fanciful to believe that we are listening to Francis himself, through the tradition handed down through Brother Leo and other Franciscan mystics. He writes:

> Push on bravely, friend, toward mystical union. Abandon the workings of the senses and the operations of the reasoning faculty, leave aside all things visible and invisible and cleave as far as possible to the One who transcends all essences and all knowledge. In this immeasurable and absolute elevation of soul, forgetting all created things and liberated from them, you shall rise above yourself and above all creation to find yourself within the shaft of light that flashes out from the divine and mysterious darkness.

'Paradoxically, it is this shaft of light that first brought darkness to Francis. He had to face the sin and the selfishness that prevented him from being perfectly fitted into Brother Jesus, in whom and through whom he wanted to experience the love of the Father. Once the purification was underway, the shaft of light, which is nothing other than the Holy Spirit sent by the Father, began to transform him into the Christ-like man that he became. Gradually he was endowed with all the knowledge and with all the wisdom that you simply cannot find in books. St Bonaventure puts it perfectly at the beginning of chapter 11 of his *Life of St Francis*, otherwise called the *Legenda Maior*:

> His unwearied application to prayer along with his continual exercise of virtue had led the man of God to such serenity of mind that although he had no skill in sacred scripture acquired through study, his intellect, illuminated by the brilliance of eternal light, probed the depth of scripture with remarkable acumen. Free from all stain, his genius penetrated the hidden depth of the mysteries, for where the scholarship of the teacher stands outside, the love of the mystic enters within.

'As the shaft of light that had first brought darkness turned to light, St Francis began to realize that he was experiencing the action of the Holy Spirit. It was the same Spirit who had conceived Jesus in Mary's womb and who had enabled him to "grow with wisdom and understanding with the years". It was the same Spirit who had come down upon him as he was baptized in the Jordan and who had filled, guided and completed him throughout his life on earth and then raised him from the dead at the end of it. The more intensely Francis experienced the love of the Holy Spirit coursing through the veins of his inner being, the more he was struck with wonder and awe. This was the same Holy Spirit, the inner love of God himself, whom Brother Jesus promised he would send at the Last Supper. Now this isn't just the sort of academic knowledge that you find in books, but the experiential knowledge of a lover experiencing being loved. It's the sort of knowledge that demands a response, and Francis responded by surrendering himself with ever-greater abandon to Brother Jesus and to whatever he wanted of him.

'Bonaventure uses the symbolism of light to describe the action of the Holy Spirit in the mystic way to express a profound truth. Once a person has been sufficiently purified, then he or she is progressively filled with a sublime spiritual wisdom that enables them to understand the meaning of the Gospel as never before. Further to this, they are empowered to live the Gospel as they have never been able to do before. This is what we see happening in the life of Francis as his prayer life deepens. Once the demons that distracted him were silenced, he could hear the word of God that he had been unable to hear before. He could hear it speaking to him personally, telling him to follow him in absolute poverty.

'When, inevitably, others came to join him, they were welcomed into a brotherhood with a unique way of life. Through prayer in this hermitage Francis came to understand that he and his followers must embrace exactly the same way of life that Jesus had lived before the resurrection. For more than a thousand years nobody had tried to do this. Before Francis, the main form of religious life was monasticism, first founded by St Antony in the Egyptian desert. However, after the age of the martyrs, when Christianity became the official religion of the Roman Empire under Constantine, the Church became "established" and everything suddenly began to go wrong. The trouble was that many now wanted to become Christians, not to die for Jesus as the martyrs had done before them but in order to live the good life. That meant a richer and more prosperous life by getting the best and most important jobs in town. Nine times out of ten these seemed to go no longer to the pagans but to the "old faithful".

'Sadly this meant that there was a sudden upsurge in people converting from paganism with questionable motives. The clergy themselves were tempted and some corrupted with positions of honor and high office that had been closed to them before. Bishops who had once been hunted down, mutilated and executed were now raised to senatorial rank, and the Pope, who had been almost permanently in hiding, was given the rank of a consul with all the attendant flummery. It soon became the custom for the laity to give large tracts of lands to the Church in their wills to ensure a certain and trouble-free journey into the next life. And so the Church became richer and richer, with huge estates that became the foundations of the Papal States and the temporal power of the Pope. In no time, the blood of the martyrs that had been the seed of the Church flowered and went back to seed again, but this time the seed was barren or bore ambivalent fruit. Now the question was what could be done to reconvert the world, which was becoming more and more secular compared to the fervor of earlier times.

'The plans for renewal involved taking the spiritual life that was flourishing with ever-greater fervor in the desert and using it as "leaven" to enable the secular world to rise from the decadence that threatened to destroy it. Far from being tainted with the laxity that was becoming endemic in the newly established Church, the nuns and monks in the desert were thriving, as whole armies of the young and the disillusioned were heading there to swell their ranks. They had not only heard about the exploits of these intrepid spiritual explorers by word of mouth, but they had also read the life of St Antony by St Athanasius, the patriarch of Alexandria, who had known Antony personally. Many had read the writings of John Cassian too, who had lived for twelve years amongst the monks in the Egyptian desert, recording their ascetical heroism, and other writings that have remained with us to this day. Now people wanted to join them, so they flooded in droves to the monasteries founded by Antony, Pachomius, Macarius and others in Egypt, as well as to those founded by Hilarion, Jerome and Melanie in the Holy Land. That's not to mention the great monastic foundations in Cappadocia, in present-day Turkey, which thrived under St Basil, St Gregory Nazianzen and Gregory of Nyssa, drawing their followers mainly from the Eastern Church.

'The plan was to encourage the monks to set up monasteries in the West on the edges of civilization or sometimes even in towns, to act like beacons of light to enlighten a secular world that was forgetting its origins. Important monastic foundations were set up in the south of France by such people as John Cassian and St Honorius and even in Rome itself and other major cities of the empire that were in desperate need of the spirituality of the desert. Then the next step was to choose the holiest and most learned of the monks and make them bishops, to inspire their clergy with the spirituality that they, in their turn, would hand on to the faithful, who were becoming all but spiritually destitute.

'When this new monastic breed of bishops found themselves alone in the world they had been asked to re-evangelize, they felt isolated and insecure after the brotherly support they had received in their monastic seclusion. So, many bishops brought brother monks with them, so that in their new surroundings they could continue to practice the way of life that had been the making of them. This inspired other bishops like St Ambrose, St Augustine and St Martin of Tours to gather their clergy around them and introduce them to a sort of semi-monastic community for mutual support in turning to God and in ministering to the people to whom they were called to serve. These priests, who were not monks, were introduced to this semi-monastic way of life and came to be known as "canons" or "canons regular", because they were committed to a regular rule or canon that determined their way of life.

'When these bishops built their cathedrals, they built monasteries next to them. Then they set aside a place in them for the sort of monastic prayer that they had enjoyed in the desert where they had been formed. What were later called "choir stalls" were built, so that each member of the monastic or semi-monastic community could sit, kneel or stand opposite each other to recite the Divine Office. The structure of this "Office" was based on the Jewish tradition – which Jesus and his disciples would have followed – of praying five times a day just as Muslims do to this day. It later came to be called the *Opus Dei* in Benedictine monasticism, which gradually became the most popular interpretation of Eastern monasticism in mainland Europe in the sixth century, mainly due to its spirit of moderation.

'Although monasticism, as such, was never specifically designed as an instrument to promote the Gospel message in the world, it was nevertheless remarkably effective. In addition to providing "holy bishops" who had imbibed the spirituality of the Desert Fathers, their monasteries became beacons of light in the Dark Ages to clergy and laity alike, disseminating both spiritual and secular learning, while transcribing the Christian and pagan classics for posterity. They provided preachers too, especially in the wake of the barbarian invasions, like Columba and

Columbanus, Boniface and Augustine to convert and reconvert Europe into the Christian continent that it became.

'However, by the eighth century Europe was awash with wandering monks, busily undoing by their behavior all that had been done by their illustrious forebears. The situation was such a scandal that when Charlemagne was enthroned in 800 AD he ordered all monks back to their monasteries and decreed that henceforth all monasteries in his empire must accept and observe the Rule of St Benedict. The vow of stability taken by every monk meant that the monasteries would never be able to provide Christendom with itinerant preachers as they had done in the past. Cluniac, Cistercian and Carthusian monks would help reinterpret and reform the monastic life in subsequent centuries, but they would do little for the laity, who were increasingly starved of the evangelical spirituality that they were denied. The various forms of canons regular which had initially developed out of monastic life had little effect. The diluted form of monastic spirituality on which they depended was hardly sufficient to keep them from spiritual starvation themselves, let alone enable them to feed those starving in the world. It was certainly not sufficient to generate with any consistency the profound contemplative prayer that animates the effective apostle with the same Spirit that animated Jesus.

'If this was true of the religious communities, what about the secular priests whose secularism was damned by the Fourth Lateran Council? This was sitting at the very moment when the first friars were doing for the laity what the secular priests had so lamentably failed to do. Other mendicant orders began to flourish with the Franciscans, all trying in their own way to respond to the needs of a Christendom which was beginning to slide back into paganism. The Franciscans originally grew out of a lay movement, the Carmelites originated from the eremitical life, and the Dominicans owed much to the monastic life that they adapted for the sake of those spiritually languishing in the world.

'Although the new form of religious life that St Francis was inspired to found was the perfect tool for the task of renewing the Church, there was serious opposition. The opposition came from within, as many of the new and more learned friars who had recently joined the Order found the Gospel way of life as Francis lived it too difficult. They approached Cardinal Hugolino to intercede for them at the Chapter of 1222. Francis was adamant. He had already turned down a suggestion made by St Dominic that their two orders should merge, so he was in no mood for compromise. He took the Cardinal by the hand, led him to where the friars were assembled, and addressed them:

> Brothers, the Lord has called me by the way of humility, and he has shown me the way of simplicity; and I do not want you to mention to me any other Rule, neither that of St Augustine, nor of St Benedict, nor of St Bernard. And the Lord told me that he wished me to be a new fool in the world and he did not want to lead us by any other way than that wisdom. By your learning and your wisdom God will confound you.

'In order to appreciate the wisdom learned through prayer that enabled Francis to found a religious order perfectly designed for effective apostolic action, let me compare it with the monastic orders that flourished at that period. They were, thanks to Charlemagne, predominantly Benedictine, or reforms of Benedictinism. Their timetable was divided into three roughly equal sections: time for sleep, time for work, and time for prayer. The early Franciscans divided their timetable in a similar way, but instead of time for work within the monastery the Franciscans left their friaries for apostolic work amongst the people. This is why they came to be called mendicants or beggars, because when their apostolic work prevented them from producing goods that could be sold for their upkeep (as was the practice of the monks), they had to depend on alms. Whilst they gave no ground to the monks when it came to time for prayer, the way in which they prayed was significantly different. Time for prayer was redesigned in order to emphasize a type of prayer that was not practiced in the same way in Benedictine monasticism.

'It was the deep personal prayer leading to mystical contemplation that Francis had first learned here at Le Carceri. Its full development needed protracted periods of time in solitude. That's why Francis founded hermitages wherever he went for himself and for his followers, so that they too could be transformed by the same Holy Spirit who had transformed him. There was no place in mainline monasticism for prayer such as this. The chanting of the Divine Office and the prayerful reading of the scriptures, called the Opus Dei and Lectio Divina, was the staple diet of monastic prayer. St Benedict made it clear that personal prayer was an optional extra when he wrote in his rule, "If you would pray privately, make it swift and ardent." Far from being an optional extra, private personal prayer of prolonged duration was the essential ingredient that opened Francis to the action of the Holy Spirit. All his early biographers echo the words of his first biographer, Thomas of Celano, many times over:

> His safest haven was prayer, not prayer of a single moment, but prayer of long duration. If he began late he would scarce finish before morning. Walking, sitting, or eating, he was always intent on prayer. He would repeatedly go alone at night to pray in lonely and deserted places.
> (Celano, chapter 27)

'St Francis was adamant that such prayer must be the mainspring that would prepare his brothers for intensive and effective apostolic action. Long before the Divine Office was introduced into the Order, personal mental prayer was the staple diet of the early Franciscans, as St Bonaventure makes clear in his *Life of St Francis*: "They spent their time praying continuously, devoting their time especially to fervent mental prayer; they had not yet acquired any of the liturgical books so they could not chant the divine office" (chapter 4:3).

'In order to make more time for prayer, Francis radically shortened the long monastic office that took monks hours to perform. For instance, in the Cluniac reform of Benedictinism it took eight hours. St Francis rejected this monastic office in favor of what was called the "Roman Office", because it was used by the members of the Roman curial officials and it was, needless to say, infinitely shorter, leaving the friars with more time for personal prayer. After they had risen to recite the Divine Office in the middle of the night, many of the friars would remain in silent personal prayer until dawn. Now Francis did not reject what the monks called Lectio Divina, the slow and meditative reading of the scriptures; indeed it was the source of inspiration for all Franciscan prayer. So much so that towards the end of his life Francis admitted that he knew most of the scriptures by heart.

'It was the genius of Francis which saw that personal prayer to contemplation had to be learned by the friars inside their friary or in the hermitage, so that it could support and sustain them as they went about their apostolic work, without the need for the sort of liturgical prayer that supports and sustains the monk in his monastic seclusion. Furthermore, if his work was going to be successful, the friar had to be trained to a high degree of personal responsibility, which was not demanded in the same way of the monk. The friar, for instance, would have to learn how to turn to this prayer daily, often without the physical presence and support of his community and away from the supervision of his superior.

'Take my brother David as a case in point. He has spent months – no, years – traveling all over the world giving retreats without the constant support of his brothers and without the watchful eye of his superior. Only God knows that he has been faithful to the daily personal prayer without which he would have degenerated into a hypocrite; laxity would have had an obvious effect on him, undermining what he said.

'After our mother died, I stayed with my brother at his friary at Woodford Green in London to sort out a few problems arising from our mother's will. The day after my arrival, David invited me to join him on a day of recollection given by Cardinal Basil Hume to the clergy of Brentwood Diocese. The Cardinal perfectly summed up the point I have been trying to make. He explained how, as a monk at Ampleforth, he had been formed and sustained by monastic spirituality. Each day, he was supported by his brother monks as together they pursued perfection through the ancient and hallowed rhythm of the monastic life, as they moved effortlessly from the Opus Dei and the Lectio Divina to their various spheres of work in the community, in their search for God. But now, he admitted, since being made Archbishop of Westminster, he had to learn a new form of spirituality. Moving towards a group of Franciscan friars in his audience, he said, 'And I have had to learn from these gentlemen here.' He went on to explain how he now had to master a different way of praying in his private chapel and in his apartment without his brethren to support him. It was also a way of praying which he needed to return to when he was out and about, serving his people through an apostolate for which he had not been specifically prepared. If he was to be supported by prayer when he was traveling by Tube or taxi or by plane or train, or while waiting at a station or in an airport departure lounge, it would have to be by new forms of prayer. These forms of prayer were those developed by the mendicant tradition, rather than the monastic tradition on which he had depended before.

'During the Second World War a well-known Cistercian

monastery released thirteen monks to man local parishes, to enable secular priests to act as army chaplains. Only one monk returned after the war! The majority lost their vocations and several lost their faith. This is not an indictment of monasticism, but merely an example of what happens when monks are suddenly asked to do work for which their spirituality has never prepared them. Block time for personal prayer each day, then, became the main way in which the early Franciscans sought the contemplative prayer that would alone open them to experience the same Spirit who sustained Jesus, so that they could become other Christs to those they had committed themselves to serve. Whenever they forgot to do this, the inevitable would follow: they would be on the steady downward slope into decline and then into decadence.

'This was already beginning to happen thirty years after the death of Francis, when St Bonaventure became Minister General of the Order in 1257. In order to arrest the decline, his first act was to send a general letter to everyone in the Order. He didn't beat about the bush or bother to pepper his criticism of the brethren with flannel – only spiritually insecure ditherers need to do that. He detailed the reasons for the decline in standards which were already apparent in the Order and they do not make pretty reading.

'He writes about

the indolence and idleness of certain friars which is the cesspool of vice. Too many are merely daydreamers, in some awful state midway between the active and the contemplative, but engaged in neither. Importunate begging is rife, which sometimes reaches the point where people are afraid to meet friars lest they be set upon as if by robbers. Then there is the multiplicity of contacts with women, which the rule forbids. From this arise suspicions, evil rumors, and many scandals.

'Then, after listing many more problems, he insisted that there was only one thing that individuals had to do in order to arrest the decline. That was to return to the primitive fervor that had characterized the early friars. In his words it was simply to return to "prayer and the spirit of devotion". In order to facilitate this, he laid down in his new constitution that total silence must be observed every night from after Compline in the evening to Prime the following day. This was not to introduce a new practice but to reiterate an old practice that went back to the time of Francis himself. In his history of the friars in England since their arrival two years before the death of Francis, Thomas of Eccleston states that it was their custom to keep silent throughout the night until after the morning office and that the friars "were so assiduous in their prayers that there was scarcely an hour in the night when some one of them was not at prayer in the oratory".

'It was of course the same in Italy. In addition to the early sources that speak of the close companions of Francis and of how long they prayed, the famous Franciscan preacher Thomas of Pavia gives us his observations. Writing in about 1245, even before Bonaventure, he tells us that many friars often spent the whole night in prayer and almost all of them spent at least part of the night on their knees.

'In order to give everyone an example, Bonaventure retired to the hermitage at La Verna where he wrote his masterwork on prayer, *Itinerarium Mentis in Deum*, to encourage and inspire his brothers. His simple recipe for effective reform was always at the heart of every subsequent Franciscan reform – back to "prayer and the spirit of devotion". Even before the great Observant reform at the end of the fourteenth century, the Chapter of Pepignan held in 1331 gives us but one more example, amongst many other provincial edicts stressing the importance of prayer:

Lest it should happen that the spirit of holy prayer and

devotion be extinguished by useless wanderings, by general restlessness, by scurrility, and much talk and finally by dissipation of mind; by this present constitution we order that from the time of compline to the first sign of prime all friars are to be restricted to the oratory, the cloister, the dormitory and the "secretae necessitatis locus". The purpose of this order is to make sure that friars do not wander about through other houses, porches or squares, so that in all prayer and supplication, with thanksgiving, in silence and quiet, let them make known their supplications to God. And he will see them praying with the door shut, and in secret, and will as Christ promised in the Gospels render them an inestimable reward.

'In an article on the history of mental prayer in the Order, one of the most respected experts on Franciscan spirituality, Fr Ignatius Brady OFM, to whom I am indebted for these quotations, continually stresses the importance of prayer. Speaking about the great Observant reform that flourished 200 years after the birth of St Francis, he writes,

At first sight the new reform might seem to be primarily a reaction to the quarrels over poverty and a return to stricter material poverty. But in reality poverty lay on the surface, the root of the divergence was deeper and it eddied around the twofold life of prayer and the apostolate. This is the key to the internal history of the Franciscan order and to the series of reforms that have marked its history, namely the observance or non-observance of the spirit of prayer and devotion.

'This insight is clearly underlined by Christopher of Varisio, one of the "superiors" of the Observant movement. In a letter to one of the friars he writes quite simply that "Holy Prayer is the key to our whole observance. When it is lost all else is lost".

'Despite the behavior of the few, the new mendicant

movements led by the Franciscans were incredibly effective at implementing the ecclesiastical reforms which Innocent III had dreamed about. In spite of their success, or perhaps because of it, many supporters of the monastic ideal began to attack the new orders, insisting that they should be subject to the same sort of monastic rule to which monks were bound. In answer to these criticisms, the great Dominican theologian St Thomas Aquinas coined the slogan that perfectly summed up the very quintessence of all the new mendicant orders. "Our calling," he insisted, "is to contemplate and then to share the fruits of contemplation with others – *contemplare contemplari aliis trahere.*"

'Now St Thomas Aquinas always explained exactly what he meant and never used a word out of place, carefully defining every key word that he used. He did not say that their calling was to pray and share the fruits of prayer with others, or even to meditate and to share the fruits of meditation with others, but to contemplate and to share the fruits of contemplation with others. For St Thomas and for St Bonaventure, who were fellow students at the University of Paris, contemplation was a specific form of prayer. It was the prayer that is experienced beyond meditation when, in the "Dark Night", God begins to infuse his inner life into the heart and mind of those who have persevered in the preceding purification. It is a pure gift of God that cannot be attained by human endeavor alone, but it is consistently given to those who have traveled on for long enough in the mystic way to demonstrate that they are more interested in God than in what they can get out of him. This is the profound prayer that was at the heart and soul of everything that Francis said and did, and the source from which he drew his unique vision, which we have come here to appreciate more deeply.

'It is not easy to pray all day long as you travel, sometimes for hours from one preaching engagement to another, nor is it easy to meditate, but contemplation is quite another matter. Precisely because it is the profound God-given experience of his all-pervading love, it requires no effort to experience it and to be sustained by it. The sources give many examples of Francis being enveloped in deep contemplation on his travels. Sometimes he would pull his hood down over his face so that nobody would see the joy that overwhelmed him. In short it is the highest and most perfect form of prayer, which is first learned in set periods of time inside solitude in such a way that it gradually begins to irrigate every moment of the mendicant's life outside that solitude. It should not be surprising, then, that in the 800 years since the death of St Francis over eighty percent of mystical writers were mendicants, not monks.

'This hermitage and all the other hermitages were built precisely so that this sublime form of contemplation could be learned in month after month of solitary prayer. Even when the friars returned to their friaries, hours were expected to be given each day to sustain the only form of prayer that would enable them to become perfect apostles. In the early days, legislation was not considered necessary to enforce what every friar knew to be the ideal, so it was over 200 years before a specific time and place was laid down for prayer in the friaries. In 1465 the constitutions of John Macriforis, Vicar General for the Nuremberg Province, laid down that "after Compline and Matins the friars are to remain in church for prayer, after Compline for an hour and more, after the midnight Office until half past three".

'This was the minimum to which all had to conform. More time was of course encouraged, to enable a friar to be empowered by the same Spirit who had sent out and inspired the apostles on the first Pentecost. The success or failure of the friars in subsequent centuries was directly correlated to the quality of the prayer that sustained them.

'Now, before I finish, I want to emphasize why Christendom had to wait so long before a saint like Francis was able to return to the simple Gospel spirituality for himself and for all who would listen to him. Hadn't there been saints who had preceded him – saints who had much to teach about prayer and the spiritual life? The answer is clearly, yes. Every man and woman who opens themselves up to receive the Holy Spirit gradually receives not only the knowledge and wisdom to see the Gospel spirituality that was so dear to Francis, but also the inner strength to live by it. However, the key word is "gradually". St Francis did not see and understand everything the very moment he experienced the love of God. It took him years of solitary exposure to that love. Other saints before him saw parts of the vision, but he eventually saw the whole vision in all its simplicity, because he spent more time than others receiving the One who inspired that vision in the first place. So before we begin to see that vision in more detail, let me make it abundantly clear that without prolonged prayer, without solitude, without the hermitage, Francis would be as blind as the rest of us. He saw so much and he saw so clearly because he saw everything in the light of the Holy Spirit, as St Bonaventure makes abundantly clear in his *Life of St Francis*: "Francis learned in his prayer that the presence of the Holy Spirit for which he longed was granted more intimately, when he was far from the rush of worldly affairs. Therefore he used to seek out lonely places in the wilderness and go into abandoned churches to pray at night" (chapter 10).

'If we want to see what he saw and receive the strength to embody his vision in our lives, we must follow him into solitude. We may not have a hermitage nearby, but as Jesus taught us we can all find an inner room, a garden, a peaceful place or a quiet church. One way or another, we all need what Montaigne called "a little back shop, untouched by others, in which we establish our true freedom and chief place of seclusion and solitude". If we don't do this then we are just playing at being Franciscans like children, merely surrounding ourselves with the outer show that shows others what we are: salt without savor, bread without leaven, as flat outside as we are within. No solitude, no

Franciscan. It's as simple as that!'

When Peter had finished speaking he put all his notes back into his briefcase and said, 'I'm sure you'll have a lot of questions to ask me, but could you leave them until this evening? I think you need more time to digest all that I've said and anyway I have to meet Father Guido in fifteen minutes. He's the Guardian here now, but he was a member of the community when I stayed at Montefalco fifteen years ago. I don't want to keep you waiting as I did yesterday, so perhaps you would like to visit Assisi and pick me up later.' Then he spoke to Emelia in Italian before we went our separate ways.

Emelia took us to a beautiful spot for our picnic, near the ruins of the old fortress on the Sasso Rocco with breathtaking views of Assisi and the valley of Spoleto below. The day was so clear that she was able to point out La Verna many miles to the north. Then, after visiting San Rufino where St Francis was baptized, the house where he was said to have grown up and San Francesco where he was buried, we picked Peter up at Le Carceri. When we all met up again after supper, Peter asked us if we had any question after his morning's talk.

'The truth of the matter is you made everything so clear that I haven't anything to say but to thank you,' said Bobbie, and Emelia and I nodded in agreement. Peter had spoken so well. When he had spoken to me in the past it had always been about my own spiritual life, but this time I had seen a totally different side to him. He was speaking to us as a teacher, explaining a subject on which he seemed to be a complete master, for although he had taken notes out of his briefcase he had hardly ever referred to them.

'There is just one thing,' said Bobbie. 'Although St Francis is so transparently humble, he was nevertheless totally confident that his vision for his own future and that of his Order came from God. How could he be so sure? Did God speak to him directly and if so how? The reason why I am asking is because history is strewn with religious fanatics who think that they have a direct line to God, when they are usually only using him as pretexts to canonize their own bizarre religious convictions.'

'You're absolutely right,' said Peter. 'No, God didn't speak to Francis as he was supposed to have spoken to Joan of Arc. Nor did he detail everything that he ought to say or do. It's far more complicated than that and yet it is absolutely simple, if you'll excuse the paradox, at least until I can explain it. You see, all God does is to love and it is through this love that St Francis received all the infused knowledge that made him certain of what God wanted him to do. When I was in Italy fifteen years ago, it was Antonio – whom you met yesterday – who explained everything to me so clearly. St Bonaventure said that in mystical or contemplative prayer God's love gradually begins to shine out of the mysterious darkness that preceded it, like a shaft of light. Now Antonio taught me that a single shaft of light contains within itself all the colors of the spectrum. They remain unseen until they strike a prism that reflects and refracts them in such a way that all the colors of the rainbow are clearly visible for all to see. Now it's exactly the same with the shaft of God's light or his love. When it is allowed to shaft down into the human heart, it first purifies it, and then it refines it into a spiritual prism that refracts and reflects that love into every part of the human personality. When it penetrates the mind, it infuses into it a wisdom and knowledge that had been denied the receiver before. It enables them to see and understand the meaning of the Gospel that they had never understood before – and with such ease and such simplicity. When it enters the human heart it fills it with a superhuman care and compassion, and with a quality of selflessness and sacrifice that they had never been able to generate by themselves. In short they are not only able to see the truth, but they are also given the inner strength to do it. That's why Francis could see more clearly than the most erudite theologian, and that's why Abbot Evagrius, the great spiritual theologian who wrote down the teachings of the Desert Fathers, said, "A theologian is a man of prayer and a man of prayer is a theologian."'

'Thank you,' said Bobbie. 'What you say makes a lot of sense.' And it did.

'There's one thing I would like to ask,' said Emelia. 'This shaft of love that St Bonaventure talks about... When it begins to enter into a person, does it feel like the human love that we have all experienced?'

'No, not really – at least not to begin with,' replied Peter. 'You see, human beings are made up of body and spirit so their love is both physical and spiritual. However, God does not have a body, so when he loves he loves with his Spirit alone. As a mark of respect, his love has traditionally been called the Holy Spirit. Now when his love begins to enter into a human being, it is primarily experienced in the mind.'

'I see,' said Emelia. 'But is it possible to describe precisely what it feels like?'

'Yes, it is,' said Peter, 'if you can bear with me. When the romantic poets try to express what they call "the numinous" in nature, they are trying to capture in verse the sort of spiritual feeling that most of us have experienced, particularly when we were young. It occurs, for instance, when we are swept off our feet by a particularly beautiful landscape, enthralled by the vibrant colors that shimmer over the sea as the sun settles down to rest, or are entranced watching an insect crawling through the undergrowth. The operative word is "entranced", because that's what happens to us. We are drawn into an inner trance that draws the mind together in such a way that it focuses on what seems to be nothing in particular, but is in fact upon a sense of presence within. Our spiritual senses have somehow extracted from the natural world the presence of the One who is the All in all, to contemplate that presence within.

'This is what I would call a natural mystical experience. Now this is precisely the same experience that engages a person at the outset of the mystic way, when what Bonaventure refers to as the "shaft of light" begins to shine through the darkness. At first the experience is soft and subtle, but in time its intensity grows, sometimes to shattering degrees of intensity, filling the recipient with joy and often resulting in ecstasy. Eventually what was experienced purely in the mind begins to overflow, causing paroxysms of delight that reverberate throughout every part of the body. When this used to happen to Francis in company, he would flee to savor in solitude what was a deeply personal and private encounter. When it happened at the time he received the stigmata, it swept him into a series of raptures and then into an ecstasy that lasted for days, as he rode back to Assisi oblivious of the crowds that gathered to venerate him along the way.'

'I'm afraid I haven't had too many ecstasies,' said Emelia, smiling, 'but I do know what you mean by "natural mystical experiences". Like most people, I've experienced them for myself and so for the first time you've enabled me to understand what mystical experience feels like, at least at the outset.'

'Good,' said Peter. 'Well, I think it's time we had an early night because we have another busy day ahead of us tomorrow. I'm pleased that we were able to begin at Le Carceri. It gave me the opportunity to show where and how a man with hardly more than an elementary school education could see and understand the meaning and message of the Gospel that had been forgotten, misunderstood or distorted for almost a thousand years. But the first touch of love that Francis experienced on his way home from his last party was but the first note, as it were, of a life that was a symphony of love. That first note developed into the major theme that grew and varied in and out of prayer until it reached its stunning and revealing climax on La Verna, with the revelation of the "Primacy of Love". This is a theme to which I must return in far greater detail later.'

Before going to bed, I took out a large exercise book that I had brought along for the purpose and wrote down as much as I could remember of all that Peter had said. I vowed that, no matter how tired I was, I would do likewise every evening before going to sleep. I didn't want to miss a word that he said.

I lay awake for hours, going over everything Peter had said that day.

Then I analyzed every word that Bobbie had said and every gesture she had made, to see if I could see anything to suggest that she wanted to relate to me in a different way, but I couldn't.

Chapter 6

Back to the Future

When we arrived for our second visit to Assisi, Peter took us to a café near San Damiano for morning coffee and small talk, before he began to speak about the Crusaders.

'I'm not here to defend the behavior of the Crusaders,' he said, 'but, in opening up the Holy Land to pilgrims, they set the scene for a new dawn in Christian spirituality in the twelfth century. It brought back the person of Jesus Christ and placed him at the heart and center of Christian spirituality where he belonged. This new dawn had two distinctive phases. The first involved a growing interest in the Jesus who had lived and died before the resurrection. A hundred years before Francis was born, the whole of Europe had been inspired by what was presented to the faithful as a noble Christian cause – to go and win back the Holy Land from the "infidels" who had held it for centuries. Encouraged by the Church, people from every walk of life set out for the East. Sovereigns and serfs, troops and troubadours, prelates and prostitutes, indeed the whole of Europe was brought to a fever pitch of excitement that is difficult to imagine a thousand years later.

'A great man like St Bernard was preaching the Crusade only a few decades before Francis was born. By the time he was growing up, the family fireside, the taverns and the market-places as well as the courts of the nobility were places where tales were told and retold of the land where the Word was made flesh and "dwelt amongst us". Pilgrims loved to tell of how they had seen the very spot where Jesus had been born, where he'd walked and talked, where he'd died on the cross and where he had been buried. No wonder it was one of the deepest desires of

Francis to go to the Holy Land himself. Nor was it surprising that when he came back he wanted to burn into the hearts of all people something of the fire that had set him alight with the love of Jesus – the one who had chosen to come amongst us as a helpless baby on the first Christmas Day. That is why he built for himself and his fellow countrymen a crib on the hillside above Greccio, high up in the Rieti Valley. It was here that he invited everyone to join him in a celebration of Jesus' birth that would stain their memories with an experience that would inspire them for a lifetime. The cribs that found their way into every Christian home from that time onwards symbolized the rebirth of Jesus Christ as the heart and center of Christian spirituality, through the inspirational genius of the poor man of Assisi.

'The second phase of this new dawn involved a new and vital understanding of how Jesus had lived, loved and animated the first Christian community after the resurrection. It was Francis, more than anyone else, who was responsible for inaugurating this second phase, precisely because he had not only heard the Risen Christ speak to him but had also experienced his love. It was the same love that had inspired early Christianity, then, which was to inspire Francis. But to avoid any confusion let me summarize the essence of the Franciscan way of life as conceived and lived by Francis.

'The physical structure of the Order that he founded was entirely based on the way of life lived by Jesus and his disciples before the resurrection. As such it involved the eremitical or solitary life, the community life and the apostolic life, as David explained in his summary. Just as Jesus spent prolonged periods of time in solitude, so Francis taught his brothers to do likewise by both word and example. It would be in solitary prayer in the hermitage or in the friary oratory that his friars would learn to embrace the Kenosis, or spiritual emptying, that would enable the Holy Spirit to possess them. It was in sharing what they received with their brothers that true community would be born as the springboard for intensive apostolic action. Then, firstly by example and secondly by preaching, they would endeavor to extend to the world outside what they had already experienced within their friaries. In this way the whole world would become a friary, so that the brother and sisterhood of "all creation" might be reborn and flourish in that world. Although the physical structure of the Franciscan way of life was entirely based on the life lived by Jesus before the resurrection, its spirituality was based on the spirituality that prevailed amongst the first Christian communities.

'Before the resurrection the apostles were beginners, learning from their new master as he traveled all over Palestine preaching to the people. They were not scholars or intellectuals but ordinary workaday folk. The few years that they spent with Jesus before his premature death was little enough time for all he wanted to say and do for them. That's why after the resurrection he sent the Holy Spirit as he had promised at the Last Supper "to make everything plain to them" – everything that he hadn't had time to explain before his death. It was under the influence of the Holy Spirit, then, that the first Christian communities flourished. They were animated by the profound spirituality that was later recorded in the Gospels, the Acts of the Apostles and the Pastoral Epistles that Francis knew by heart. It was from reading these scriptures, inspired by the same Holy Spirit who had first inspired those who wrote them, that Francis was inspired to embody the spirituality that they taught in his own life and in the lives of his brothers. This profound spirituality first began to penetrate his heart and mind with immediate effect here at the Church of San Damiano.'

Peter gestured to the church in front of us, then led us inside to see the cross before which Francis had heard Christ speak to him.

'Before I go any further, I would like to say two things. Firstly, I want to point out that this is not in fact the actual cross; it is a copy, albeit a good copy. The original is in the Church of Santa Chiara in the town where the Poor Clares have their convent. Secondly, I want you to notice that it is not the dead or the dying Christ on the cross but the Risen Christ. He stands out from the cross; his eyes are open and you can see the tomb from which he rose behind him. So it is not the dying but the Risen Christ whose words Francis heard speaking to him.

'When Bonaventure wrote about the incident that took place here, he not only tells us that Francis heard the words of Christ telling him to rebuild his Church, but he tells us that he experienced his love too. It was the same love that was unleashed on the first Pentecost Day – the Holy Spirit. The experience so overwhelmed him that he lost consciousness as he was caught up in a profound ecstasy. It is one thing to believe with your mind that Jesus Christ is alive, bursting with creative energy and life, but it is quite another thing to experience his love enveloping your heart and soul with such intensity that you are temporarily taken out of your senses. What happened here gave Francis the strength to abandon his life to Christ. In the years that followed he allowed his love to transform him in such a way that he was able to bring back Christ once more, placing him at the heart and center of Christian spirituality. But he didn't just call people to remember the Christ who had once lived in the past, but to open themselves to receive the Risen Christ who is living and loving now in the present.'

'But that seems strange,' remarked Bobbie. 'How could it be that Christ was not at the center of Christian spirituality?' Bobbie was mystified at what seemed to her a paradox, as it seemed to Emelia and to me too for that matter.

'Because,' said Peter, 'in the centuries that followed the resurrection, the profound spirituality that had bonded the first Christian community together, with Christ at its center, gradually disappeared due to a series of heresies. However, it was precisely because of Francis' experiences in prayer here, at Le Carceri and elsewhere that it came into view once more.'

'But how did it all disappear in the first place?' asked Bobbie, still a little mystified.

'Let me explain,' said Peter. 'Early Christianity was dominated by a world-shaking event and an undeniable fact. Jesus had risen from the dead and was alive and well. Many people had seen him alive again and all had experienced his love. It was this Love, his Holy Spirit whom Christ had promised to send at the Last Supper, who bonded the early Christians together into a unique caring and loving community, firstly in Jerusalem. It was here that, for a time, all that the community owned was owned in common and those who held anything back were punished (Acts 2:42–54; 5:1–6). It may not have technically been a democracy, but decisions were always first discussed collectively and even reversed when an "inspired outsider" like St Paul showed the believers they were wrong. In the mother of democracies, Athens, it was only the Athenian males with a prescribed portion of land who were full citizens. Women and slaves were not citizens, but in the new Christian community all were included. St Paul made it clear that in this community there would be no more Jew and Gentile, no more male and female, no more slave and freeman, but all would be one in Christ (Galatians 3:28). In him there was total equality, as people exercised their unique priesthood to offer themselves through him to receive the otherworldly love that bonded them together (1 Peter 2:5).

'In the early Church the word "priest" was used only when applied to Christ himself, or to the Christian community as they offered their "spiritual sacrifices" in, with and through him to the Father. Gradually this Spirit-filled community spread to every town and city in the Roman Empire. For them, Jesus was their brother who was still alive and living amongst them, reaching out to them and permeating them with his love, gradually transforming them into his own image and likeness. In short, the first Christians were mystics, because they experienced the self-same life and love that had animated Jesus throughout his life on earth and raised him up at the end of it.

'Their contemporaries were stunned to see a quality of selfless loving that they had never seen before. They saw it not only reaching out amongst the Christians themselves but also extending to others who did not belong to their community, and even to those who ridiculed them, imprisoned them and put them to death. Time and time again, jailors, torturers and executioners who persecuted them saw what they had never seen before: men, women and children actually forgiving them as Jesus had done before them. And so did countless hundreds and thousands of others who had come to mock at their public executions. They not only saw such loving forgiveness for themselves, but they also witnessed other supernatural signs that regularly accompanied the martyrdom of Christians. The pagan crowds who had originally come to scoff at them were deeply moved by a quality of love that they had never experienced before and many were moved to ask to be received into their community. Then, like Jesus himself, they were plunged three times into the mystic waters to receive the Holy Spirit, and when they rose from "the womb of the Church" they were consecrated as other Christs with sacred oil. The threefold immersion symbolized that they were now able to receive the threefold love that bonded together the Father, the Son and the Holy Spirit to the measure of their openness to receive it.

'The speed with which Christianity spread all over the Roman Empire and beyond was because Jesus their brother was still alive at the heart and center of their communities, bonding them together like a radioactive isotope bursting with creative life and vitality. They were convinced that he was still amongst them, filling them with the love that had filled and animated all he had said and done, so that his work could be continued through them.

'For several centuries the love of Jesus guaranteed that those first Christian communities continued to spread the Good News that promised to transform the world, until corrosive and pernicious heresies rose to destroy them. The heresy that first began to spread at the beginning of the fourth century was called Arianism after its founder Arius, a Berber priest from Alexandria. It maintained that Jesus was not divine, but purely human and a later creation of God. To use the technical language of the day, he argued that Jesus was not consubstantial or coeternal with God the Father and that there was a time when he did not exist in any form. The heresy was so successful that at one time over eighty percent of Christendom became Arian, with disastrous effect.

'In the days before mass media the only thing the Church could do to stop the heresy was to coin a slogan and then beat it incessantly like a drum to impress the truth into people's minds. The slogan was quite simply "Christ is God", "Christ is God", "Christ is God". Orthodoxy finally won the day, but at a price. The divinity was emphasized so much that Christ and God were hardly distinguishable in people's minds. Jesus Christ "our brother", who had been at the heart and soul of the Christian community, suddenly vanished from view. It was as if Jesus had ascended into heaven again, but this time it was a psychological ascension that raised him up and out of people's minds and hearts. Jesus the brother, who had once been the vital and dynamic source of Christian spirituality, was all but lost to view. In future, even the foremost Christian writers used the word "Christ" for God and the word "God" for Christ, without feeling it necessary to distinguish one from the other.

'Then another heresy called Macedonianism began to spread alongside Arianism. Like Arianism, it was called after its founder, the Greek Bishop of Constantinople, Macedonius I. Macedonianism was the logical consequence of Arianism. It did for the Holy Spirit what Arianism had done for Jesus: if Jesus was not divine, then neither was his love – the Holy Spirit. So the brotherly love of Jesus, the bond that had united the first Christian community, seemed to disappear from Christian spirituality, if not in theory then at least in practice and that's what really matters. With God and Christ far away in heaven – and the Holy Spirit with them – it's no wonder that Christian community life suffered. Rip out the cog from a bicycle wheel and see the effect that it has on the spokes; you'll see that without Jesus Christ at its center, Christian spirituality was disastrously damaged, until Francis came to repair it.

'Although I've heard of Arianism before,' said Bobbie, 'I'd no idea that it had such a devastating effect on the early Church.'

'No,' replied Peter, 'most people don't. And yet without an understanding of the effects of Arianism, it's impossible to appreciate just what Francis did to return Christianity to it origins. Perhaps it would help if I gave you a few examples. Let me show you how Arianism radically changed the way Christians prayed and worshipped, how it affected the very buildings they worshipped in – what they looked like and even how they were adorned. You see, by the time Francis was born, the gulf between the way his generation prayed and worshipped and the way the first Christians had prayed and worshipped was simply immense. But I will leave that until after supper, as I have to visit Father Joseph, an old friend of mine at St Mary of the Angels. I'll leave Emelia to show you around and make my own way back to Montefalco.'

Emelia knew every nook and cranny so we missed nothing. It seems that Francis installed St Clare at San Damiano in 1212, where she and her sisters remained until her death in 1253. Seven years later, the sisters moved to Santa Chiara inside the city walls for safety. Some years later, the friars moved in and have remained there to this day. I was particularly moved by the choir stalls in the church, although they only go back to 1504 when the Observants were in residence. There was an ancient grille in the apse that we were assured was original. It was through it that St Clare and her community received Holy Communion. There were of course many dubious relics, but Emelia insisted that the pectoral cross of St Bonaventure was genuine.

Then Emelia took us to see the Church of Santa Chiara. It was built over the Church of San Giorgio where Francis had learned to read and write and where he had delivered his first 'official sermon'. We were privileged to see the original cross from which Francis heard Jesus speaking to him and from which he had experienced the brotherly love that had transformed his life. I wasn't so impressed with St Clare's 'incorrupt' body. I couldn't see it very well and what I could see of her face seemed very dark and shriveled. I must say that, as an Anglican, I've never been particularly impressed by relics of any description and I always want absolute proof before I am prepared to believe in any of them.

When we all gathered together after supper, Peter apologized for having to leave us all so abruptly, but he had made his date with Fr Joseph before he knew that he would have to take his brother's place. He came straight to the point.

'I said this morning that the way Christians worshipped at the time of Francis was radically different from the way the early Christians worshipped, thanks to the effects of Arianism. Let me explain what I mean by showing you firstly how the early disciples of Jesus prayed immediately after the resurrection. To begin with, they still went to the synagogues for prayer and to the temple too, as they had done with Jesus whilst he was on earth. There was no reason why they shouldn't. It was only when the Jewish authorities "excommunicated" them as "heretics" that they were banned from the synagogues. When this happened they still came together for their own synagogue services twice a week. These services were rather like the first part of the Eucharist as we celebrate it today – that is, up to the Offertory. However, the readings would all have come from the Old

Testament until they were eventually supplemented with readings from the New Testament, as and when it was written.

'It was the custom for the Jews at that time to hold their midweek services on Tuesdays and Thursdays, so the Christians began to hold theirs on Wednesdays and Fridays. Then on the first day of the week, later called the "Day of the Sun" or "Sunday", as the rising sun became a symbol of the resurrection, they celebrated what came to be called the "Breaking of the Bread". This was to commemorate the sacred meals that they had celebrated with Jesus in the past and, most of all, the last and most sacred meal of all that they had celebrated on the night before Jesus died. It was probably persecution and the dangers of meeting too often that led the first Christians to put these two religious services together as one. So, gradually they began to meet just once a week on Sundays in each other's houses, not in churches, where they would celebrate these two services together: first the synagogue-style service called the *synaxis*, immediately followed by the "Supper of the Lord". From the beginning and to the present day this combined celebration is called the Liturgy in the Eastern Church. In the West it came to be known as the Eucharist, the Communion Service, or the Mass.

'When the synaxis had taken place they would gather around an ordinary dining table where they celebrated the Breaking of the Bread, as Jesus had done with his disciples on the night before he died. When they had received Christ within them, they were all able to offer themselves in and through him to the Father. He was now the new "temple" in and through whom Christians were able to participate in a new form of worship, which he had promised to the Samaritan woman: "The time approaches, indeed it is already here, when those who are real worshippers will worship the Father in spirit and in truth. Such are the worshippers that the Father wants. God is a spirit and those who worship him must worship in spirit and in truth" (John 4:23–25).

'This new form of worship did not involve physical sacrifices, because it was the offering of oneself; this would always be acceptable if it was offered with a pure heart in, with and through Christ's own offering to his Father. So exclusion from the temple did not affect the Christians nor did the destruction of the temple in 70 AD when the Romans utterly destroyed it. Then, as now, Christ was the temple in and through whom they continued to worship God "in spirit and in truth".

'When the Church became "established" under Constantine, Christians no longer needed to practice their faith furtively and the influx of new converts resulted in the building of larger purpose-built places of worship. They were originally called basilicas, because they were copies of contemporary all-purpose buildings of the same name. They were commonplace in all major cities in the Roman Empire and they usually opened onto the forum. They were used especially in poor weather for business transactions, for markets, for the equivalent of council meetings and sometimes they were used as courts. They were easily adapted for worship because they were rectangular in shape with columns of pillars on each side.

'Now at the very moment that Constantine proclaimed that Christianity would henceforth be the official religion of the Roman Empire, the heresy of Arianism began to spread like wildfire. In no time at all, the emphasis on the divinity of Christ began to influence the new churches that were being built to accommodate the converts who came flooding in. The wooden table was gradually discarded in favor of an ever bigger and grander stone table that soon came to be called an altar. Very soon it was venerated as God's throne where, after the conse-cration, he came down to dwell for a time in the sacred bread and wine. Now emphasized as God's throne on earth, the altar was seen as so holy that it was moved further and further away from the common people. Slowly but surely the emphasis changed. The wooden table that had once enabled the faithful to receive

Brother Jesus into their lives through the bread and wine had now become a sacred altar, the very throne of the all-holy God before whom all must prostrate themselves.

'The priest, who had once presided at the Breaking of the Bread, sitting at the Eucharistic table with the faithful gathered around him, now stood in front of it, usually with assistants who hid what took place on the altar from everyone else. Only consecrated clergy or monks were allowed to take their place immediately behind them, further separating the people from the sacred mysteries. They now took up their position at a distance in the main body of the church, men on one side, women on the other. Then another development took place to separate the people even further from the mysteries. The action that took place on the altar/throne was thought to be so holy that reverence demanded that it should be all but screened off from the "vulgar gaze" of the laity.

'In the East an *iconostasis* or decorated screen was used to separate what came to be called the "sanctuary" from the people. The "rood screen" or "holy screen" fulfilled the same function in the West. When pictures or mosaics began to be used to decorate the apse immediately behind the altar, they depicted the distant Christian God, Christ the "Pantocrator" – the Ruler of All – who would come to judge the living and the dead. These dramatic mosaics, many of which can still be seen today, symbolize the new spiritual ethos that began to determine the character and design of Christian churches, thanks to Arianism.

'As Christianity grew and grew and the Goths and other barbarians were converted, new developments were incorporated into far larger churches and cathedrals. These may well have owed much to Euclidian geometry and Roman building techniques, but their external and internal design owed more to the builders' own Gothic heritage. They were inspired by the craggy mountain strongholds where for years the barbarians had felt safe from the Roman legions. The design of these cathedrals and churches was used to dramatic effect to express the new emphasis on the divinity of Christ and the utter transcendence of God, with whom Jesus was for all practical purposes identified. The great Gothic cathedrals that were being built just before and after the birth of Francis perfectly embody in "bricks and mortar" the spiritual ethos of the world into which he was born. They symbolize, too, a Eucharistic spirituality that was eons away from the simple Christ-centered liturgies that had prevailed amongst the early Christians.

'When the ordinary faithful went to Mass it was primarily to encounter the all-holy and transcendent God who, after the consecration, came down on his altar/throne to be worshipped and adored by his people. It was for this reason that at the end of the twelfth century, shortly after Francis was born, the practice spread of elevating the host at Mass. This was to enable ordinary people to adore and worship their God the moment after the consecration. However, the sense of awe and even dread was such that ordinary people, who were weighed down by a sense of sin and guilt, felt totally unworthy of receiving the sacred host. Sometimes they went years without doing so. It was for this reason that at the Fourth Lateran Council, when Francis was about thirty-five, everybody was told that they must go to Communion at least once a year as part of what came to be called their Easter duties. In the early Christian Church it would have been all but unthinkable for believers to take part in the Supper of the Lord without eating and drinking the sacred food that enabled Christ to be continually reborn within them, so that they could offer themselves through him to the Father.

'The wholly new emphasis that prevailed in the medieval Church, the antithesis of that which was emphasized in the early Christian Church, was changed by Francis. He was neither an intellectual nor a great liturgical scholar whose study had inspired him to return to the spirituality of the Gospel as practiced by the first Christians. He was simply a mystic filled and inspired by the same Holy Spirit who was unleashed on the first Pentecost Day. Filled with his love and guided by his wisdom, he was able to inspire others to embrace the simple spirituality of the Gospel that had animated the first Christian community.

'I want to show how Francis was able to do this in many different ways in the rest of my talks, but let me just end this one by showing you how he did it for the Mass. For him, the ultimate mystery that he could never get over was not just that Brother Jesus had become man, but that he had become common bread and wine. The reason for this act of self-abasement was for Francis far greater than the abasement itself. He saw with absolute clarity that Jesus freely chose to become bread and wine, not primarily so that he could be worshipped, but so that he could enter into our very beings, so that, as he promised at the Last Supper, he could make his home within us.

Francis' letter to the General Chapter couldn't be clearer:

Let mankind tremble, let the whole world shake, and the heavens rejoice when Jesus Christ, Son of God, descends onto the altar in the hands of his priests. Oh how wonderful is his dignity and how amazing his condescension. Oh humble sublimity, when the Lord of the universe, God and the Son of God, so humbles himself as to conceal himself beneath the simple form of bread for our salvation. Acknowledge the humility of God, my brothers, and lay the homage of your heart at his feet, humble yourself that he may exalt you. Withhold no part of yourself from him, so that he who has given himself so completely to you may take complete possession of you.

'In his *Life of St Francis*, St Bonaventure described the effect that it had on Francis the moment he received Communion: "He felt a glowing with the devotion that consumed the very marrow of his bones, as he marvelled at the most loving condescension and condescending love. He seemed like one inebriated in Spirit and rapt out of himself in ecstasy" (chapter 10).

'He was totally consumed with the realization that he was being possessed by the love of Brother Jesus entering into his human being, then into his human acting, fusing it with his own. In this way he was caught up into Christ's action, into his love of his Father, so that he could experience something of the mutual love that binds the Father to the Son. This enabled him to experience the ecstatic joy and bliss that ensued as he was drawn into love unlimited, as it relentlessly revolves between the Father and the Son to eternity. He wanted all to share in these ineffable experiences, most particularly his own brothers for whom he wrote in his first rule: "Let nothing hinder us, nothing separate us, nothing disturb us from enshrining the most high supreme eternal God in our hearts. Let us honour, adore, praise, and bless, glorify, exalt, magnify and thank him, who is Trinity in unity, the Father, the Son and the Holy Spirit, creator of all things" (*Regula Non Bullata*, chapter 23).

'Francis couldn't change the physical fabric of the "new order" – churches could not be knocked down and rebuilt – but he did change the Eucharistic spirituality that had been obscured, and returned it to its origins. For Francis, for his brotherhood and for all who were influenced by them, the sacred mysteries took on once again their original meaning. He would do the same, as we shall see, for all the essential characteristics that had epitomized primitive Christianity.'

Peter characteristically paused for us to take in what he had been saying. Although I had been extremely interested in everything that he had said, a misgiving occurred to me.

'I found what you've just been saying very interesting,' I said, 'but I'm wondering how much the early Christians realized the profound implications of participating in the sacred mysteries. After all, I hadn't fully appreciated them myself until now and

I'm a university lecturer.'

'Our problem,' said Peter, 'is that we are far too far away from understanding and appreciating the scriptures as the first Christians did. After all, they were predominately Jewish and had imbibed the Old Testament with their mothers' milk. What I have been trying to say, and what Francis came to understand through his mystical encounters with Jesus, was understood by all of them, precisely because the scriptures were their spiritual meat and drink.

'Let me explain what I mean by imagining one of them going to offer sacrifice at the temple before Jesus had begun to preach. Let's suppose it was St John. It's Passover, so he takes a young lamb with him and gives it to one of the priests as a sacrifice. The lamb is slain and then burnt on the fire. The smoke rises high into the sky, where it was believed that it would attract God's attention by its sweet savor. Then, if God saw that the offering was made by someone with a pure and humble heart, he would send down his Spirit to penetrate the lamb, filling it with his presence. Now what was once John's lamb becomes "God's lamb" or the "Lamb of God". Then, when he and his family, or his friends, sat down to eat that lamb together at Passover, they knew that they were doing something more than just sharing a meal together. They were doing something far more profound. They were being drawn into a mystical union with God, who entered into them through the meat that had been penetrated by his Spirit. His Holy Spirit united them not only with God but also with each other. Now this was something every Jew would have understood, so it would only have been a simple step to under-stand the new sacrificial meal to which Jesus would introduce them.

'When St John heard John the Baptist calling Jesus the "Lamb of God", and then heard Jesus calling himself the "Lamb of God", it could mean only one thing. It meant that God's Holy Spirit possessed Jesus as surely as he had possessed the lamb that John had sacrificed in the temple. So at the Last Supper, when the Lamb of God told John and the other disciples that he would always remain with them through the bread and wine into which he would enter, they all knew exactly what was meant. They knew, not because they were mystics or intellectuals, but simply because they were Jews. They knew that whenever they celebrated sacred meals in commemoration of him in the future, he would not only be present amongst them, but he would also enter into them as they ate the bread and drank the wine that would contain his very presence. Furthermore, he would enter, not just into their human being, but into their acting too. Those who placed no obstacles to him would be caught up into his love of God in heaven and his love of everyone on earth, in what came to be seen as the sacrament of love.

'Now perhaps you can see that what might appear to be complex theological dogmas – to later Christians who did not inherit Jewish culture and traditions – were understood by the early Christians with the greatest of ease. Once Christianity lost its links with its Jewish roots, ignorance became the breeding ground for later heresies that disfigured and distorted the spiritual heritage left by Jesus. But I have said more than enough for one day. I have a few things to do tomorrow morning, so would you mind if I leave you to yourselves until twelve o'clock when we will leave again for Assisi?'

Chapter 7

Turning Pyramids into Circles

The others seemed to have disappeared after breakfast, so I went for a walk around Montefalco, only to bump into Bobbie coming out of a shop with a bundle of postcards in her hand.

'Hello!' she said warmly. 'I'm just about to go for a walk – do you want to join me?' We spent the morning walking around Montefalco before returning for our afternoon excursion.

We set off at midday and took the road to Ponte San Giovanna to visit the site of the battle of Collestrada where Francis had fought against the Perugians. It was here that we stopped for lunch, almost halfway between Assisi and Perugia. It didn't take as long as usual; Peter was eager to get us back on track after the break.

'Jesus made it clear that he had not come to "lord" it over other people but to serve them,' he said. 'This was always the way authority was wielded in the early Church too, until things gradually changed. It was with the establishment of the Church under Constantine that leaders soon assumed positions of power and influence. So by the time Francis was born, the Church that had once seemed like a warm, all-embracing circle of light with Jesus at its center began to look more like an austere pyramid of power. The Pope ruled from the top, followed by cardinals, patriarchs, archbishops, bishops and canons, all the way down to priests and deacons at the bottom. The vast Papal States gave the pontiff immense secular power, something that Jesus would never have accepted because, as he insisted, his kingdom was "not of this world". The Pope may well have styled himself the "servant of the servants of God", but that was all it was – style. The title bore no semblance to the way he acted or to the absolute obedience that he demanded from his subjects. The way he exercised his temporal power inevitably affected the way he exercised his spiritual power and so his spiritual authority was weakened.

'The papal pyramid of power mirrored another pyramid of power called feudalism, which almost totally dominated the secular world. This time it was ruled by the Emperor from the top, followed by kings, dukes, earls, counts, sheriffs and knights, all the way down to the villains and serfs at the bottom. However, events happened in the town of Assisi that were to ensure that Francis would be caught up in the new movement towards democracy that was in its infancy.

'Already many of the major towns in Italy were bent on overthrowing their feudal lords to set up free towns like Florence, Bologna, Genoa and Venice which were ruled by the people and their freely elected leaders. From his infancy Francis would have heard his father ranting and raving at table about Duke Urslingen and his German henchmen who ruled Assisi with a fist of iron. He was fed up paying their taxes and bowing and scraping to him and his flunkies. He was sick of hearing of the cruel and inhuman fate of those who tried to stand up to or speak out against them. Urslingen's dungeons were full of those who had dared to thwart him and they were the lucky ones – at least they would be freed, "come the revolution".

'The citizens were just waiting for the chance that came when the Duke left Assisi to do homage to his new feudal overlord, Pope Innocent III, at Narni. Seizing the opportunity, Bernadone, with his sons Francis and Angelo, joined the rest of the insurgents, razed the Duke's fortress to the ground and built a wall around the town to make sure he couldn't come back. After months of civil war the aristocrats who had sided with the occupying tyrant were routed. Those still alive fled into exile to Perugia where they raised an army. The inevitable happened when, two years later in 1202, the two rival armies met near here at the battle of Collestrada. The Perugians and their collaborators may well have won the battle, but they didn't win back Assisi. Sadly Francis ended up a prisoner of war. Although he was released a year later, his health had been seriously impaired and he never enjoyed good health again for the rest of his life. But thanks to his efforts, his hometown became a free town, free of the pyramids of power that ruled in the rest of Europe. Long before his conversion Francis had played his part and risked his life to bring democracy to his own town. To the Germans he would have been seen as a terrorist, but to his own he was a freedom fighter. It was thanks to him, among others, that Assisi was proclaimed a "commune" with its own freely elected mayor or *Podestà*. These events would have given him a different attitude to power and authority which would prepare him for the future.

'Francis might initially have been dazzled by the chivalry practiced by the knights who had once inspired him, but his heroes were predominantly the Arthurian knights – seen through rose-colored spectacles – and those who followed in their footsteps. Their time was spent fighting for justice, for what was right, and to protect the downtrodden. When they sat down to eat and drink or to take counsel, it was at a round table, for they were all equal in their chivalric brotherhood. But once Francis had experienced the brotherly love of Jesus and read about the way of life he had lived with his disciples, he cast aside his adolescent fantasies. Now he began to dream about living in another form of brotherhood where the bond that bound it together was nothing other than the love that he had already experienced for himself. This Gospel way of life made the democracy that was rising in his hometown and elsewhere look little better than the autocracy that it had displaced. Once his father's cronies took power, Francis soon saw for himself that although all "pigs" were equal, some pigs were "more equal than others". At least the class that they had just usurped had had some sense of the chivalry that Francis had once admired and courtly manners. But these were totally unknown to the new bourgeoisie, who seemed to know only "the price of everything but the value of nothing".

'By the time it was founded Francis was quite clear about his Order; it would be a democratic brotherhood, not another pyramid of power. He totally rejected the way monasticism had copied the pyramid of power in the Church, with its abbots at the top, followed by priors, sub priors, cellarers, and choir monks, all the way down to the minions at its base. That's why he refused to accept the rule of any other previous religious order, whether it was the Rule of St Benedict, the Rule of St Augustine or the Rule of St Bernard. The only rule that he would accept was the rule of life as lived by Jesus and his disciples and in it there would be total equality, as he believed there had been around Arthur's round table. He insisted that it would not have superiors: he would not have abbots nor would he have priors. In his Order a brother would be elected to serve the needs of the brethren for a while as a "mother" or as a "minister", as a "guardian" or as a "warden", before returning to the ranks. Those who were raised to serve the brotherhood for a while would return to their place as simple friars, before power could corrupt them. Their service was not to lord it over anyone, but to create the environment in which everyone had the space and time to receive the Holy Spirit. It was he alone who could create a loving, caring brotherhood from a group of sinners, as he had done in the early Christian Church. Only he who could bring about the unity in the world that Jesus had prayed for at the Last Supper.

'If the Church had to be rebuilt, how better than by a brotherhood of men who lived exactly as Jesus and his disciples had done before the resurrection, and who were filled with the same Spirit who had animated the apostles after the resurrection. Nevertheless Francis never criticized the way that authority was wielded in the Church, any more than he would criticize the scandalous way all too many of the clergy behaved. He knew that there was only one way to change them and that was by the example of his own life, and the lives of those who would follow him.

'Francis made his intentions clear from the very beginning. The moment the fledgling order set out for papal approval, it was Bernard of Quintavalle who was chosen as leader, not himself. The principle set by Francis has continued to this day. Within the brotherhood there was to be total equality, no matter what a man's status had been before. A knight would sit with a nobody, a lawyer with an erstwhile layabout, a general with a private soldier. It was the ultimate desire and hope of Francis that what was seen as successful in his brotherhood would be embraced by others. Then gradually, what Brother Jesus prayed for at the Last Supper would be brought about – all would become as one and peace would reign everywhere on earth, where tyranny had reigned before.'

After Peter had finished speaking we had a break for half an hour or more before going for tea to a quiet restaurant with panoramic views of Assisi, not far from the Basilica of St Mary of the Angels. As we sipped our tea, Peter seemed to be lost in a sort of trance as he gazed at the town in front of him, tumbling down the Sasso Rocco. When he gradually came to his senses he drew our attention to the ruins of the castle at its summit and to the circular wall at its base that Francis had helped to build.

'Look!' he said. 'A perfect pyramid with a circle at its base. I can't help thinking that, without realizing it, Francis spent his life turning pyramids back into circles. There was yet another pyramid that Francis was able to topple that was all but invisible, because it dominated the minds and the imaginations of medieval men and women. It was presided over by an austere and awesome God. He may well have been presented as a Father, but he was a fearsome Father who had demanded the cruel and barbarous death of his only Son to redeem sinners who languished at the base of the pyramid. If he had demanded this of his only Son, what demands would he make of his adopted sons who felt far from him, floundering in the mud and mire of their human helplessness? The demands that were made of them, by the commandments, by the rules and regulations of the Church and by the latest fanatical lay preachers seemed impossible to satisfy. With the departure of Jesus and the Holy Spirit from their personal spirituality, ordinary people felt that they had been left alone to scale the heights from where their awesome God ruled. With no one else to help them, they were left to fend for themselves. This predicament was the perfect breeding ground for yet another heresy to flourish, imported from Greek philosophy. It was called Pelagianism after a Welsh monk called Morgan who was given the Latin name of Pelagius. It was Pelagius who propagated this heresy, which had been derived from Stoicism.

'Although Aristotle was able to argue to a supreme being who created the world, he couldn't see how he could have any interest in that world, as such a being couldn't contemplate anything less than himself. It would be metaphysically impossible. If, therefore, a person wanted to become virtuous or seek communion with God, he was on his own; he could expect no help from God. This was the position of perhaps the greatest moral philosopher of all, Socrates, and of his later disciple Zeno the Greek who was the founder of Stoicism. His ideas were propagated in Rome by Seneca, Epictetus and Marcus Aurelius. They all maintained that if anyone wanted to be perfect, he or she would have to seek perfection and union with God by their own unaided efforts. It's not difficult to see how this heresy soon began to thrive amongst Christians, who, thanks to Macedonianism, seemed to have been deprived of the strength previously given by the Holy Spirit to do what is impossible without him.

'Stoicism never worked for the Stoics, any more than did Pelagianism for Christians, but it didn't stop people trying and believing that they could be the architects of their own perfection – they still do! When those who eventually came to realize the hopelessness of their plight still wanted to reach out to God, they had to look elsewhere for help. Aware of their failures and of the sinfulness that held them back, they began to turn to others more worthy than themselves to intercede for them. So gradually the gap that separated people from God was filled by others more worthy to whom they turned for intercession. First in order of holiness was Mary the Mother of God, then St Joseph, then the martyrs who had died for Jesus, then the saints who had given their life for him. Then many turned to all sorts of superstitious practices, imported from paganism, which promised to do for them what they couldn't do for themselves. This practice was later called "religion by proxy" by the Protestant reformers. It was another pyramid that Francis tried to turn into a circle. However, it was to be a difficult task, because everyone was not only deeply conscious of their sinfulness as flawed human beings but of their guilt too, which grounded them to the earth when they wanted to reach for the heavens.

'This guilt was mainly due to yet another heresy, Neo-Platonism, which had seeped into Christianity. Yet again it had its origin in Greek philosophy. The Neo-Platonists taught that every-thing that was made of matter was evil, especially the body that imprisoned the spirit – the spark of the divine. For them, salvation involved freeing this spirit from every material thing that imprisoned it, so that it could rise to be united with the divine spirit from where it had originally come. And, as man was on his own, it all had to be achieved by his own unaided human endeavor.

'Whilst Neo-Platonism tended to appeal to the more intel-lectual believers, another heresy, Manichaeism, with its origins in the East, tended to appeal to less sophisticated Christians, although St Augustine was one of its adherents before his conversion. Mani taught that there were two Gods: one good, who was responsible for all things spiritual; the other evil, who was responsible for all things material. Both heresies had the same "bottom line" – all things material were evil and an obstacle to salvation. The way to the practice of true virtue and union with God, therefore, involved freeing oneself from everything made of matter. This was the opposite of early Christian spirituality which had taught quite clearly that God had created all things in the beginning and that they were good, precisely because they were made by God in and through his own Word, who was made flesh, not just to live amongst us, but to enter into us. This involved inhabiting every human being open enough to receive him – to the very foundations of their being. So as Arianism became ever more rampant, so too did its offsprings Pelagianism, Neo-Platonism and Manichaeism, and these began to invade every aspect of Christianity spirituality.

'It has become customary for us to look back to the Desert Fathers with a certain reverence and awe, as if they were the founders and guardians of the first expression of authentic Christian spirituality. But the truth is that many of them practiced a bizarre hybrid spirituality that was unheard of in the Gospels. Thanks to the influence of these pagan philosophies, asceticism was often seen as the primary means to free the human spirit from its bodily prison. Inevitably this led to an unhealthy attitude toward the body: it had to be beaten into submission, sometimes by literal beatings or by deprivation of food, drink and sleep.

'If this asceticism was hard enough in the Egyptian desert, it was even harder in Syria and Mesopotamia where the renowned Simon Stylites lived half-starved to death on top of a thirty-foot-high pillar. Even those who found his asceticism extreme nevertheless tortured their bodies into submission with mortifying fasts, often broken only with meals of freshly cut grass. As if this weren't enough, they made liberal use of other means of grinding their bodies into submission with "prolonged scourging, spikes, chains, weights and other instruments of penance" – practices that were never used by Jesus, nor enjoined upon his followers. Many of these disciplines – flogging, for instance – were not just left to the whim of individual monks but were often imposed by superiors on monks who had sinned against the monastic way of life. This practice was even commonplace in Benedictine monasticism, otherwise known for its moderation, and practiced for many subsequent centuries by other religious orders too. However, all this was nothing compared to the floggings imposed on the early Irish monks, not by choice but by statute: "Six strokes for the monk who broke the silence, twelve for leaving the monastery without permission, fifty for gossiping and one hundred for speaking to a woman!"

'Inevitably women, who were believed to be more responsible than any other "material thing" for luring men away from the "life of the Spirit", were seen as the enemy of both monks and laymen who wanted to seek perfection. They were looked upon as, at best, unwitting temptresses and at worst as jezebels who would lead even the best of men to perdition. In the words of St Augustine, "nothing is so powerful in drawing the spirit downward as the caresses of a woman". It should not be surprising, then, that the Fathers at the Council of Nicaea actually debated whether or not women had souls. It was in this sort of climate that priests, for whom marriage was originally the norm, were progressively pressurized into accepting virginity, so that their sacred ministry would remain untarnished by the sins of the flesh that would inevitably result from contact with the daughters of Eve!

'Sex then became the single most serious sin that threatened to prevent, not just priests, but everyone from attaining union with God. An attitude to sexuality and marriage began to flourish that had no place anywhere in the Bible. Even a great mystical writer like St Gregory of Nyssa, for instance, referred to marriage as "a sad tragedy", one of the regrettable results of original sin. St Ambrose called it "a galling burden". St Jerome believed that its only positive significance was that it raised virgins with which to adorn the Church. Although Saint Augustine's view is well known – that sexual intimacy is always sinful except for procreation – it is not as well known that St Gregory the Great went one step further, condemning all sexual intercourse, for whatever reason, as inevitably sinful.

'What was holy and sacred for Jesus and the Jewish tradition into which he was born suddenly became suspect, ugly or even evil, through alien pagan heresies that desecrated the Christian spirituality which still prevailed in the world into which Francis was born. In the Bible sex was the single most important means by which God's promise to Abraham was to be fulfilled. It was only through marriage and sexual intercourse that God would make Israel a great nation and the place where the Word would be made flesh to dwell amongst us. So in the Old Testament, virginity was not seen as a sign that a person was virtuous, but a sinner whom God was punishing by excluding him or her from his covenant with Abraham. Once again, distance from the roots of Christianity and the insidious effects of paganism muddied not only the spirituality of monasticism but that of the wider Christian community too.

'However, it was in Albigensianism, which was flourishing at the time of Francis, that the logical consequences of Platonism and Manichaeism were to be found. The Podestà of the new democracy that Francis had fought for was an Albigensian. The Albigensians argued that, if attachment to material things prevents one from attaining perfection, then total abstention should have the desired effect. Therefore, for the Albigensian who was impatient for perfection, the so-called *endura* was the only course of action. This entailed a sort of ritual suicide. Once he had committed himself to such a "holy enterprise" his brothers would support him with prayers. Then, just in case he had second thoughts when the end drew near, leather straps would be kept handy to make sure he remained true to the "holy desire" that had first inspired him!

'Once again it was in experiencing the love that he received from Brother Jesus, in whom all things were created, that Francis saw that all things were good in themselves. He did not ask his brothers to deny themselves the good things that God had created because such things were flawed but because they themselves were flawed and therefore greed could dissipate and corrupt them. Even then, he always counseled moderation and scolded those who fasted or mortified themselves immoderately. In his *Life of St Francis*, St Bonaventure insisted that "Francis did his utmost to encourage the friars to lead austere lives, but he had no time for exaggerated self-denial which excluded tender compassion or was not tempered with discretion" (chapter 5).

'Francis clearly saw the difference between the sacrifices that are necessary to wean people from all that prevents God possessing them, and the sacrifices of a person who just wants to express the joy of being possessed by the love that surpasses the understanding. The first must always be kept within the bounds of moderation, but the second is bound only by the love that must express itself. It was this love that drove Francis to express his feelings in ways that would seem at times extravagant to those who have never experienced the superfluity of love that enthralled him. This was the love that he wanted to share, not just with his own brethren but with the whole of humanity, so that the whole world could become bonded together as one into the unity for which Jesus had prayed at the Last Supper.'

All of us remained still for several minutes, gazing at Assisi bathing in the sunlight, which made it look like a fairytale town with a fairytale story to tell. It was a story that we all thought we knew. But without Peter's historical sweeps and profound spiritual insights we wouldn't have known the half of it. As we passed the great Basilica of St Mary of the Angels on our way home, I felt aggrieved that, though we had passed it half a dozen times or more, we hadn't been in to visit the place more special to Francis than any other. Peter must have read my mind as I gazed at the great dome out of the window.

'Don't worry,' he said. 'We'll be going there first thing tomorrow morning – I promise.'

I smiled and Peter smiled back.

It was Emelia who posed the first question that evening. 'Why was virginity seen as a sign of separation from God in the Old Testament, when it was seen as a sign of consecration to him in the New Testament?' she asked.

'Well,' said Peter, 'in the Old Testament there could be nothing worse than to be barren. It meant that you were excluded from the first part of God's plan. This was that Abraham would father a people to inherit the Promised Land and all the promises that he had made through the prophets. However, in the New Testament, once Jesus had sent his Spirit out to bring about the second part of God's plan, everyone could transmit it to others. This would enable everyone, married and unmarried alike, to take part in bringing about what St Paul called "God's Secret Plan". Its contents were only hinted at by the prophets in the Old Testament, but it was fully revealed in the New Testament. Now interestingly enough, the word St Paul used for "God's Secret Plan" is the Greek word *Mysterion* from which we derive the word "mystic" (Ephesians 1:9 et seq.). The Secret Plan or the Mysterion was simply this – that the Holy Spirit sent by Jesus, working through his followers, was to unite all people together with the whole of creation into a vast all-embracing brotherhood and sisterhood.

But let the words of St Paul speak for themselves:

He chose us in Christ, before the world was made, to be holy and faultless before him in love, marking us out ... to be

135

adopted sons through Jesus Christ ... He has let us know the mystery of his purpose ... which he determined beforehand in Christ ... that he would bring everything together under Christ as head, everything in the heavens and everything on earth.

(Ephesians 1:4–10)

'Those most able to bring this plan to perfection are mystics, in other words those Christians who have received and experienced for themselves the Holy Spirit, who alone can draw all things into one – into the All in all. In this new world order inaugurated by Jesus, virgins who were rejected as barren in the Old Testament were to have a unique role. By choosing to forgo the "sacrament of love", they were able to dedicate every moment of their lives to opening themselves directly to the reality of Love. This is none other than the Holy Spirit, whose love they then transmitted to others through a spiritual motherhood denied to their counterparts in the Old Testament.

'When the Fathers of the early Church wrote treatises, usually called *Ad Virgines*, to encourage women in their vocations, the message was always the same: they would be as barren as their forebears if their virginity did not lead them into inner Kenosis, where they were to wait with the "wise virgins". Then, ready and waiting, they would come to experience the same Pleroma, the "fullness of love" that filled the Risen Christ. Now they could become spiritual mothers, living channels through which his love could be transmitted to others so that God's Hidden Plan, his Mysterion, could be brought about on earth.

'I've answered your question at length, so that you can see that it was by entering into what Francis called Lady Poverty and what the early Fathers called Kenosis, that he was ready and open for the moment of truth. The moment of truth came when he received the Pleroma which enabled him not only to experience the love of the Holy Spirit but through that love to receive the wisdom given to true mystics. This wisdom enabled him to see in its entirety God's Hidden Plan, his Mysterion.

'In a letter to the General Chapter shortly before he died, Francis begged his brothers to show reverence for Christ's Body and Blood, precisely because it is the Body and Blood of the one in whom all things have been brought together as one and reconciled with God: "Kissing your feet with all the love I am capable of, I beg you to show the greatest possible reverence for the most holy Body and Blood of our Lord Jesus Christ through whom all things have been brought to peace and reconciled with Almighty God."

'Although these words were written toward the end of his life, it was at the beginning of his spiritual transformation that he had first come to see and understand that all things were created in and through Brother Jesus. It was his love that he felt penetrating every part of him, and his wisdom that enabled Francis to appreciate what was happening to him and what God wanted of him. This was the sacred task that God had given to Francis and his followers. His mystical brotherhood was to be totally dedicated to bringing about God's Mysterion so that all creation could be brought back into loving communion with himself. Radical poverty and prayer without ceasing would open them to be filled by his relentless loving. Then, by their humble presence in the world, that loving would spread to do again what had been done over a thousand years before. Winter was over, a new spring had dawned, and the plan conceived by God and forgotten by man was to be resurrected again, thanks to a poor little man who never stopped loving.'

'I find what you say most inspiring,' I said, 'but what happened to this vision after Francis died?'

'The vision continued and many of his followers have lived and preached it to the present day, but it has to be admitted that not all followed Francis as faithfully as they should. You see, after his death many of his followers became so entangled in disputes about the interpretation of the rule, the size of the houses that they lived in, or the meaning of the poverty that they professed, that they forgot to go to the hermitages. The inevitable happened. The Mysterion and the Christ-centered spirituality on which it depended gradually lost the breadth and the depth that only the true mystic sees. Eventually a new spirituality emerged that spread all over Europe. Although it would not have been possible without Francis, it sadly diluted his vision.

'This new spirituality emphasized a personal piety, full of feeling and sentiment, that made Jesus a friend and personal savior. This was not of course bad in itself, so long as it was a starting point, as it usually is anyway. However, when it became the "be all and end all" of Christian spirituality it easily degenerated into nothing more than a self-indulgent personal piety. It turned a blind eye to the social needs of others and to the brotherhood of all in God which is the goal of all authentic Christian endeavors. The name given to the best-known expression of this piety was the *Devotio Moderna*. It was particularly associated with a certain Geert Groote and the Brethren of the Common Life in the Netherlands. Most of us are familiar with it, thanks to a member of that community, Thomas à Kempis, and his book *The Imitation of Christ*. The flowering of this new spirituality coincided with the rise of humanism at the Renaissance and many Christian intellectuals like Erasmus tried to fuse the two together. The marriage was not a happy one, for their offsprings inherited unwelcome genes from their parents. Manichaean tendencies, with its rather self-indulgent piety, were inherited from the Devotio Moderna. Then Pelagian tendencies were inherited from humanism, which began to see Christ as a sort of Christian Socrates, so that he came to be viewed more as a moral teacher than as a mystic.'

'So I suppose you could say that these were the seeds of the spirituality that came to characterize the Protestant Reformation?' I suggested.

'Yes, I think that's true,' said Peter. 'But they are also the seeds that fed the Catholic piety that we were brought up on too.'

'My parents were originally English,' I went on, 'so they sent me to an English public school where the spirituality that they fed us on was exactly as you have described. It was a fusion of the Devotio Moderna with Anglican Humanism.'

'Yes,' said Peter, 'you're absolutely right, but let me explain why. Way back at the beginning of the sixteenth century there was an extremely erudite priest called John Colet. He had been brought up on the spirituality of the Devotio Moderna, but when he spent time in Italy he not only fell in love with the glories of the Renaissance in general but also with the teachings of Socrates and their descendants, the Stoics. He came back to England full of enthusiasm to share his ideas with others. He wanted to share them not only with his peers but with the younger generation too – so he founded St Paul's School in London. The perfect product of this school would be embodied in a true English gentleman, in whom the teachings of Socrates and Christ would be perfectly harmonized. The other eight major public schools modeled themselves on St Paul's. The grammar schools followed suit. Later, public schools that arose to accommodate the sons of the nouveau riche – who were born of the Industrial Revolution and the exploitations of empire – modeled themselves in their turn on the "big nine". The same aims and ideals could eventually be found in more diluted forms in the secondary and compre- hensive schools of the twentieth century, and I do not exclude Catholic schools either.'

'So really,' said Bobbie, 'one way or the other, we have all inherited a spirituality that may well owe much to Francis for its origins, but owes much more to the Devotio Moderna and Christian Humanism.'

'Exactly,' said Peter as he turned to Emelia, who wanted to say something.

'Our Third Order chaplain,' she said, 'told us that the instigators of the Second Vatican Council were in fact trying to do in our day what St Francis had done in his day. So I suppose he was right.'

'He was absolutely right,' said Peter, 'but sadly it only had a limited success because it didn't have a Francis to embody and spread the biblical spirituality that is its heart and soul. It had more than enough intellectuals who had studied biblical theology for years to make the council possible, but it needed saints like Francis to implement it and spread it to ordinary people. Remember the point made by St Bonaventure: "It is only those who have been purified by prayer who can penetrate the hidden depth of the mysteries for, where the scholarship of the intellectual stands outside, the love of the mystic enters within." Most revolutions fail because the revolutionaries are flawed by human weakness and their idealism cannot be sustained. When he was dying, Lenin saw that his revolution had failed to fulfill the ideals for which he had fought and suffered so much. His dying words were that it would only have been possible to achieve with ten Francises of Assisi.'

That night, I went to sleep the moment my head touched the pillow. Peter had given us a great deal to think about, but my poor head had had enough for one day. I didn't even have enough energy to think about Bobbie. Our little adventure the day before had certainly drawn us closer together. Could it be the beginnings of what I believed Peter wanted for us?

Chapter 8

The Prayer without Ceasing

Strange, but the moment I entered the great Basilica of St Mary of the Angels I felt at home. It wasn't the Basilica itself that affected me – far from it: I found it vast and vacuous. It was rather the little church that nestled beneath the great dome.

'Now,' said Peter, 'I want you to close your eyes for a moment and imagine away the Basilica with all the other buildings that surround it. Imagine yourself back 800 years ago. Then imagine this little church completely restored by the hands of Francis, but without the later embellishments that decorate the façade. And there you have it – the pride and joy of the Poverello of Assisi! He loved it most especially because of where it was, on worthless land too poor to cultivate. For the soil was too marshy to support anything other than weak and sickly woodland. It was not worth the time and energy to drain it so the monks left the land to fester and the church to fall into ruins. It was simply ideal for Francis. The "woodland" bore an abundance of wispy branches and twigs, ideal for making hurdles that could be daubed with mud from the marshland and made into primitive cells to house his first companions.

'It was, he felt, divine providence that this poor little church was called after Mary the Mother of God. If ever Lady Poverty was to have a physical embodiment then it was in her. Although Mary was of noble birth – a direct descendant of David, the first king to rule over Israel – she was born as poor as Francis had been born rich. However, it was another form of poverty that characterized her inner soul: a "spiritual poverty" that Francis wished to imitate with all his heart. She was totally empty of all the human frailty that could possibly mar her simple docility and openness to God. If only Francis could be as open to God as she had been! Then perhaps Jesus could be conceived again in him and grow in him so that like her he could become a spiritual mother and give Jesus to the world. This was his deepest desire for himself and for the brothers who would join him. That is why Francis wanted this miserable barren little property; it was to speak to all who lived in it or visited it of the physical and spiritual poverty that he wanted embodied in all who followed him. That's the reason why he loved this grubby wasteland, this Portiuncula, more than any another place on earth and this poor little oratory at its center more than any other church in the world. To him, St Mary of the Angels was to be the hub and headquarters of his Order that would spread all over the world and all down the centuries. He would repeatedly say to his friars, "My sons, see that you never abandon this place. If you are driven out of one door, re-enter it by another, for this place is holy indeed. For it is the dwelling place of Christ and his Virgin Mother."

Peter didn't tell us to open our eyes, but we did, one by one. We did not, however, forget those pictures that we had conjured in our imaginations, for they were left to stain our memories for the rest of our lives. He led us up and into what was for Francis and his followers one of the holiest places on earth. I can't hide the fact that I felt a certain pride that I had chosen to become one of his followers; I also sensed that, in coming here, I had come home. I knew for certain that I would return many times for the rest of my life (and I did).

Our visit had already been prearranged, for as Peter gestured to us to be seated, one of the friars cordoned off the entrance to the little church so that he could speak to us without being disturbed. Then the friar sat at the back so that he too could listen to Peter. We all rightly assumed that it was his friend Fr Joseph.

'You all know,' he said, 'what happened here on the Feast of St Matthias on February 24th 1208. Francis was so moved by the words of St Matthew's Gospel that he abandoned what little he still had. He threw away his staff, took off his sandals and in future wore only one tunic, which he now tied with a simple cord instead of the leather belt that he'd discarded. He never again carried a haversack, which was superfluous anyway, for he had nothing to put in it.

'When the priest explained what he had just read, Francis said, "This is what I long for with all my heart." Now he went out with joy to proclaim the same Good News that the apostles had been told to proclaim by Jesus himself. Henceforth he would always begin his preaching with the words "God give you peace". Then, after explaining that God's love was as present today as it had been on the first Pentecost Day, he called upon his listeners to repent. This was the only way to receive that love, so that the Father, the Son and the Holy Spirit could find a home within them, as it had found a home within him. This was the only way that they could come to experience the God-given peace with which he had first greeted them.

'Francis was not the first person in medieval times to preach repentance, but he was the first to do it as St Peter had done over a thousand years before. Peter was so filled with the love of God that people thought he was drunk. It was the same with Francis. But once his listeners came to realize that he was inebriated, not with alcohol, but with the love of God, they began to listen with respect. Then, when he told them that by repenting they too could receive the same love that animated him, they began to take him seriously and then they began to respond to what he asked of them. When you see someone embodying the pure unadulterated goodness that you want for yourself, you'll do whatever they say to receive it – and they did. Hundreds and thousands wanted to join his new Order to receive what he promised them and many thousands more chose to change their lives while remaining in the "world". God's plan was not just back on the table again; it was being implemented once more by a new brand of apostles inspired by the same Spirit who had inspired the first apostles. And oh, how these apostles were needed!

'There was certainly more than enough need for radical reform in the Catholic Church and, to be fair, Innocent III had openly admitted it. He had even detailed the evils that needed reforming, in particular the evils that galvanized many of the traveling preachers who swarmed over medieval Europe before Francis was born and whilst he was growing up. Many looked poor, dressed poorly and many *were* poor, but all too many of them were bitter too. They preached against the clergy and they preached about the wrath of a vengeful God who ruled from on high, threatening hell fire and eternal damnation.

'When we came into the Basilica,' said Peter, 'I asked you to close your eyes so that you could imagine the Portiuncula as it was over 800 years ago. Now I would like to ask you to do the same so that I can imprint on your imaginations something of the ethos that prevailed in medieval Europe, to help you to appreciate the world that gave birth to these disparate sects. Then you may see why Francis, though he was born into that same world, was so different.'

Peter paused for a moment until we had all closed our eyes, then continued.

'Picture in your imaginations those great medieval churches, those vast cathedrals. They still move us today, but imagine how they must have moved medieval men and women, how they must have spoken to them, as they were meant to, of the *Rex Tremendae Majestatis*, the "Utterly Transcendent God" who ruled from on high. He was the Pantocrator – the Ruler of All – and he ruled with an inflexible iron fist. The very liturgy that people celebrated reinforced the distance of the God who came down amongst them briefly so that all could prostrate themselves before him. He may well have been called a Father but he was predominantly a spiritual lord and master. Those who disobeyed him would be punished with eternal flames. And just to make sure everyone understood the message, the walls of the churches were vibrant with vivid paintings of the horrors of hell hereafter. The back wall of the church was a favorite place to terrify the congregations with the fear of eternal punishment as they left.

'No wonder medieval men and women felt small and insignificant, aware of their sinfulness, their guilt and their powerlessness. No wonder they turned to others more holy than themselves to intercede for them. No wonder they turned to superstitious practices from their pagan past to induce God to forgive them for the sins that would banish them to eternal damnation. This was particularly true of their so-called "sexual sins", which seemed to besmirch what little human consolation they could turn to. This spirituality, seeping into them by a sort of pernicious osmosis each time they went into the church, was reinforced from the pulpit if they were unlucky enough to understand Latin, or by the latest batch of itinerant preachers if they couldn't. The prevailing atmosphere was one of fear. The same atmosphere that permeated their religious practice inside the church permeated their daily lives outside the church too. This time it was the fear of punishment at the hands of their feudal lord or at the hands of their ecclesiastical lords and masters who could exact terrible temporal punishments too. Those who questioned the conventional wisdom of the Church would receive little mercy – the punishments were harsh, from excommunication and confiscation of property, to exile or even death. Even God appeared to them as a person of little mercy. Hadn't he commanded that his own Son should suffer an ignominious death to pay off some infinite debt incurred eons ago?

'This, then, was the world in which Francis had grown up. It was exactly the same world in which the lay preachers who preceded him had grown up too. Now these radical firebrands fell into two main groupings: those who were within the Church, like the Waldenses or the Humiliati, and those who had set up their own church like the Cathari and the Albigensians. Although the Cathari publically embraced Manichaeism, all the other sects were tainted by its teaching too.

'Why was Francis so different and why did the same call to repentance sound so much softer and prove to be far more effective when it came from his lips and from the lips of his followers? There was certainly a completely different tone and texture about his preaching that endeared him to his listeners. It inspired them to embrace his invitation to repent because it was preached with softness and with a compassion that was invariably absent from those who had preceded him. And it spoke of a completely different God. The same distant God who had first frightened the young Francis had been revealed to him as a tender, loving Father. First it was the love of Jesus that enveloped him, sweeping him up into an ecstasy which taught him instantly and experientially that if he had such a loving Brother then he had a loving Father too. That's why he was given the strength to make the break with his own father in open court before the Bishop of Assisi and declare that henceforth he had only one Father. In the years that followed, Francis experienced this Fatherly love ever more deeply, preparing him for the day when he would be commissioned, in this little church, to go out preaching the Good News that he had already experienced for himself.

'The Good News was that, contrary to what everyone had been brought up to believe, God was a tender, loving Father whose main concern was not to damn people to hell but to fill them with the same love that had filled Jesus. This would enable them to experience, even in this life, something of the fullness of love that was in store for them in the next. Thanks to Francis, the verb "to repent" was given back its original meaning. In the Old Testament it was derived from the Hebrew word *shub*, which means "to return". Isaiah used the word to describe prodigal sons who returned to their Father. This is precisely how Jesus used the word except that, with him, the Father to whom we are called to return is described not by the Aramaic word for "Father" but by the Aramaic word for "Daddy", namely *Abba*. The word "Father" can be ambivalent in any language, but this is never true of the word "Daddy". Who is a daddy? What is a daddy? In any language he is the one who gives life to his children. It was from this loving Father that Francis received exactly the same life and love which animated Brother Jesus and which drew him up into the familial love that he continually experienced.

'So the repentance that Francis preached was more an invitation to return home like the prodigal son to a doting father, rather than a threat of eternal damnation for those who would not listen to him. The firebrands seemed to be more interested in frightening people into performing punishing penances for their sins with threats of terrible tortures to come if they didn't. Francis was far more interested in filling them with the Fatherly love that he knew from personal experience would make all things possible that are quite impossible without it. This does not mean that there was anything soft about practicing what he preached. He knew full well what repenting involved, because he had practiced it himself for several years before he preached it to others. Through continual practice in and out of prayer, Francis learned that returning to God meant continually turning and opening his heart and mind to his loving Father. This enabled his Fatherly love to empty Francis of everything that prevented him conceiving Christ within him.

'The Holy Spirit instantly entered into Mary because she was totally pure and open to receive him. But for Francis and the rest of us, that is not the case. The process of being emptied of the sin and selfishness that was never in her is at times very painful. It involves a profound inner purification. It was comparatively easy for Francis to embrace a life of physical poverty, but it was far more exacting for him to embrace a life of spiritual poverty. Yet this was the only way that he could enable the Holy Spirit to bring about in him what had been brought about in her.

'As he persevered in trying to turn to God in prayer, no matter how dark and exacting it became, Francis discovered that he received strength that he had never received before. It enabled him to turn to God outside of prayer too – in those who were poor and needy. The first time that he realized this was when, instead of running away from lepers, he kissed them on the mouth and tended their wounds.

'Gradually he came to realize that practicing repentance inside of prayer is the way to observe the first of the new commandments, which is "to love God with all your heart and soul". Only then was he given the strength to observe the second commandment outside of prayer, which is "to love your neighbor as you love yourself". It was in this way that Francis came to practice what the scriptures call the "prayer without ceasing" as every moment of every day became a time for turning to God. As he wrote in his rule, "Idleness is the enemy of the soul and so those who serve God should always be busy praying or doing good" (Rule of 1221).

'When he began to invite others to turn to God, they listened, because they could see that he had practiced what he preached and had already received for himself what he promised to others.

'The firebrands who were calling people to repent before and after Francis had a far harsher edge to their preaching. They didn't last for very long, for the stoical demands that they made on themselves could not be sustained. However, there were always new generations of bitter rabble-rousers ready to fill their sandals, so the movements that weren't condemned by the Church did last much longer than human frailty would have allowed. After all there's only so much blood that you can lose marching from town to town, flogging yourself to exhaustion. Many later saw the errors of their ways thanks to the preaching of Francis and his sons, and some even joined them to embrace a teaching that was the very antithesis of the one from which they had so recently departed.

'It would be wrong to suggest that Francis was not a man of his time or that he was totally unaffected by a spirituality that, thanks to the grace of God, he was able to supersede. Although he was ultimately freed from the Neo-Manichaeism that no doubt affected his early years, he was nevertheless so strict with himself that he felt it necessary to apologize to Brother Body once he finally saw the error of his ways. However, it is always important to remember that with Francis, as with all the great saints, there is a clear distinction between the acts of self-sacrifice that are practiced in order to control whatever prevents union with God and those that follow such a union. Whenever a person experiences the joy of being loved, they want to express their love through sacrifice and this is what you see Francis doing over and over again.

'When followers see such sacrifices and mistakenly think that they are the way to sanctity, they are deceived. It is only a matter of time before the inevitable failure that makes them renounce all asceticism for good and settle for apathy instead. That's why Francis always taught his brothers to practice moderation from the very beginning. He went out of his way to ban "penitential shirts", the use of "iron rings" and other forms of metal "disciplines" to torture "the naked body". And he did this at a general chapter so that nobody could be in doubt about his feelings in the matter. He made it clear that moderation should always be used in all forms of asceticism, especially when it came to food and drink, and he chastised those who wouldn't listen to him. He even insisted that they should always eat whatever was placed before them when they were on their travels. Nevertheless the asceticism that we might find repulsive today was not exceptional by the standard of his day nor was it seen as an attempt to free the spirit imprisoned in an evil body. The flesh that he shared with Brother Jesus was not evil in itself, but it did have a wayward tendency; that's why it had to be kept under control.

'In practicing repentance before he preached it to others, Francis was in fact copying Jesus who did likewise. You see, while he was on earth Jesus spent his whole life repenting. Before you write me off as a heretic, please hear me out. The letter to the Hebrews states quite clearly that "he was tempted in all things just as we are tempted". However, unlike us, he never succumbed to temptation. He repeatedly turned away from it and turned his attention back to God – in other words he *repented*. It is only because we are sinners that we always assume that repentance means turning away from sin after we have fallen, and we usually associate it with feelings of guilt for what we have done. The meaning of repentance is far wider than that – it also means to turn away from temptations too and from anything that would turn us away from God. This is the sort of repentance that is learned by endlessly turning away from the distractions and the temptations that always assail anyone who seriously tries to pray for any length of time.

'When Jesus went into solitude to pray at the outset of his work on earth, he was repeatedly tempted to turn his attention away from God. Despite the powerful temptations that were hurled against him in the desert, he nevertheless repeatedly turned his attention back to God to receive the love that he needed to support him for what lay ahead. In other words he was tempted in prayer just as we are, but he repeatedly turned back to his Father without the long hesitations that continually flaw us. In the same way he had to practice repentance outside of prayer too as his enemies continually tried to prevent him from speaking the truth and doing good. His final act of repentance was made on the cross when, despite the terrible pain and suffering and the temptations to end it all sooner rather than later, he finally turned to God with the words "Father, into your hands I commend my spirit". He never needed to repent again because at that moment he was caught up in the ecstatic joy that resulted from receiving the Pleroma – the fullness of love that he had temporarily abandoned to come and teach us how to receive it.

'When Francis had prayed before the Risen Christ in San Damiano, he knelt there as a bystander. That's how he prayed to begin with, but as his prayer changed from meditation to contemplation his relationship to Christ changed too. As the Holy Spirit progressively purified him, as he repeatedly repented, he gradually became less and less of a bystander. The more his contemplative prayer deepened, the more he was taken up into Christ, not just into his life but into his action – into Christ's endless love of his Father. He became a participator now in Christ's love of his Father and a sharer in what Christ received from God. If we can only learn from Francis and do what he did, what happened to him can happen to us too. Then if a sufficient number do for our world what Francis did for his, I think you'll find that Lenin was right, even if his communism was wrong.'

When Peter had stopped speaking he quietly walked out of the little chapel and left us all lost in prayer. I couldn't help thinking that I was praying in the very place where Francis had cut off the hair of St Clare and received her as the first member of a new order of poverty for women. It was the very place too where he had shared a meal with her and the very place where he had received Jacoba de Settesoli when she came to visit him shortly before his death. Emelia took us to the little chapel built over the place where Francis had died and where he had written the verse in praise of Sister Death shortly before what came to be called his Transitus. We couldn't help but smile when we saw the famous statue of Francis with the doves nesting in his hands. After we had visited the ancient *convento* built by San Bernardino of Siena, we drove to a beautiful garden nearby where we ate our packed lunches. We had all been so moved by what we had seen and heard that we said very little on the journey back to

Montefalco.

When I saw Emelia knocking on Peter's door after supper I realized why he had said that he would be engaged. He had said at the beginning of the pilgrimage that he would be available for private consultation, so Emelia was taking him at his word. After a walk in the surrounding countryside to the sound of gunshot – the local hunters were shooting everything in sight – I retired to the church before going to bed. I was just leaving when I bumped into Emelia. She looked radiant.

'He was absolutely wonderful!' she said.

'Who was?' I asked, a little disingenuously.

'Peter,' she replied. 'I asked to speak with him privately this morning before we set off. Then when I heard his talk this morning I felt I'd be making a fool of myself because he had really answered the questions that I wanted to ask him. But he was so wonderful – I'm so pleased I didn't cancel. You see, for some months now I've been tempted to give up the daily time for prayer in our little chapel. I just didn't seem to be getting anywhere at all. I seemed to be spending all my time fighting against distractions and temptations that seemed to make a mockery of what I was supposed to be doing. When I explained my problem, Peter gave me a wonderful reply. He said that St Teresa of Avila had said that you couldn't really pray without distractions. If you didn't have any distractions then you were either asleep or in an ecstasy. If you were asleep then you weren't doing anything and if you were in an ecstasy then you weren't doing anything either because God was doing everything. Prayer, he said, takes place in the middle between the sleep and the ecstasy, and there you will always have distractions of one sort or another. The essence of prayer involves endlessly trying to turn back to God despite them.

'Then he said that's how St Francis finally became a saint: by endlessly turning away from distractions or by repeatedly repenting – it's the same thing. By continually practicing repentance in this way, he learned how to turn and open himself to God to enable his love to empty him of all that caused the distractions in the first place. This didn't mean that they would ultimately go away for good, but that he would have ever more quality time inside of prayer to contemplate God in peace and receive from him the stuff that saints are made of.

'But I must go,' said Emelia suddenly. 'Peter has agreed to put together a summary for me. I'll give you a copy when I've finished.'

She was true to her word, but the truth of the matter is that I had heard it all before; after all, Peter had been my spiritual director for years. However, I have inserted her little memorandum below because it may be of help to you, particularly as it perfectly complements the talk Peter gave in the morning.

Emelia's Memorandum

Francis first practiced what he preached and he practiced for several years before he started preaching to others. The essence of prayer consists in repeatedly turning to receive the love that continually pours out from God. Like everything else, responding to love has to be learned.

Learning to pray, then – learning to open ourselves to God – is like anything else: it needs practice and it takes time. There is no accomplishment of any worth that I know of, that you can attain merely by desiring to have it. We think nothing of spending hours a day and working for years to get a degree, pass an examination or attain certain qualifications. And we quite rightly accept as a matter of course that the time we give and the energy we expend is necessary. Somehow we seem to think that prayer is an exception, but believe me, it is not. Like any form of learning, then, responding to God's love is initially difficult and burdensome until, with continual practice, it becomes easier and easier until 'practice makes perfect'. Practice eventually makes perfect because as we turn to God we enable him to enter into us, permeating our being with his being, fusing our acting with his.

Let me give you an example of what I mean. When I set up home in my cottage on the island of Calvay, I found an old mangle in one of the outhouses to help me with my washing. It was so old and rusty that I had great difficulty in using it until the parish priest came to my aid with a can of oil. As I tried to turn the handle, he poured the oil onto the cogs and gradually they began to turn with ever-greater ease and facility. The action of the oil symbolized for me the action of the Holy Spirit in prayer. As a person tries to turn to God, the Holy Spirit enters into the process, gradually giving ever greater ease and facility to do what would be quite impossible without him. Now notice that I used the word 'tries' because we can do no more than *try* to turn to God. If we ever succeed it will be thanks to him. This is true not only of prayer but of everything else. The Jewish philosopher Simone Weil said, 'A person is no more than the quality of their endeavor.' That's how God will ultimately judge how we have prayed – and how we have done everything else for that matter.

However, the way we try is crucial. Initially I found it so hard trying to turn the handle of the mangle that I lost my temper with it. I was depending totally on my own efforts and this got me nowhere until the oil came to my rescue. It's exactly the same with prayer: if we act as if everything depends on us, we will get nowhere. In prayer, then, the way a person tries must demonstrate their deeply held conviction that success ultimately depends, not on their action, but on the action of God. If we find that we are getting angry it's because we think everything depends on us and it doesn't depend on God. When we have learned this and the patience that humbly awaits his action, then he will begin to act within us like never before. That's why I like to qualify the word 'trying' with the word 'gently'. The word 'gently' describes the way we ought to try. In other words, in such a way that we know that without God's action entering into ours, failure will be inevitable. Harness these two words together and you have what I think is an ideal definition of prayer: 'gently trying to turn and open the heart and mind to God'.

Now in order to help a person keep turning away from distractions and back to God, Christian tradition has devised many different forms of prayer. There are no perfect means of prayer. There are just different means to help a person to keep turning and opening their heart to God. The important point to remember is that there is no magic formula, no infallible method or technique. There are just hundreds of different ways of prayer to do one and the same thing. A means of prayer is good for you, if it helps you here and now to keep turning your heart back to God. What might help you at the beginning of your spiritual journey may be of no use later on. What helps you in the morning might not help you in the evening. What helps you one minute might not help you the next. So please move from one method to another with complete freedom. Remember that these methods are only means. Beware of the 'here today and gone tomorrow' gurus who have a fixation about a particular means of prayer which they enjoin upon everybody without question as a 'panacea'. They know nothing about the spiritual life. If they did, they'd know that methods of prayer change as people change and as prayer develops with the years. Remember the words of Dom John Chapman: 'Pray as you can, not as you can't.' However, the first Christians found that meditating on the sacred scriptures was the preferred means of launching them into prayer and this was also true of Francis. Through the scriptures, he came to know and love Brother Jesus and in him and through him he came to experience the love of his Father.

Nevertheless, whatever forms of prayer a person chooses, there will still always be distractions, so don't be discouraged. Let me reassure you by explaining the psychological dynamics that underpin all prayer, no matter what form it takes. The journey into God can be described as a journey from selfishness to selflessness. When we become selfless there's nothing to prevent God from totally possessing us. Whenever you choose to turn away from any distraction, you are in fact performing an act of selflessness. If you turn away from fifty distractions in fifteen minutes, you are in effect performing fifty acts of selflessness. As the only way you can learn to become a more selfless person and therefore more open to love is by performing selfless actions, then prayer is a school for love. It is the school where the essence of loving is learned.

The logic of this is such that even an atheist should be able to appreciate the importance of putting aside time for practicing selflessness. It is only by practicing selflessness that a person is open to receive the love that will alone make them fully human, whether it comes directly from God or from anyone else. A 'saint' is just a word used to describe a man or a woman who possesses a quality of love denied to the rest of us. When we say that they are invariably men and women of prayer, we are merely saying they must have spent years practicing the selflessness that opens them to love., If you didn't have distractions in your prayer, you couldn't practice the one indispensible ingredient that can open you to receive what you yearn for more than anything else. By first practicing repentance himself, Francis was in effect learning the selflessness that opened him to receive and experience the love that made him into such a unique saint. When he began to call others to repent, people listened to him, because they could clearly see the love that they wanted for themselves already embodied in everything he said and did.

Chapter 9

The Revelation of the Primacy of Love

Peter had told us to get an early night because we were setting off at first light without breakfast; our lunches had been prepared the night before by brother cook. However, we didn't take the main road for La Verna; once again we headed out towards Assisi.

'I have a surprise for you all,' said Peter. 'My good friend Father Joseph, whom you saw briefly yesterday, has permission to say Mass for us all inside the little church of St Mary of the Angels. I have asked him to say a few words to you about Francis and the Eucharist too, as he published a book on the subject only last week.'

I was still half asleep but his words had the desired effect – I was fully awake in no time at all. Nowhere in Franciscan Italy had touched me quite like the little church of St Mary of the Angels and the thought that we were going back there for Mass simply thrilled me.

So it had indeed been Fr Joseph who had sat at the back listening to Peter's talk the previous day. We hadn't really seen him afterwards because he had disappeared before we could be introduced to him. But we saw him well enough that morning as he opened the great door to the Basilica to greet us. He was about six foot four and quite oblivious of his stunning Mediterranean looks. He spoke in soft whispers as he led us into the little church before retiring to the sacristy to get ready for Mass. There was something quiet and peaceful about him and the way he said the Mass that somehow drew you into the mystery that he was celebrating like an irresistible magnetic force. After he had read the Gospel he came away from the altar to within a couple of feet of us and began to address us in a quiet monotone. I don't know whether it was what he said or what he was that gave his words such power, but they had an almost hypnotic effect on all of us.

'Nobody will ever understand Francis or Franciscan spirituality,' he said, 'until they can realize just how important the Mass was to him and to all who followed him. It is a subject that he returns to again and again in his writings. The Mass is the sacrament or sign for him of the continual outpouring of love that will alone enable a person to enter fully into Brother Jesus. He did not take part in the holy mystery with the frequency that is commonplace today, for in his day reverence was shown more by the quality of the inner disposition of heart with which one approached the sacred table. This is why the whole of Francis' life was punctuated by protracted periods of solitude, so that in silence he could prepare himself to receive the sacred mysteries; then, after he had received them, he could savor and assimilate the graces poured out through them. He saw so clearly that without time set aside for this solitary assimilation, the Mass would be fruitless, not in itself but in himself. You see, love can't be forced on anyone – not even God's love – because forced love is a contradiction in terms. So if a person does not create space and time to allow that love to enter into them then that love can't possibly touch them, never mind change them. Anyone who thinks that merely going to Mass, no matter how often, changes them, without putting aside set time to receive the graces poured out in the Mass, is treating the Mass as magic. Francis saw so clearly that personal prayer is the time we freely choose to set aside, to digest, to assimilate and to interiorize the personal love of God, which is available at all times to the person who's got time – for what time was made for in the first place.

'I often used to stay with a small community of sisters who live in a little house in London, from which they engaged in various forms of social apostolate. Every day the main concern seemed to be how to "get their Mass in". They had no resident chaplain and so they had to go out to different places, depending on the demands made by their workload. The strange thing is that though they would never think of missing their daily Mass, and would have terrible feelings of guilt if they did, they could nevertheless go for months without solid block time for personal prayer, and they wouldn't have the slightest twinge of conscience. The Mass does not automatically dispense grace – it's not a magic rite. Christianity is an end to magic. It inaugurates a new age. It is the age of love. Its message is simple: human beings are not saved by magic, but by love. Now loving must be learned, and prayer is the place where that learning takes place, in such a way that the love of God is able to enter into human loving, gradually bringing it to perfection. So it's pointless to keep celebrating the Sacrament that is signifying the outpouring of love, without setting aside time after that the Sacrament to assimilate, to digest and to interiorize that love through a process of deep interior prayer.

'I find it quite frightening when I see so many contemporary priests and religious endlessly getting worked up and excited by experiments with all sorts of new ways of presenting the Sacrament – in modern ways or returning to old ways – without seeing what is really important. What is really important is to understand that, however the liturgy is celebrated, these celebrations will be pointless unless they point the participators to personal prayer. Too many still think that personal prayer is an optional extra for the extraordinarily pious, for the young, for the novices passing through their first fervor, or for the aged who are too old for anything else. They seem to think that it is a luxury that simply cannot be afforded by the busy religious butterflies who have got the whole world to change by their intensive apostolic endeavor. If they can't afford time for prayer, to personalize the love unleashed in the sacred mysteries, then they won't be able to give it to others, because they will be spiritually bankrupt themselves. If a person is merely content to "get their Mass in" each day, and say their prayers of obligation before rushing out to change the world, then it's the red light. And if they regularly ignore the red light, spiritual disaster is inevitable.

'You see, there will never be an effective apostolate outside of prayer unless that apostolate is transformed by a Christ-like selflessness that has first to be learned inside of prayer. Don't be deceived by all the pretentious gobbledygook that is peddled today by the purveyors of a so-called "apostolic spirituality", who talk of contemplation in action in such a sophisticated way that the undiscerning hardly notice that it's just another way of conning the overworked and the undernourished into believing that they are "mystics in the marketplace". There has never been a "mystic in the marketplace" who hasn't first learned in the desert-place to die to the old self-centered egotist within. If the lesson is not first learned there, then the would-be apostle will only shape their apostolate to suit their own needs and promote their own honor and glory, though they'll kid themselves it's for God's.

'Now the selflessness that is practiced inside of prayer must be put into practice outside of prayer, so that it suffuses every-thing we do. Inside of prayer a person may use the rosary, a meditation, the slow meditative reading of the Scriptures or some other means to help them keep turning their hearts to God. Outside of prayer they may use teaching techniques, home-making skills or medical expertise, and in doing this they are in fact continuing to turn to God by turning to him in the neighbor in need. This is how a person finally comes to practice what the Gospel calls the "prayer without ceasing".

'The self-sacrifice learned in this daily prayer without ceasing is the only acceptable offering that is made when they next take part in the sacred mysteries. This is the offering that unites them with the offering made by Jesus, and it opens them to the super-natural life that he received without measure on the first Easter Day. So in a lifetime of practicing self-sacrifice through daily trying, a believer is progressively opened ever more fully to the love that will alone fashion them into the person they have committed themselves to follow.

'Now let's see how this profound mystical giving and receiving is worked out in the life of Jesus, whom Francis continually tried to imitate throughout his life. It can be seen most clearly at the final moments of his life on earth, although it took place at every moment. When he knew that his hour had finally come, he knew the terrible ordeal that he would have to endure at the hands of those who wished to destroy him. He felt afraid, he felt insecure and he felt in need of support – after all, he was human. He therefore called upon those whom he loved most in this world for their support. Then he told them to prepare a meal that would reaffirm their mutual love, but it would do something further. It would at the same time provide the opportunity for all of them to receive the help of the Father, whose strength and support was needed for what lay ahead.

'The sacrament celebrated at the Last Supper unleashed in an unprecedented way the fullness of love that Jesus would receive in an unrestricted and abiding way the following day. It would give him the strength to face the ordeal that awaited him with unlimited courage and fortitude. Now, notice that once the sacrament had been celebrated, Jesus went into the Garden of Gethsemane. It was here that he began to assimilate and digest the love that he had just received; it was here that that love was personalized through deep interior prayer. The angel of consolation symbolized the help and the strength given to him to help him turn away from the temptation to flee from the ordeal that he knew lay ahead of him. That help and strength filled his heart with the supernatural power and energy that overflowed into every part of his body, so that the will of the Father could be done, not just in his heart but with every part of his human personality.

'Now he could stand with poise and dignity before Annas

and Caiaphas, and discuss the nature of authority and kingship with Pilate when he was half flayed alive. Even on the road to his death he found time to stop and sympathize with the women of Jerusalem, to forgive the soldiers who battened his hands to the cross, and to promise the good thief the same Paradise to which he himself was going.

'When the last act of surrender was made, it was a sacrifice made with the whole of his human personality – from the depths of his dark and depressed mind to his cut and bleeding body. It was an act that had been rehearsed time and time again throughout his life through practicing the prayer without ceasing. The moment the final surrender was made was the moment when the divine love that he had received in part was given in full measure, to overflow forever onto all who would turn to him to receive it. Any believer who would follow Christ must learn to undergo something of what he underwent, and experience something of what he experienced, even though their match-wood crosses may seem at times more than they can bear. This is the only way to the human transformation that is everyone's deepest desire.

'True imitation of Christ, then, does not primarily mean copying his outer behavior but rather the way in which he endeavored to turn, open and surrender himself to the Father with his heart, his mind and with his whole person. This is the only way we will be able to welcome into our hearts the same Spirit who animated him, so that everything can be done to death in us that prevents the perfect love of God and the perfect love of neighbor being embodied in all we say and do. The inner peace and joy that was lost by sin is then restored, and is experienced as the harmony of mind and spirit. This is the psychological expression of the in-dwelling promised by Christ himself on the night before he died. This is how the perfect disciple is formed; his or her very body gradually becomes the place where the Father and the Son and the Holy Spirit make their home.

'May God bless you all and give you a safe journey to the place where St Francis came to experience the fullest possible union with Brother Jesus that anyone can have on earth!'

We all listened intently, though I had heard much of what was said before – after all, both Father Joseph and I had the same spiritual mentor. We remained quiet for the rest of the journey to La Verna, mulling over his every word. As we made the final approach Peter began to prepare us for our arrival.

'Shortly after St Clare was settled in San Damiano,' he said, 'Francis set out for Morocco in April 1213. When he arrived at Montefeltro in Romagna he stopped at the Castle of San Leo where there was a party in full swing to celebrate the investiture of a new knight. Francis addressed the assembly and so impressed a young nobleman, Count Orlando dei Cattani, that he asked to speak to him in private. It was after this meeting that the Count offered to give to Francis the mountain of La Verna as a place of solitude for prayer. After sending two of his brothers to see if it was suitable, Francis gratefully accepted his offer. He was too busy to go there himself at the time, as he was on his way to North Africa to seek the martyrdom that he believed would enable him to follow and imitate Brother Jesus all the way to Calvary. This was his second attempt, which failed, as did the third. Little did Francis realize at the time that Count Orlando had just given him the place that would later be called the "Franciscan Calvary", where he would achieve the martyrdom that he had sought elsewhere.

'After he celebrated midnight Mass in Greccio in 1223, the health of Francis seemed to improve as the following year moved from early spring to summer. So in August he left Rieti with brothers Leo, Angelo, Masseo, Sylvester and Illuminato and set out for La Verna to celebrate the Feast of the Assumption and then to prepare himself for the Feast of St Michael with a fast of forty days. After the feast Francis withdrew from his brothers on the far side of a deep ravine. Only Brother Leo was to visit him once in the day with bread and water and once at night for Matins, by walking across a bridge over the ravine. If Francis didn't answer his call from the bridge, he was ordered to go back and only return at the next appointed time, because Francis was often rapt in ecstasies for hours at a time and privacy was paramount. But on this occasion, when Francis failed to respond, curiosity overcame Brother Leo and he crossed the bridge to witness the beginning of St Frances' mystical transformation.

'But more of that later – it's time to eat.'

With perfect timing Peter guided us to a deserted picnic area in full view of La Verna. I was so interested in what Peter had been saying that I hadn't noticed how hungry I was until the food was spread before us. Nor, it seemed, had the others, judging by the way they tucked in. It was hardly eleven o'clock but we'd had no more than a cup of coffee and a biscuit after Mass since our early departure that morning. When we had finished eating we were ready for Peter to continue his story and miraculously we remained unmolested until he had finished, when a whole army of pilgrims arrived for lunch.

'Before I continue the story,' said Peter, 'I want to let you into a secret. It is the secret of sanctity. St Paul was the first to pen it. It is simply this: "God's power works most perfectly in weakness." That's why God always seems to choose the wrong person for the job, the person we would all think was not fit for purpose. Take Abraham and his wife as a case in point. He was a hundred years old and his wife was ninety yet Abraham was chosen to become the father of God's chosen people. Moses had a speech impediment yet he was the one God chose to be his spokesman before Pharaoh. The stripling David was chosen to fell the giant Goliath. The whole point of God choosing someone who we would think was unfit for purpose was to make it quite clear that it was not this man's potency, or that man's eloquence, or this boy's strength that triumphed but God's power working through human weakness. It was the same in the New Testament.

It was Peter the weak ditherer – the one who was always getting things wrong, always putting his foot in it, the one who finally denied Jesus – who was chosen to be the rock on which the Church was founded. It was the narrow-minded bigot Paul who was chosen to become the apostle to the Gentiles and to free early Christianity from its slavish adherence to the law that he had once upheld with such zeal. Over a thousand years later, God chose a small, insignificant draper's son who Brother Masseo thought was quite unfit for purpose, to inaugurate a Christian renaissance that was to save a Church that had itself become quite unfit for purpose. The truth of the matter was that Brother Masseo was everything that Francis wasn't. He was so tall, good-looking and eloquent that when he arrived at a new destination, people who had never seen Francis before assumed that it was Masseo who was *Il Santo*.

'It must have made Masseo wonder why God hadn't chosen him to do what he was far better equipped to do than Francis. He was to learn, and Francis was to teach him the humility that he was wanting, but that was for the future; for the present he couldn't help voicing his misgivings. He didn't mince his words; he came straight to the point: "Why is everyone running after you?" he asked his master. "Why does everyone come running to see and hear you? You are nothing to look at, you are not learned, and you haven't a drop of noble blood in your veins."

'Far from being annoyed by his words, Francis was sent into an ecstasy of delight as he saw more clearly than ever before what he already knew. What he already knew was this – that it was precisely because he was so unfit for purpose that God had chosen him in the first place. He knew this because, as Bonaventure tells us, God spoke to him when he was praying and told him in words that could not be misunderstood, "The very reason why I chose you was because you had nothing to boast of, and so what I did in you would be attributed to divine grace and not to human effort." (*Life of St Francis*, chapter 8).

'So, like his illustrious predecessors, nobody, least of all Francis, could be in any doubt that it was God's power that would be seen working in his weakness. Of himself he was nothing. That's why Bonaventure continually emphasized more than anything else his total dedication to prayer:

> Prayer was his sure refuge in everything that he did; he never relied on his own efforts, but put his trust in God's loving providence and cast the burden of his cares on him in insistent prayer. No one, he declared, could make progress in God's service without it. Whether he was walking or sitting at home or abroad, whether he was working or resting, he was so fervently devoted to prayer that he seemed to have dedicated to it, not only his heart and soul, but all his efforts and all his time.

'Francis wasn't initially aware of quite how weak and useless he was, so God had to show him. The more the light of God's love bore in upon him, the more God was able to show him his weakness with all his personal sins and inbred selfishness. As prayer develops, the Holy Spirit first shows a person what is keeping him out and then the process begins of emptying every vestige of sin and selfishness which is preventing the sublime indwelling that Jesus promised.

'I have been corresponding for some time now with an old and saintly Cistercian monk from the Cameroon. He told me that for many years he had been undergoing the emptying process at the hands of the Holy Spirit and it was at times so dire and so painful that he all but lost his faith. Only what he called "naked faith" kept him going, until he fell ill and was moved into the monastic infirmary. Then he suddenly experienced what he could only describe as a "weak ecstasy" that remained with him at all times. On three separate occasions when Holy Communion was brought to him, he heard words that he insisted were clear and distinct, but only heard by him. The words were simply these: "Only you have been keeping me out."

'Whoever perseveres, repenting in prayer, will come to the point when the light of the Holy Spirit shafts deep down to highlight the weakness within. Then the process begins of emptying the sin and selfishness that prevents a person experiencing the peace that surpasses the understanding. Gradually, as this purification is brought to its completion, the Jesus who was once physically conceived in Mary is spiritually conceived within that person. However, this profound spiritual purification can go on for years.

'But let me now return to the story I was telling you about Brother Leo, to see what happened to Francis when his purification was brought to completion. When he failed to respond, Brother Leo crossed the bridge to search for Francis. He was lucky – it was a full moon so he could easily see that Francis was not inside the hut that had been built for him. As he searched for him on the mountainside he heard a distant murmuring. Following the direction of the sounds, he found Francis lying prostrate in prayer; his arms were spread out in the form of a cross. Brother Leo came as near as he dared, hiding himself behind a tree but close enough to hear what Francis was saying. Over and over again it was the same prayer that he heard: "Dearest Lord and God, who are you? And who am I? A little worm of a servant." Eventually Brother Leo moved, trod on some twigs and the game was up. Francis was not amused. It had always been his way to hide himself away when he received special graces in prayer; even when he was traveling he would put his cloak over his head or cover his face with his hood and, if all else failed, simply put his hands to his face. But his love for Leo was so great that he forgave him. Reassured that he was forgiven, Leo fell to his knees and begged Francis to explain the meaning of what he had heard. Francis told him that he had seen two lights shafting down: one enabled him to glimpse into the utter poverty of his own wretchedness, and the other enabled him to glimpse something of the transcendent glory of God. Brother Leo never again disobeyed his master.

'Soon it was mid-September and time to celebrate the Feast of the Exaltation of the Cross on the 14th. The feast had been inaugurated to celebrate the finding of the true cross by the Empress Helena in 326 AD and the recovery of that same cross by the Emperor Heraclitus in 626 after it had been captured by the Persians. Francis was again praying with his arms outstretched in the form of a cross, immediately after Mass and before sunrise. It was to be an eventful day, the most eventful day in the whole of his life. His prayer was twofold. Firstly, he wanted to experience as far as possible something of the pain that Brother Jesus experienced in his passion. Secondly, he prayed that he might, as far as possible, experience again something of the love that drove Jesus to accept such an ignominious death. His purification was all but complete; through a life of repentance he was as empty as any human being ever can be of the stuff that keeps God out. The stage was set for something that had never happened before.

'At first all he saw was an angelic form with six wings, gradually coming closer. He was given to understand that it was a seraph, but as he looked more closely he saw that it had the figure of a man. He could hardly contain the mixed emotions that all but tore him apart. The initial fear and dread was softened as he realized that the figure was in fact Brother Jesus coming to him, but that initial joy was turned to compassion when he saw that his dearest friend bore the terrible marks of the crucifixion. It was at this moment that Francis received a revelation that would determine the very essence of Franciscan spirituality and the profound theology that it would inspire. Whether it was imparted through words or by some sort of interior conviction that was impressed upon his mind, we do not know, but it matters little. What does matter is the content of the revelation that he received when he was swept up to experience what St

Paul had called the love that surpasses the understanding. The revelation was simply this – he was given to understand that although he had prayed to experience something of the sufferings that Jesus had experienced on the cross, believing that that was the way to union with him, it was in fact not by suffering but by the inner flame of God's love that Francis would be transformed into Brother Jesus. The very moment that the vision faded, he began to feel that flame within him, whilst at the same time he began to notice the marks of the crucifixion looming large on his poor emaciated body. The sublime union that was now taking place, however. was not caused by the wounds that he could see as they became ever more visible, but by the invisible flame of love within that consumed him.

'For those who could see, this revelation represented a shaft of light that pierced the thick pall of gloom which had hung over medieval spirituality, giving hope where all seemed hopeless before. A new spirituality was born with a new theology to explain its profound implications. It was Francis who inspired this new spirituality that proclaimed the Primacy of Love. And it was John Duns Scotus who made it the starting point for the most profound and spiritual theology of love ever written.

'Initially Francis wanted to hide this latest gift from God, as was his custom, until Brother Illuminato intervened. He said that such gifts were not just given for the receiver but for others too, so that they could be inspired by how God's love works in weakness. Francis could hardly keep the stigmata a secret anyway, so he told his close companions what had happened to him, and through them his experience was passed down to posterity. However, there were certain secrets revealed to him that he kept secret and resolved never to divulge to anyone this side of the grave.

'After celebrating the Feast of St Michael he set off from La Verna for his beloved Portiuncula with Brother Leo, by way of Borgo San Sepolcro and Monte Casale. Far from being in pain,

Francis was initially transported into a rapturous joy that repeatedly lifted him out of himself and into ecstasies that raised him into another dimension. Now in, with and through Brother Jesus he was experiencing something of what was in store for him hereafter. Although crowds came out to greet him on his way with cries of *"Ecco il Santo!"*, he was rarely aware of them. The donkey that carried him carried a man who was not of this world but totally lost in another. However, once back at Portiuncula his experiences seemed to have revived him and he set out preaching again, sometimes in as many as four or five towns a day. Sadly his newfound vigor was illusory – it was not to be for long. Death gradually began to claim his poor body, which could no longer sustain him. In the last months of his life the prayer he had made before sunrise on that fateful day would be granted over and over again as agony and ecstasy alternated in the last days of his life on earth.'

By the time we arrived at La Verna, we got out of the car like little children arriving at their favorite funfair with pockets full of money. We wanted to see everything and we had Emelia to show us every nook and cranny. We did see everything – from the so-called "bed of St Francis" deep inside a crooked ravine to the great Sasso Spicco, the immense rock under which St Francis used to pray. We visited the little church built for St Francis by Count Orlando, called St Mary of the Angels to make him feel at home. We went into the little chapel built over the very spot where Francis received the stigmata and so much else, and into the cell where St Bonaventure had written the *Itinerarium Mentis in Deum*. On the way back we made a detour to Monte Casale for tea with an old friend of Peter's, Fr Bernardino, and arrived home late for supper.

Just as I was getting washed and cleaned up, Peter knocked at my door.

'So sorry to interrupt you,' he said, 'but time has been passing so quickly that I had forgotten to ask a favor of you.'

'By all means,' I said as I sat on my bed to finish wiping my face.

'You see, tomorrow was supposed to be a free day to rest in preparation for the three days that I've arranged for us to spend in solitude in various different hermitages, but things have changed. Bobbie and Emelia want to go and visit Foligno to see places associated with the great Franciscan mystic Angela of Foligno and this would give me the opportunity to go somewhere that I have always wanted to visit. High up in the hills above Foligno is Brogliano where the great Observant reform began and where St Bernadine of Siena spent years in prayer in preparation for his preaching. So the favor I want to ask of you, James, is to take this letter for me to the Eremo Franciscano where a very dear friend of mine, Sister Françoise, has spent years living in a community dedicated to the eremitical life. There she will introduce you to another friend of mine whom I would like you to drive back here. I've asked Father Guardian to lend me a car for the day to go to Foligno, leaving our car for you. I'll give you the directions tomorrow. Is that OK?'

'Sure,' I said. 'No problem at all.'

Peter left as the bell rang for supper so I had no time to think, but I thought a lot before I went to sleep that night. Françoise! So I'm to meet the enigmatic Françoise! I said to myself as I made my way down the stairs for supper.

Although we were all tired, we met up afterwards to reflect on the busiest day of our pilgrimage.

'I really think I've said enough for one day,' said Peter. 'I think we all need a good night's sleep, but there is just one thing I would like to draw to your attention. The further Francis traveled on his mystic way, the more we are able to see how his prayer is most usually directed to God the Father. It is powerful and effective precisely because it is made in, with and through Brother Jesus. That's why at La Verna he is seen praying with his arms outstretched in the form of a cross. This symbolizes his oneness with the one through whom he prays. The Trinitarian dynamic of his prayer is symbolized too by the shafts of light as the Holy Spirit radiated outward from the Father. One inflamed Francis with the fire of love that enabled him to glimpse briefly within the inner recesses of the Godhead; the other showed, in comparison, the utter misery of his own worthlessness.

'After he had received the stigmata he felt himself brimming over with joy in the realization of his new and intimate union with Brother Jesus. It was then, as he was reveling in this ecstatic joy that the "Praises of God" simply burst out of him. Notice they are all directed to God the Father. In the same way, so are the praises in his "Canticle to Brother Sun" written on his return to Assisi. The clear understanding of the "Three-in-One" which determined the very nature and inner dynamics of early Christian spirituality were rescued from the heresies that had distorted them by the mystical experiences of the Poverello. No one had denied the Trinity, but it tended to be viewed as a piece of mystical mathematics if it was viewed at all. It did not seem to have any relevance to the ordinary believer, save as a test of their blind faith in the utterly incomprehensible.

'Like so much else that was lost to sight in the Dark Ages of Christian spirituality, the Trinity was restored to his rightful place by Francis. But this did not just mean that in future his prayer tended to be "politically correct" – addressed to God the Father in, with and through Brother Jesus. The truth was far more profound. It meant that his new oneness with Jesus drew him up into the vortex of supernatural life and loving that endlessly revolves between the Father and the Son. This is precisely the sublime love that he asked to experience just before he received the stigmata, the same love that drove Jesus to give his all for all on the cross. In the months that followed, Francis would sometimes experience nothing but the cross, sometimes nothing but the glory. At other times he would experience both together, when it became his greatest joy to suffer and to sacrifice. For those of us who only travel in the foothills of the spiritual life, this is beyond comprehension, but for Francis it was the fullest possible way that he could respond to and express the love that surpasses all understanding.

'When he finally opened his arms to welcome Sister Death, it was the expression of a tremendous lover yearning for what came to be called his Transitus. This was the moment when the ecstasy of loving and being loved that he had experienced on earth was seamlessly transformed into its completion in heaven. It was to be an utterly fulfilling, if ever-expanding journey into love unlimited. In describing heaven, St Gregory of Nyssa said that it involved not just ecstasy but "epecstasy". He made up a new word in order to try and express the inexpressible. Ecstasy means to go out of oneself into Love; epecstasy means to go out of oneself endlessly into Love, for there is no end to the journey into Love without measure. To be drawn up into the life of the Three-in-One is to be caught up in a journey that has a beginning but no end, a journey where we return whence we came, to have the same love lavished on us that is lavished on Jesus. The reward of the traveler is to go on traveling into an endless abyss of eternal loving in the company of everyone and everything born into the one Francis called "Brother Jesus". It is here in him, in his Cosmic Friary, that all who do not resist are eventually caught up to see and experience the fulfillment of God's Hidden Plan, the Mysterion for which all things were created from the beginning.'

I was weary when I went to bed that night but my mind was fully awake. Peter was asking me to take a letter to the woman he had fallen in love with years before. Their parting had caused agony to both of them, as Peter had explained to me on Lake Trasimeno. However, he made no reference to that conversation – perhaps he was regretting telling me something so personal. Perhaps, after telling me that they had both chosen to part and follow their different vocation in life, it was embarrassing for him to ask me to be the bearer of a letter to her. What could it all mean? Was it to arrange a meeting between them before Peter returned to Calvay? I simply had no idea, but one thing was for sure: I was to meet the beautiful Françoise de Gaye whom I had read about in Peter's private papers without his knowledge.

I didn't sleep much, but in the morning I bounced out of bed with a spring in my step. I'd have bounced much higher had I only known what that day held in store for me. I'm going to meet the famous Françoise! I kept on saying to myself with delicious anticipation as I took the road to Foligno.

Chapter 10

Francis and the Primacy of Love

Eremo Franciscano was miles from anywhere, perched up on the hillside overlooking Clitunno. I approached it along a small donkey trail with magnificent views of the Spoleto Valley below. This, I was told later, was the only way that the hermitage could be supplied with what little sustained the sisters. The hermitage proper was preceded by an enclosed grove with a small gate. I rang the bell as Peter had instructed me – and all hell was let loose. A huge hound raced towards me, snarling and baring its teeth. I was absolutely terrified. Then to my horror the sister porter came running after it, shouting 'Hide, hide!' I looked behind me and there was simply nowhere to hide. Even if there had been, I couldn't move – I was riveted to the spot. Then, instead of putting the beast on a chain, the sister opened the gate to allow it out. I'd never been so close to death before. I just closed my eyes and prayed that it wouldn't be long drawn out and painful. I seemed to wait a millennium before I heard the sister saying '*Pronto, pronto!*' Then when I opened my eyes, it was to see the sweet angelic little sister smiling at me and the beast looking up at me, panting with its tongue out and its tail wagging, willing me to throw the ball that it had dropped at my feet.

It took me more than a moment to come to my senses, which had been preparing for the hereafter. Eventually I did manage to force a smile, but I didn't dare risk bending down to pick up the ball. Instead I booted it into the garden and followed the busy little sister as she bustled down the path in front of me. She didn't seem to have a word of English, or so I thought, until I discovered that she had at least two when she called the beast to heel, this time with the word 'Jekyll'. So that was it! She hadn't been telling me to 'hide' after all – she had been calling the beast to guard the place! One of the more literary hermits had evidently given the dog two names: Hyde when it was guarding the sisters and Jekyll when it was told to revert to what appeared to be its true self. I saw the transformation back to Hyde once more when we were leaving the hermitage.

I was led into a dark and rather dreary parlor. After about five minutes the door opened and in came Sister Françoise.

Despite Peter's description of her, I had prepared myself for the worst – after all, beauty is in the eye of the beholder. But there is, I believe, something called "objective beauty" and, believe me, objective beauty was embodied in her more perfectly than in any other woman I had ever met. Peter's description of her was simply perfect: she really was beautiful – 'Not just with the made-to-measure beauty of the model that demands perfect symmetry of shape and form; she had all that, but she had much more. She was no mere mannequin but a woman in full bloom, a bloom that was suffused as if by some inner light that radiated the warmth, the wit and the well-being of a mature and vital personality. Every feature of her face spoke, whether it was the way she tilted her head, arched her eyebrows, parted or pursed her lips, and they all spoke of a highly intelligent and articulate woman in her prime.'

So this is how solitude sensitizes the soul, I thought, to assimilate what it receives, and reflect outwards a new and unique embodiment of the One who is the All in all.

I'm sure that in the fifteen or more years since Peter had seen her, Françoise had grown even more beautiful, as years of dedication to the eremitical life had added a further spiritual dimension to her physical beauty. Peter had said that at their first meeting he'd thanked God for the dark and gloomy room that hid the blushes that would have betrayed his feelings. I thanked God too and for exactly the same reason. I was so confused that when she offered me her hand I took it and kissed it. I was later relieved to hear that in the society in which she had moved in Paris before her 'conversion', this would have been the accepted etiquette. She smiled easily when I gave her Peter's letter and, for someone so used to solitude, the conversation flowed naturally, enabling me to recover my composure.

She laughed when I told her about my encounter with Jekyll and Hyde, and confessed that she was responsible for naming him. She didn't apologize for his behavior – after all, a group of women living all alone needed a guard dog. If it had been up to me I'd have had a den of deadly dragons lurking in the grove to ensure that this damsel would never be in distress. She wanted to know about the pilgrimage, but most of all she wanted to know all about Peter and in particular about his health and how he was coping after the death of his father. She enquired about David too, whom I didn't know she had met, and I could see that she was deeply concerned about him overdoing things. After about half an hour she suddenly seemed to look rather concerned and said that she had better go and find my passenger so that we could be on our way.

She returned ten minutes later to introduce me to Ellena. It was so strange, because the moment our eyes met I knew that I had seen the woman I wanted to be my future wife. At least I hoped I had. I hoped she wasn't thinking of becoming another member of the community. I'd always been an unbeliever when it came to love at first sight, but I had an instant conversion experience that very day. There was no ring on her hand so I had to assure myself that she wasn't thinking of the unthinkable. My very first words to her were, 'You're not thinking of becoming a hermit, are you?'

Françoise picked up on the anxiety in my voice. I felt she could read my soul, but you didn't have to be a seer to see what had just happened to me.

'No,' replied Ellena. 'I must admit that I've thought about it long and hard, but with the help of Sister Françoise I've come to realize that the eremitical life is not for me.'

Did I sigh with relief? It must have been almost audible. I was so relieved and thankful that I felt like kissing Françoise on both cheeks. I think she knew it too because she took one step back and then kissed Ellena on both cheeks and made her promise to keep in touch, as she ushered us both out of the door. This time it was Françoise who took us to the gate to see us off. The moment the key turned, Jekyll reverted. My last view was of Françoise waving her hands and laughing as Hyde snarled, growled and howled, attacking the gate like the wolf of Gubbio before his 'conversion'.

I said that there's such a thing as objective beauty and there is, but it wasn't embodied in Ellena. Oh, she was beautiful to me and that was partly why I fell in love with her at first sight, but I have to admit that not everyone would find the beauty in her that they would certainly find in Françoise. If there is such a thing as objective beauty then perhaps there is such a thing as objective friendliness too; if so, it was certainly embodied in Ellena, particularly in her open and transparent face. She was slightly taller than Françoise with the sort of 'girl next door' looks that I found irresistible. I know this sounds a bit corny but it just happens to be true – it just happens to describe exactly how I related to her from the beginning: it was as if I'd known her all my life and suddenly realized that it was time for her to come into my home. No, to *be* my home. I read her bubbly sense of fun and her mischievous sense of humor in her face the moment I set eyes on her. It made her look much younger than she was, for she was twenty-nine years old, almost ten years younger than me.

No man could look at Françoise without finding her utterly ravishing, but the way I related to Ellena was totally different. Françoise was almost on a sort of spiritual pedestal. She was so otherworldly that I couldn't really relate to her as a man would relate to a beautiful woman. I couldn't see myself feet up in front of the fire watching *Fawlty Towers* with Françoise, but I could with Ellena, despite her exotic name. We were halfway down the hill before she told me who she was. I was utterly flabbergasted. She was the eldest daughter of Sheila Watson whom I had met at a retreat house in Scotland many years before. It was Sheila who had introduced me to Peter in the first place. She had in fact come from Woodford Green in London, where she still lived. Ellena had been educated at the local convent school and had come to know David well when she went on retreat with her class every year to Walsingham House. It was through him that she came to join the Third Order of St Francis. It was through him too that she had spent the last seven years teaching at a mission school at Bambui in the Cameroon. She liked it so much that the years just seemed to pass by without her realizing it. Then when she saw the 'Big Three-O' on the horizon, she realized it was time to take a break to review her life and see where she should be going.

It was Peter who suggested staying for a month at Eremo Franciscano because he knew no better place and no better person than Françoise to help her. Ellena did admit that she had been tempted to stay several times, but Françoise had helped her to see that her vocation was elsewhere. It was only just over a week ago that she had come to realize that her future was not in religious life but in married life and she had written to Peter to tell him. When I asked her the precise time she had written that letter, I could hardly believe it. That was the letter Peter had received as we were leaving Emelia's home. That was the very same day that I had opened my heart to Peter on Lake Trasimene. In other words, within hours of hearing that Ellena would be looking for an 'ideal husband', he was assuring me that before the pilgrimage was over I'd be finding an ideal wife – if he had anything to do with it. So Peter wasn't a prophet after all! He couldn't see the future any more than I could; he was just a common-or-garden matchmaker. He had sent me with a letter for

Françoise to meet my future wife – well, well, well!

However, it takes two to tango. Peter had done his part; it was now up to me to do mine. When Ellena had finished telling me all about herself I told her all about me, and I was deeply moved by her compassion when I spoke about my wife's premature death. We'd already taken the road to Montefalco when she asked a favor of me. She wouldn't have another opportunity to visit Assisi again before we left for home so could she pay one last visit to St Mary of the Angels? She felt exactly the same about it as I did, so I was only too delighted to visit it for the last time with her.

When we entered the little church I stayed at the back and let her go on to the front where she knelt down in prayer. I couldn't pray. I simply couldn't take my eyes off her. Then I suddenly came to my senses and fell to my knees to thank God for finding for me the only woman in the whole world whom I wanted to marry. But what was she praying for? Could it be for the same thing? Could there really be similar feelings in her for the man she had just met? It hardly seemed possible, and anyway I was ten years older than her.

She was just getting up to leave when I saw Fr Joseph coming into the chapel. He went straight over to Ellena and kissed her on both cheeks, before leading her out of the chapel to who knows where. I was mortified. How did he know her? And where were they going? As he ushered her out, Ellena raised her hand, fingers splayed out to indicate that she would only be five minutes. I was overcome by the green-eyed monster as I saw him touch her on her back as he allowed her to leave first. The green-eyed monster did more than touch me: when they hadn't returned after twenty-five minutes and when they still hadn't returned after forty-five minutes, I was fully in his power. I had always prided myself on never having experienced jealousy at any time in my life. Until that moment, I simply didn't know what it meant to be jealous, but I knew then and I will never forget how it completely took me over. I knelt there, apparently lost in prayer, when I was in fact lost in blind green rage as I imagined those two closeted in some small room together. Of course it was ridiculous – jealousy usually is and it usually makes a complete fool of the person who suffers from it, as it nearly did for me. I actually bit my lip when Ellena finally came back fifty-five minutes later, full of apologies. I didn't want her to see my childish feelings, and anyway what right had I to be jealous? I had only known her for a couple of hours! She noticed a little blood on my lips, but when I assured her that it was nothing she didn't pursue the matter, though she drew more blood later as she talked about Fr Joseph and what a wonderful person he was, all the way back to Montefalco.

I spoke only once to allay my worst fears by asking her what they had talked about for such a long time – as if it was any of my business anyway. I wish I had never asked, for her reply caused only more pain, both spiritual and physical.

'He spoke to me about love,' she said, 'in a way that nobody has ever spoken about it before, and then I took the opportunity for him to hear my confession.'

How on earth we ever got back to Montefalco in one piece, I'll never know. Although I did all I could to keep a poker face, I felt as if a red-hot poker was burning inside my stomach. I didn't know what to do or what to say, so I was eternally grateful to the others, who arrived back at exactly the same time as us, brimming over with news of their adventures.

After the introductions we all sat down for a cup of tea. My inner turmoil was only partially quelled when it transpired that Fr Joseph had actually been sent to Eremo Franciscano at Peter's request to help Ellena make the decision that she had finally come to. Emelia and Bobbie were full of Angela of Foligno. I had no idea that she had been married with a son before she entered the religious life after her husband's death. Peter didn't say much about Brogliano – it seems there wasn't much to see – but he spoke a lot about a chance meeting that they had all had with another old friend of his. Fr Giovanni was a conventual friar who had only recently been moved from Padua to the Basilica of San Francesco in Assisi and he insisted that we should all visit him there the following day for the 'grand tour'.

Peter was delighted. He had said at the beginning of our pilgrimage that everything would be left open-ended just in case an eventuality like this should present itself. It was an opportunity that couldn't be missed, so Peter left us to make a series of phone calls to rearrange the program. He returned with good news: he had spoken to his brother David, who was feeling much better and was looking forward to meeting us all again the day after tomorrow at Fonte Columbo. We would still have three days of solitude in various hermitages, but instead of going back to Castagnoli we would catch the train directly to Pisa for our flight home, after spending the final night together at San Fortunato.

After tea I went straight to my room to pull myself together before supper. About half an hour later, I saw Peter sitting next to Ellena in the garden, deep in conversation. Peter was no doubt asking after Françoise and how Ellena felt about her decision. Could I have featured in their conversation?

After supper we all met as usual, not really expecting there to be any questions, but Ellena spoke out. She wasn't exactly asking a question but rather musing out loud about the conversation she had had that afternoon with Father Joseph.

'Although I've been a member of the Third Order for over ten years now,' she began, 'I've been so busy teaching in Africa that I really haven't had the time to read much about the Franciscan spirituality that turned me on at school thanks to David's retreats at Walsingham House. So it was so wonderful listening to Father Joseph explaining how love was the central theme that links together every aspect of Franciscan spirituality.'

'He is so right', said Peter. 'What he said is so important that I would like to end my talks to you on this pilgrimage by saying a little more about the love that Francis injected into the spirituality of his day, which would have remained dark and gloomy without it. I don't need to remind you again that, before heresies deformed it, Christianity was a close-knit community of men and women bonded together by the love unleashed by Christ's victory on the first Easter Day. As his Kenosis was followed by Pleroma, the love that he received was poured out to bring about God's Hidden Plan on earth – what St Paul called the Mysterion.

'Although the symbol of the cross was not as commonplace as it is today, in the early Christian Church it was nevertheless used as a sign of Christ's victory, but it had no figure on it until much later. After the battle of Milvian Bridge in 312, when Constantine saw a cross in the sky promising victory, its use as a symbol of victory spread throughout Christendom. Its popularity as a Christian symbol was sealed forever with the finding of the "true cross" by the Emperor's mother, St Helena. Nevertheless it was still a long time before it became customary for the cross to be adorned with a figure. When a figure did begin to appear on it, it was of a victorious Christ – a king or a cosmic ruler like those mosaics of Christ the Pantocrator, who was often depicted in the apse of contemporary churches. The Christ who spoke to Francis in San Damiano, however, was not, as we have seen, the dying Christ but the risen and victorious Christ. It was one of the last vestiges of an older tradition that was about to be superseded.

'When the Crusaders opened up the Holy Land to pilgrims in the century before Francis was born, they were not only able to see where Jesus was born, where he walked and talked, but the very place where he died too. There was a new fascination with the human nature of Jesus and the horrors he had to endure, and this new emphasis encouraged more realistic crosses with "Christ crucified" depicted upon them. These in their turn helped to encourage, more than ever before, the significance of suffering in the spiritual life for religious and laity alike. By the time Francis was born, it was perhaps the dominant prevailing feature that deeply influenced Christian spirituality. Francis himself was so deeply affected by the sufferings which Jesus had to endure on the cross that for years he was seen weeping whenever anything reminded him of them.

'Medieval Europe was a harsh and difficult place to live; human joy was hard to come by. To the right and to the left there seemed to be suffering everywhere. There were all sorts of terrible illnesses that afflicted people regardless of rank. In Europe alone there were 20,000 leprosariums and many more primitive hospitals for "the lucky ones", and when eventually the plague struck, it annihilated more than a third of the population. But even with good health, times were still very hard. Infant mortality cast a pall of suffering over virtually every woman's life and most men had to face the horrors of war, with their physical and psychological consequences. Even in peace, the harsh reality of living under the heel of some feudal overlord was exacting in the extreme. It was not surprising, then, that spiritual leaders encouraged their people to seek solace in Christ – and Christ crucified.

'He was someone with whom they could identify; he understood their sufferings because he had suffered before them and had even shown how suffering could be redemptive. It helped the plethora of religious cults, as well as authentic religious communities, to give deeper meaning to their asceticism and spurred them on, as it was believed that suffering was the only way to fully identify with Christ and achieve union with God. Now Francis was, as I have stressed before, a man of his time, and as a man of his time he most certainly believed with his contemporaries that suffering bravely borne or rigorously applied to oneself was the way to union with Christ and through him with the Father. That's why he relentlessly sought out martyrdom. It was this belief that was finally revealed as false on the Feast of the Exaltation of the Cross on September 14th in the year 1224.

'In his *Life of Francis* Bonaventure was adamant, as were many other early writers, that at the precise moment when Francis was receiving the stigmata he received a profound revelation. Once again the revelation that he later shared with his close companions was this: union with Jesus and with the Father who sent him does not come about through suffering but through the "flame of love" burning within. If Francis had known this explicitly before, this revelation would have been quite unnecessary.

'It must be realized that progress to the full human awareness of a truth can be a subtle and complex journey. In our own experience, for instance, we have often known and believed in certain truths of the faith that may have played an important part in our lives; yet it can be a long time before we suddenly realize *explicitly* what we had known implicitly all along. When I had a heart attack in my little boat in the Minch, I lay there totally helpless for hours on end. I had learned how God's power can work in weakness long before I was rescued that day. I had known this truth all along, but I came to know it in a new way when I discovered how my weakness enabled me to experience and be sustained by God's love as I had never experienced it before.

'Now we have already seen the fire of God's love progressively penetrating Francis in those early years, bringing wisdom with it and the strength to do what wisdom showed him. We have seen too how that love finally enabled him to understand and penetrate the meaning of God's Hidden Plan in a way that his contemporaries couldn't. Nevertheless it was only at the moment when he was receiving the stigmata that the absolute primacy of love was revealed to him – God's love, of course, not man's love, as his favorite Evangelist insisted.

'Henceforth this realization dominated his every word and action until the day he died. It was as if his whole life was a unique symphony to love. The central theme was already there after the first introductory bars. As the symphony progressed, it gradually developed, becoming more and more dominant while endlessly manifesting itself in endless variations until, in the fullness of time, this central theme was dramatically revealed in all its simplicity. It finally extricated itself from all that had been hiding or obscuring it before and announced itself with a massive crescendo in such a way that it could not be misunderstood. Sometimes it is not until a person has heard the clear presentation of a central theme toward the end of a work that they can then go back to see that it was in fact there all the time. It had been pervading everything and inexorably developing towards its final and unmistakable manifestation.

'This was certainly true for Francis, once the revelation of the absolute Primacy of Love was dramatically revealed on La Verna. Once he had seen "the light", he could see, as never before, that it had in fact been the central leitmotif of the whole of his life. It was God's love that, as St Bonaventure explained, came to him as "a shaft of light that flashes out from the divine and mysterious darkness". It contained within it everything that was necessary for forming Francis into another Christ. It strengthened his weak human love in such a way that he was able to respond in kind as the love of Jesus born in him fused with his own. The more this love grew, the more it became a mystical pathway through which the Father's love continued to penetrate every part of him. Just as Antonio explained, his heart became, as it were, a prism that enabled the divine love to be transposed into human thought and action, progressively suffusing it with the divine. The story of his life is the story in which you can see this love permeating everything that he did and reaching out to others with what had transformed him. It is at the moment when he attained the most perfect union possible with Christ on earth that the revelation of what had indeed been happening throughout his life on earth was made clear to him, ready to be announced to a world that needed to hear it.

'His yearning to have ever more space and time to receive this love was satisfied in a way he had never before thought possible, at the Christmas following the revelation on La Verna. Thanks to an edict signed by Pope Honorius III, Francis would now be able to have Mass said in the hermitages. With Brother Leo as his constant companion, he would never have to leave his chosen solitude to receive within his poor and dying body the sacrament of love. This would enable him to be touched again and again and set alight by the same flame of love that had touched him on La Verna.

'Through Francis the gloom that shrouded contemporary spirituality was pierced by a ray of light and then lit up, bringing hope where hopelessness seemed to have reigned before. However, something further has to be said. It was not wrong to encourage people to dwell on the sufferings of Christ and to seek solace from one who had experienced extreme suffering himself, nor to show the value of redemptive suffering. It was then, and is now, an indispensible characteristic of authentic Franciscan spirituality. Nevertheless it is only half the story, and authentic Christian spirituality is distorted when it is presented as the whole story. Christianity is not exclusively about Good Friday; it is about Easter Day too. In fact St Paul said that if Christ had not risen then our faith would be in vain. And without the emphasis on the love that was unleashed on that day, our spirituality would be seriously flawed and shrouded in what Horace Walpole was the first to call "gloomth".

'The myriad hellfire preachers who preceded Francis with their vicious asceticism and their apocalyptic warnings were not a merry bunch of bedfellows, but Francis and his brothers were. Come what may, they preached about a loving God whose warm embrace they had experienced for themselves and they reveled in inviting others to experience it for themselves too, to bring light where "gloomth" had suffocated them before. Francis wanted the very demeanor of his brothers to speak to others of the Good News that they proclaimed, before they even opened their mouths. If gloom was written all over the faces of the prophets of gloom, joy must be written in capital letters on the faces of his brothers. In *The Mirror of Perfection* Brother Leo perfectly summed up what Francis felt about the matter:

Why do you make an outward show of sorrow and sadness for your sins? Keep such sadness between you and God and pray to him that, by his mercy, he spare you and restore to your soul the gladness of his love which you have lost through sin. But before me and before others try always to be joyful, for it is not fitting that a servant of God should show before his brother or others, sadness or a troubled face.

'And Francis felt so strongly about this that he wrote in his rule how he felt his brothers should conduct themselves: "They should let it be seen that they are happy in God, cheerful and courteous, as is expected of them, and be careful not to appear gloomy or depressed like hypocrites."

'St Bonaventure's spirituality was shot through and through by the revelation that Francis received at La Verna and the most profound part of it was written within a matter of meters from the place where he received it. What St Bonaventure did for Franciscan spirituality, John Duns Scotus did for Franciscan theology.

'But sadly,' said Peter, looking at his watch, 'we have no time to go into the theology of John Duns Scotus tonight. Thanks to my chance meeting with Father Giovanni today, however, I will be able to speak to you again tomorrow evening.'

When Peter retired to the friary chapel the four of us sat down to share more of what had happened to us during the day. Then, after I'd told the story of my encounter with Jekyll and Hyde, we all listened with rapt attention as Ellena told us about Eremo Franciscano and her newfound friend Sister Françoise de Gaye.

I was walking along the corridor on the way to my room when

I heard Ellena running along the corridor to intercept me.

'Oh, James!' she called after me. 'I haven't thanked you for going to so much trouble to fetch me and then take me to St Mary of the Angels. It was so good of you.'

'Not at all. It was a pleasure,' I replied.

'Tell me,' she said, 'have all Peter's talks been so good?'

'Oh, yes,' I said. 'Every day, I think he won't be able to better what he said the previous day but he usually does.'

'I thought what Father Joseph had said to me was so wonderful, but what Peter said this evening was even better. If only I'd joined you from the beginning as had been originally planned! I would have loved to hear his previous talks.'

'I've taken some notes if you'd like to read them,' I offered.

'I'd love to – if you don't mind,' she replied.

'Here they are. I was just taking them to my room.'

She thanked me profusely and turned to go to her room. Suddenly she turned back to me and said, 'Thanks again for everything.' Then, with just a moment's hesitation, she kissed me on the cheek, wished me good night and was gone.

I rushed for my room before I went into orbit, and lay for hours on my bed, going over and over everything that had happened that day. Thank God for my swollen lip! If I hadn't bitten it to blood I would have made an utter fool of myself and maybe permanently set back the relationship that I wanted to resume the following day.

I suddenly woke with a start in the middle of the night with the realization of what I had done – I had been so taken off my guard when Ellena asked for my notes that I had forgotten about my doodles! I am an inveterate doodler and I had embroidered the margins with different versions of the letter 'E'. What on earth would she make of them?

Chapter 11

Scotus and the Primacy of Love

There were now five of us to fit in the car so it was going to be a bit of a squeeze – which suited me fine so long as I had to squeeze next to Ellena! This wasn't too difficult to engineer as Emelia would be driving as usual and Peter would be in the front passenger seat to accommodate the iron caliper on his leg. To ensure that I sat next to Ellena I made sure that I was the first in the back seat, sitting in the middle. For the first time I didn't want to arrive at Assisi. I felt as if there was a surge of electricity flowing between Ellena and me, making me feel radioactive with joy. I may have been totally deceiving myself; the electric current that turned me on was most probably solely generated by me – but so what! I was too busy enjoying the intoxication of being in love again to analyze whether or not the current was two-way, at least at the time.

Fr Giovanni met us at the door to the great Basilica that in fact incorporated three churches: the upper church, the lower church and the crypt where the body of St Francis was buried with the bodies of Brothers Leo, Rufino, Angelo, Masseo and Blessed Giacoma dei Settesoli (to give Brother Jacoba her proper name and title). The foundation stone for the Basilica was laid by Gregory IX a few days after he had canonized St Francis on July 17th 1228. His body was transferred from San Giorgio two years later. Then it was hidden so well from any roving relic robbers that it was only rediscovered after fifty-two days of intensive digging in 1818 and after innumerable previous attempts to find it. The irony of burying Francis in the largest and most lavishly embellished Gothic cathedral in Italy at the time would have been lost on Brother Elias who built it. He would no doubt have argued with some truth that he had buried Francis exactly where he had asked to be buried. It was certainly true that, as a final tribute to Lady Poverty, Francis did ask to be buried outside the city walls – at a hill called the *Collis Inferni* ('Hell Hill') where criminals were buried – but he would have been mortified to see how his final wishes had been so cynically eschewed. The moment the foundation stone was laid, the name Collis Inferni was changed to Collis Paradisi!

The building of this grandiose mausoleum required vast sums of money. So, in addition to other fundraising schemes, Brother Elias placed a large marble shell outside the Basilica to collect donations. It was this, above all else, that angered Brother Leo and his faithful companions. Despite the fact that Brother Giles warned them of the consequences, they smashed it to pieces. Enraged, Elias had them all flogged and exiled from Assisi. Most factions in the Order were united against this brutal response to the Zelanti by their General, a man who had a vast retinue of servants including his own personal chef. It was only a matter of time before Elias was thrown out of office. Meanwhile, as the years passed, he became more and more authoritarian with an ever-grander lifestyle that raised him up as the perfect antithesis of the man in whose name he ruled. By the time he was buried in Cortona, he had been stripped of office, exiled, excommunicated and welcomed as a turncoat by the Pope's arch-enemy, the Emperor.

Fr Giovanni welcomed us into the church with open arms. He told us that the great paintings that he was about to show us marked the dawn of the great artistic Renaissance. Almost every nook and cranny of the two higher churches was crammed with frescos by Giunta Pisano, Pietro Cavallini, Lorenzetti, Cimabue and of course Giotto. Our host was a mine of information. We were all especially impressed with the twenty-eight frescos by Giotto in the upper church, depicting the life of Francis. In the sacristy he showed us the original bull of Honorius III approving the Rule of St Francis, the habit in which Francis died and the handwritten blessing given to Brother Leo by the saint on La Verna. He was wearing it close to his heart on the very day that he was flogged by Brother Elias for doing what his master would have done for him if he had still been alive. It was a fitting end to our visit to Assisi to spend half an hour in prayer before the tomb of St Francis. Sadly for me, prayer was all but impossible. My heart and mind were on other things, or to be more precise on Ellena. I couldn't stop thinking of her and wondering whether or not there could be some spark of response to the fire in me.

The unalloyed bliss of sitting next to her on the return journey was rudely interrupted when, after thanking me again for the notes that had kept her up most of the night, she asked me a question. Why, she wanted to know, were different doodles of the letter 'E' used to decorate the margins? Like a flash I lied through my teeth, telling her that they were symbols of the new word 'epecstasy' to which Peter had introduced us two days before. Although I tried to remain as composed as possible as I explained the meaning of the word, my complexion gave the game away. I had turned as scarlet as I used to do as a teenager whenever embarrassment caught me out. Whatever Ellena was thinking I have no idea, but I think I know what Bobbie was thinking because, although our eyes didn't meet, I could sense she was looking at me side-on as I stared into the mid-distance, trying to give nothing away. She gazed at me for just long enough for there to be no doubt that she knew quite well why I had turned pale beetroot. The way Peter was uncharacteristically making small talk with Emelia made me realize that he knew too.

The tour only took about three hours so we were back at Montefalco for lunch, where I kept myself to myself. Peter suggested that we all meet again at teatime. I didn't hang around; I spent the time in my room, only to see Peter talking to Ellena again in the garden for a very long time. I was happy enough when tea was over and Peter was ready to begin his final talk on someone I'd never heard of before. It seemed that John got the last part of his name from Scotland, the country that he came from, and the middle part of his name from Duns in the border country where he was born. But before Peter began his talk he first apologized for not telling us the arrangement for the following day, but he had been awaiting a phone call that he had only just received. He said the Father Guardian would have lent us the friary car but he had to attend a conference in Rome, so the plan would be as follows: Peter, Emelia and Bobbie would go to Greccio in the Rieti Valley and would stay in the hermitage there for three days. Peter would drive on a little further to Fonte Columbo, high up above Rieti, where he would meet up with his brother David and spend three days in solitude there.

Then, turning to Ellena and me, he said, 'I've arranged for the two of you to spend your solitude at the hermitage of Lo Speco di Narni. Now the problem is transport. I've been unable to borrow a car for you but, if you don't mind, brother cook has offered to lend you his Vespa for three days.' My heart leapt and when I exchanged glances with Ellena it was to see her nodding vigorously. My heart leapt again, so that for one moment I thought I was going to levitate. I simply could not believe my luck – or was it luck? There was something about Peter's smile at our enthusiasm for his plans that made me realize that it wasn't luck at all. My head was spinning and my heart was doing somersaults, so it took me almost a quarter of an hour before I could concentrate on Peter's final talk and start taking notes as usual. So I'll never know how he started.

'Medieval piety,' he was saying when I began taking notes, 'was so deeply affected by Manichaeism that perfection was seen in terms of freeing the soul from its imprisonment in the wicked body. Only then could the soul rise to be united with the transcendent God who was a pure spirit. Suffering, then, whether it was self-imposed or dutifully accepted, was seen as the primary way to bring about union with God.'

'Where did this idea originally come from?' asked Bobbie, suddenly interrupting.

'I believe it came from a misunderstanding about the significance of martyrdom that was almost commonplace before the reign of Constantine,' Peter replied.

'But let me begin at the beginning. If you were to reread the end of the four Gospels and the beginning of the Acts of the Apostles, you would see what Jesus expected of his followers after his departure. They were to continue the work that he had already begun by spreading the Good News that God had planned from the very beginning of time. Although they were warned that what happened to him could happen to them, suffering was not their calling. Their calling was to call others to accept and enjoy love unlimited by opening their heart to receive it. When many of his followers did, however, suffer for speaking the truth as Christ had done, their deaths often bore witness to what they died for, even louder than the words they'd used before.

'It was not just the fact that they were prepared to die for what they believed, but also the way they died that won over hundreds of converts to the new religion. That's why the word "martyr" comes from the Greek word meaning "witness", because the very way Christians died bore witness to the one in whose name they died. Time and time again, Christ made his presence felt in the martyrs as they were dying for him. Most commonly it was in the way they died with such fortitude and bravery, forgiving their executioners, who were used to being cursed and damned by their victims. But there were other more dramatic signs that bore witness to the belief that Christ himself entered into the martyr as he or she was dying. It might have been the smile on the face of an old man like Polycarp as he was slowly being burnt alive or the unalloyed joy on the face of the deacon Carpus as he was being crucified. Like Stephen before him, he already saw the glory that was awaiting him so he cried out, not in pain but in joy,

"I see the glory of the Lord and I am in joy!" Whilst the slave girl Blandinia was being roasted alive she appeared to be in a continual ecstasy. Perhaps the best example that perfectly embodies how the early Christians viewed martyrdom was the death of the servant girl Felicity. Whilst awaiting martyrdom with her mistress Perpetua, she was screaming with pain as she gave birth in her prison cell.

'"If that's how you behave now," said her jailor, "how will you behave when you're thrown to the wild beasts?"

'"Now it is I who suffer," Felicity replied. "Then it will be another who will suffer in me."

'When her time came to die, she was flogged as she was made to run the gauntlet between two files of soldiers armed with scourges. Then she was thrown to wild beasts in the arena. There was neither screaming now nor any other sign of the atrocious pain that she had to endure. As she had promised, another was suffering with and in her.

'When the story of the heroic deaths of the martyrs was retold to successive generations, many began to see a causal effect between the union with Christ and the suffering that the martyr had to endure. This link was further underlined as monastic spirituality began to seep into secular spirituality. The monks began to distinguish between what they called "red martyrdom" and the "white martyrdom" of those who chose to suffer and die through a life of daily asceticism that promised to bring about the same union that the first martyrs experienced at the moment of their death. When, at the end of the eleventh century, Pope Urban II inaugurated the First Crusade, he called the pilgrims not only to arms but also to martyrdom, which, thanks to a full or plenary indulgence, would guarantee instant union with Christ the very moment they died. It is hardly surprising, then, that in the popular piety that prevailed when Francis was born, suffering was seen as the way to union with God.

'This understandable misconception was not, however,

expressly taught by the Church, for which there was a far safer and surer way to union with God. Like all authoritarian institutions it believed that obedience is far more importance than suffering. After all, hadn't the Bible been clear about it? "Obedience is better than sacrifice" (1 Samuel 15:22).

'In contemporary feudalism the oath of fealty was the cement that held the whole structure together under the authority of the Emperor or the king. Take that away and the pyramid of power would come tumbling down. The same was true of the Church, which gave obedience a spiritual significance that St Paul had questioned a thousand years before. For the medieval Church, obedience to legitimate authority was the surest and safest way to union with God. To underline its importance, men and women whose lives were committed to obeying their superiors, even when they were wrong, were praised for their sanctity. Those who were obedient to them, not just when they were wrong but even when they were persecuted by them, were singled out for their heroic virtue and canonized as an example to others.

'We have already seen how Francis had had problems with this conventional wisdom. He wanted it to be written in his rule that, if a superior commanded something that was patently opposed to his Gospel way of life, a brother could refuse to obey it. When that wasn't acceptable he gave personal permission to Brother Leo and others to refuse orders that were quite clearly in opposition to the authentic Franciscan way of life that he had taught them from the beginning. Despite opposition he did finally manage to insist on putting a "conscience clause" into his final rule. This had never been done before and, seen in the context of the times in which he was living, it was a remarkable achievement, not only to see the necessity of such a clause but to get it past the canonical censors and into his final rule. In its tenth chapter, where he commands his brothers to obey their superiors, he goes on to say that they should obey in everything that "is not against their conscience and our Rule". Although this was a remarkable achievement, it was for Francis a compromise – the absolute minimum. It is quite evident from his own preliminary work that he wanted it to be stated quite unequivocally that, in the name of obedience, his brothers should disobey their superiors if their commands in any way militated against obeying the rule. Francis saw clearly that the rule is above the ministers and that the brothers' vow of obedience is made to the rule and not to them. Perhaps the clearest expression of his feelings in this matter can be found in the rule that was rejected by the ministers of the Order, the so-called "First Rule of 1221". No wonder the ministers rejected it:

A friar is not bound to obey if a minister commands anything that is contrary to our life or his own conscience, because there can be no obligation to obey if it means committing sin. Moreover the friars who are subject to ministers who are their servants, should examine the behavior of their ministers and their servants in the light of reason and in a spirit of charity. If they see that any of them is leading a worldly and not a religious life, as the perfection of our life demands, they should warn him three times. Then, if he fails to amend, they must denounce him to the Minister General not withstanding any opposition.

'When, in his letter to the Duke of Norfolk, Cardinal Newman said that he would readily drink a toast to the Pope, he immediately added that first he would drink to conscience. Francis committed himself and his whole Order in obedience to the Pope and wouldn't have thought of adding "... as long as he doesn't order anything that is against conscience". After all, the Pope was the Vicar of Christ on earth, and in his simplicity Francis couldn't conceive it possible that he could order anything that was against the Gospel. Not so with some of the new ministers who took office after Brother Elias became Minister General.

Francis had already seen them living, and allowing others to live, in a way that he considered quite contrary to the Gospel way of life that had been revealed to him. It was to safeguard them against the scandal given by such people that Francis wanted to give special permission to his faithful followers to refuse to obey any command that contradicted the way of life that he had taught them. Some would make use of that special permission and of that conscience clause, but as Brother Leo and his followers found, they would have to suffer for their tender consciences – as would many others in years to come.

'Although Francis' obedience to and respect for Christ's Vicar on earth (as Innocent III called himself) is evident throughout his writings, he nevertheless came to see with St Paul that it is not blind obedience to the law that leads to union with God. It is love. The authoritarian theocracy that ruled when Jesus was born had reduced religion to a vast mosaic of myriad rules and regulations that promised union with God to those who obeyed them. In addition to the Ten Commandments there were 613 petty rules and regulations that blighted the lives of ordinary people. For instance, the number of paces that you were permitted to take on the Sabbath was prescribed precisely. Then, if you chose to travel by donkey you were only permitted to sit side-saddle. The extra effort involved in sitting astraddle was considered an infringement of the injunction to do no work on the Sabbath. If, when you arrived at your destination you were offered an egg for your supper, you had to make sure that the hen hadn't infringed the law by laying that egg on the Sabbath. If it had, you had to make do with bread alone – so long as that wasn't baked on the Sabbath. Nor were you allowed to light a fire on the Sabbath to cook anything else. These rules are still in force today, though they have been brought up to date. For instance, the spark fired by turning a car's ignition is tantamount to lighting a fire on the Sabbath and so traveling by car is prohibited on that day, unless of course the driver is a Gentile. No wonder St Paul attacked those first Christians who were still wedded to the laws and traditions of their religious forebears. Hadn't they seen and heard that Jesus had inaugurated a new era, a new world order, where love, not the law, would reign supreme? Or to be more accurate. there was a new law and it was the Law of Love. Henceforth everything else would be subordinate to the Primacy of Love.

'This was the Love that Francis had experienced from the very outset in San Damiano, though it would take time for it to possess him in such a way that he would see that this alone was to be the primary tool that he would use to rebuild the Church. The more Love possessed him, the more he became the instrument that God would use to lift the gloom that had descended on the medieval Church. Wherever there was hatred he would sow love; wherever there was injury he sowed pardon; wherever there was doubt he sowed faith; wherever there was despair he sowed hope, changing darkness into light and sadness into joy.

'All this was the fruit of what became, for him, the Primacy of Love. Since that first "touch of love", he had known by instinct what he finally came to know by revelation on La Verna. It had once been the guiding and governing principle of early Christianity; now, for all who would listen to Francis, it would become the guiding and governing principle of medieval Christianity, as it should be for any authentic Christianity to the end of time. The unique vision that Francis had seen for his time was for all time, because it was simply the Gospel of Jesus Christ. It was developed into a profound theological synthesis by his most brilliant disciple, John Duns Scotus. It is important to remember that he was a Franciscan first before he developed his theology, so he would have known and assimilated the very essence of Francis' unique vision first. What I have been able to say has only scratched the surface of what he would have been able to penetrate with one of the greatest philosophical minds of all time.

'His theological synthesis begins with the revelation on La Verna. Union with God can only come about through love. Why? Because God is love. He had been deeply influenced by Aristotle, who had argued to the existence of God through reason alone, though this did not enable him to discover what God is in himself. However, Francis' favorite theologian was able to make that discovery – "God is love," St John had taught him. And in teaching him that, he was teaching him something that was unique to Christianity. No other religion had taught or teaches such a sublime truth. Scotus is more precise: "God's very essence is love; that's what he is, and that's what he does." In Irish there is a tense called the "present continuing tense" that can best express St John's simple revelation. In doggerel English it goes like this: "God has been loving, he is loving, and he will continue to love." To keep it simple let's just say that "God *is* Loving". Aristotle put it this way: God is pure act. In short there can be no distinction in God between his being and his acting. In other words he must be what he does, and he must do what he is. This is not true of human beings. What they are and what they do can be two different things. They may well call themselves Christians, but they do not necessarily act in a Christian way. They may well call themselves fathers or mothers, but they do not necessarily act as fathers or mothers. God is love – that's what he is and that's what he does; in short, God is Loving.

'Now before I go any further let me make it quite clear that Scotus didn't just wear a Franciscan habit; he was Franciscan through and through like "Franciscan Rock". Unlike many priests and intellectuals who became Franciscans after their initial training, Scotus was firstly grounded in Franciscan spirituality from the age of fifteen by his uncle Elias at the friary at Dumfries where he joined the Order. As he was born around 1266 and we know that he went to Oxford in about 1289, he must have spent about eight years living and imbibing the spirit of Francis first. The works that would have had the greatest influence on him would have been the writings of St Francis himself, most especially his *Rule and Testament* and his *Admonitions*, then St Bonaventure's *Life of Francis* and his two great spiritual works, *The Tree of Life* and the *Itinerarium Mentis in Deum*. It would be difficult to say how many of the other early lives or writings about Francis would have been available to him, possibly none of them as they were all ordered to be burnt by the Chapter held in 1266 in the interest of fraternal unity, once St Bonaventure had completed his authoritative *Life of St Francis*. Above all other works, then, this work became mandatory reading for all prospective friars. It was in this work that he first read about the revelation of the Primacy of Love that was to dominate his theological thought. Bonaventure explains that it was just after Francis had seen the seraph approach and just before he received the stigmata that this revelation came: "Eventually he understood by a revelation from the Lord that divine providence had shown him in a vision that, as Christ's lover, he might learn in advance that he was to be totally transformed into the likeness of Christ crucified, not by the martyrdom of the flesh, but by the fire of his love consuming his soul".

'Like any novice, John Duns Scotus would be taught how to pray, beginning at the beginning – and the beginning was meditating on the life of Jesus on earth. There was simply no better companion to the scriptures than Bonaventure's *The Tree of Life*. Once an experienced director (perhaps his uncle Elias or another) discovered that his meditation had led John into contemplative prayer, he would have placed in his hands the *Itinerarium Mentis in Deum* and explained how he was now being led into the mystic way. This would explain why he wasn't interested in theology just for the sake of purely theological speculation, or for academic preferment like many of his contemporaries, but for something more important. For Scotus, the very raison d'être of all theology is to love God and through love to seek communion with him. This he discovered firstly by reading Bonaventure's *Life of St Francis* and secondly through reading the *Itinerarium* inspired by the revelation of the Primacy of Love and written at the very place where that revelation had been received. That is why his theological inspiration didn't begin at Oxford or Paris but at La Verna where he learned, from the revelation that Francis received there, the absolute and fundamental importance of the Primacy of Love. This key revelation, then, was the inspiration not only for St Bonaventure's *Itinerarium Mentis in Deum* but also for the mystical theology of John Duns Scotus.

'Realizing that you cannot love someone unless you know them, Scotus then turned his attention to knowing as much about God as reason and revelation could teach him. Anybody who takes the trouble to make something must have a reason for making it or they are simply mindless. So God must have had a reason for creating the universe and everything in it. Now, bearing in mind that God is self-sufficient and needs nothing to add to his own personal happiness, why did he need to create anything? The only reason he would have created something was for someone else's happiness, so that someone else could enjoy the pure unadulterated bliss of experiencing what it's like to love and be loved all the time. If, yet again, you ask why someone loves another, I can only answer that I do not know – not because love is irrational but because it is super-rational and therefore above the understanding of a rational animal. Rousseau put it this way: "The heart has reasons that the mind knows nothing about."

'But when all else fails, I usually end up telling a story.

'When I was studying in London in the early 1950s I stood for hours to get a ticket to see Maria Callas singing at Covent Garden. She was then in her prime and everyone was talking about her stunning performance as Norma. Even though I only managed to get a standing ticket at the back of the stalls, I considered myself lucky. At the first interval a man saw my leg and, assuming that it must have been hard for me to stand for so long, insisted that I should take his seat in the front row. It was the closest thing that I had ever experienced to heaven on earth. But would you believe it, I still wasn't totally happy. I felt that I would be fully happy only if I could share my happiness with others whom I loved. I wanted my mother and father to be with me, and my brothers and my dearest friends – only then would my cup be overflowing.

'I know it's rather silly to try and project our feelings onto God but, disagreeing with other great theologians of his time, Scotus insisted that we do share our "being" with God. Further to this, we have been created in his image and likeness, so I don't think that it is utterly outrageous to suggest that something like my petty feelings might also have been experienced by God – if one can talk about a pure spirit having feelings as we do. What I'm trying to say is this: just as I would have loved to share my little human ecstasy with others, God must have loved to share his divine ecstasy with others too. Anyway that's what John Duns Scotus meant when he said that love, and only love, impelled God to create us. When I said love impelled God I don't mean it forced him, because forced love is a contradiction in terms; it's an oxymoron and only a moron would think otherwise. You might threaten someone; you might even torture them; but you will never be able to force them to love. Love is totally free and so is God's love. That's why it makes what he is so totally and literally adorable.

'Although Aristotle argued to the existence of a god and even to a god who was responsible for creation, reason would not allow him to believe that his god would take any interest whatsoever in that creation, let alone love it. God couldn't possibly contemplate anything less than himself. This logic was found to be flawed by St John 400 years later when he wrote, "In the beginning was the Word. The Word was with God and the Word was God. He was with God in the beginning. Through him all things came to be, not one thing had its being but through him" (John 1:1–3).

'God could, and indeed does love us, because he loves us all in his other self whom St John describes as the "Word", the perfect expression of himself, "in whom all things are created". When, in order to implement what was God's plan from the beginning, that Word is made flesh, St John calls him "the Son", whose name on earth is Jesus. Although St John's Gospel was the last to be written, his profound teaching about the *Logos* (the Word) was not new; it was central to the teaching of St Paul, written down almost a generation earlier, and he in his turn insisted that all that he taught about Christ had been handed on to him by his predecessors:

He is the image of the invisible God; he is the primacy of all created things. In him everything in heaven and on earth was created ... The whole universe has been created through him and for him. And he exists before everything and all things are held together in him ... For in him the complete being of God came to dwell.

(Colossians 1:15–19)

'Although Scotus was a student at Paris only a few decades after Thomas Aquinas and Bonaventure, he differed from both of them in this. From all eternity, eons before and quite independent of man's fall from grace, God's plan was to create all things in the Word, and then the Word would be made flesh as his masterwork, to be the King of Creation – Christ the King. He would rule with a love powerful enough to permeate everyone and draw them up into his mystical body. There – in, with and through him – they would be caught up into the life and loving that endlessly surged to and fro between the Father and the Son.

'There was only one thing that could sabotage this plan. Just as God had freely chosen to love in order to share his life with others, these others would have to be made free to choose to love him in return, so that they could share in the fruits of the mutual loving for which they were created. As their failure was not part of God's initial plan, it did not stop Christ coming, because he was coming anyway. Unlike his contemporaries, then, it was quite unthinkable for Scotus to countenance for a moment that God's sublime plan, conceived for others to share in his own glory, should be scuppered by creatures made from the slime of the earth.'

Emelia suddenly burst in: 'But we were taught at school that Christ *had* to come, because Adam had committed an infinite sin in being disobedient to God. We were taught that this was the reason why Christ came in the first place.'

'This is precisely the theory that Scotus rejects,' insisted Peter, 'making God's plan to manifest his glory, in space and time and in flesh and blood, dependent on human sinfulness.'

'But don't we have to believe that as Catholics?' asked Emelia, still a little perplexed.

'No, we don't,' answered Peter. 'What we have to believe is that Christ saved us from the sin and selfishness that prevents us from taking part in God's original plan. We don't have to believe that God's grand design was caused or even prompted by what Francis would describe as the behavior of a couple of miserable worms.'

'But that's what I was taught at convent school!' said Ellena, sitting on the edge of her seat. 'I thought all that infinite sin, infinite debt stuff was the teaching of the Church that we had to believe.'

'No, not at all,' replied Peter. 'It's just a theological explanation of one of the truths of our faith that we do have to believe. And that is that Christ was the Word made flesh and that he died and rose from the dead, and by his love he can save anyone who chooses to receive that love. You don't have to believe any of the theological explanations of how this all happened any more than you need to believe in transubstantiation.'

Ellena almost fell off her seat this time. 'Sister Mary Michael said that Catholics had to believe in transubstantiation and she said that many of the English martyrs died for believing in it!'

'I do hope they didn't,' said Peter, looking genuinely concerned. 'Once again there's all the difference in the world between what actually happens and a theological explanation of what happens. We have to believe that Christ is truly present in the bread and wine after the consecration, but we don't have to believe in transubstantiation, because that's a theological explanation of what happens. There are other explanations such as transignification, but you don't have to believe that either, or any other explanations for that matter. Theological explanations are usually devised by good, well-intentioned people who try to explain to their audiences deep truths in such a way that their current knowledge will enable them to understand them. So what makes sense to Jewish Christians at the dawn of Christianity might not make sense to medieval Christians and what may have made sense to medieval Christians might not make sense to twenty-first-century Christians.

'The deep truth, namely that Jesus came to unite us once more with God through love – what is sometimes called "redemption" – has been explained in myriad different ways that can simply confuse modern believers. If you want to understand how it was explained to early Jewish Christians, for instance, you will have to immerse yourself in the Old Testament and in its rites and rituals. Just as it was Moses who led the Jews from slavery to freedom, Jesus was seen as a new Moses leading his people from the slavery of sin to the freedom of love. Almost every New Testament writer explains this same truth by using the different signs, symbols and sacrifices surrounding the celebration of the first Exodus to explain the second Exodus or Passover of Christ. It's taken me half a lifetime to study this and I still get confused!

'If you want to understand how it was explained to medieval

men and women, you will have to immerse yourselves in the medieval world and in its rites and rituals too. I said at the beginning of this talk, for instance, that in the medieval world popular piety believed that union with God would be brought about through suffering, whereas the Church, being authoritarian, said it would be brought about by obedience. Now both these beliefs were brought together by St Anselm of Canterbury a hundred years before Francis; Anselm wrote down his theological explanation of redemption, which he thought would make sense to a world that seemed to understand the meaning of suffering and the importance of obedience. Forgive me if I summarize what he said, because his explanation has been used to explain redemption up to the present day – at least if your questions and my experience are anything to go by:

'Man's first sin was an infinite offense against God. This infinite sin incurred an infinite debt that could not be paid by a finite man. Hence God sent his Son, who was both finite and infinite, so that on behalf of finite humankind he could pay the debt back and also make the satisfaction that justice demanded. In order to do this, his Son had not only to come amongst us to apologize, as it were, for man's sin, but to make satisfaction too. For this satisfaction to be made, God ordered that his only Son should undergo terrible suffering and an ignominious death. When I was at school our religious education teacher, Father Rylands, explained it to us by telling us a rather improbable story.

'We were asked to imagine that the king came to the school production of *The Mikado* and whilst His Majesty was addressing the audience at the end of the performance, a boy from the fifth form stepped out of the chorus and gave him a kick in the pants. Although the boy and the headmaster later apologized, it was not enough to redeem the school from what had shamed it, for the gulf between a king and a commoner was far too great. It would take another royal to make up for a sin committed against a king. Happily the king came up with a plan to forgive the school and remove its shame. He would send his own son as a day boy who would make up for the sin by receiving "six of the best" from the prefect every day for a week. Thus, through some sort of contorted justice that I didn't understand then and still don't understand now, the school would be "redeemed". For only then would the punishment not only fit the crime but also be acceptable to the king because his son had suffered it.

'In the hymn that we used to sing at assembly we were happy to call God "Our Heavenly Father"; now I was asked to see him as some sort of supernatural sadist who was not content with just sending his own Son to suffer the same penal servitude as Adam and sons, but also required him to undergo capital punishment at the end of it. And just to show he didn't go in for half measures, the punishment would take the form of the cruelest and most humiliating death the ancient world could devise, preceded by prolonged torture in which the victim was half flayed alive. So you see, I was taught exactly the same thing that you were taught, with a rather bizarre story of which St Anselm would no doubt have approved. You can almost imagine him nodding in agreement and saying, As it was by obedience and suffering that we were redeemed, what better way for us to share in Christ's redemption than by our own obedience and suffering!

'The greater the suffering and the blinder the obedience, the better – this was the conclusion that many drew from Anselm's explanation. Francis was amongst them, to begin with. If he wasn't and if this wasn't his deeply held conviction, he wouldn't have needed such a dramatic revelation to convince him otherwise. We still need the content of that revelation, because a thousand years after St Anselm we are still being sold his misleading explanation of redemption, which presents us with a cruel God. He could hardly demand less of us than he demanded of his own Son. This is not the God of love that St John told us about, the God of love who revealed himself to Francis and who inspired the mystical theology of John Duns Scotus.'

A deathly silence followed when Peter had finished speaking, lasting far longer than ever before. Everyone was trying to understand all that had been said, to come to terms with it and work out the implications. Strangely enough, even though I was a Protestant I could see how Protestants too had been deeply influenced by what now appeared to me as Anselm's totally erroneous and spiritually stifling explanation of salvation. Although I hadn't really anything to say, I quickly asked a question to make sure that Peter didn't suddenly get up and go, when we all wanted to hear more.

'So according to Scotus,' I said, 'Christ wasn't firstly sent by God to suffer an awful and bloody death to redeem humankind; he was sent to crown God's creation as its King and to reign over paradise on earth. But when human beings rejected God, he sent Jesus to turn back the clock and give them another chance. Then those who would listen to him could receive what they'd lost in the first paradise.'

Peter smiled.

'Yes, I suppose you could put it that way,' he said. 'Let me tell you another story. It's the story of a family who lived only a few doors away from our family when I was a boy. Anthony, Charles and Caroline were all of primary school age when their mother died. Although their father was a doctor with his own busy practice, he managed to bring up all three of them by himself. Despite the fact that they were all close to their father and loved him as a father and a mother, they'd all left home by the time they were thirty to take up lucrative jobs in California. All of them married and had eight children between them. To begin with, they begged their father to come and visit them but, without help in his practice, he never seemed to get round to it. However, he promised that he would do so as soon as he retired. His long-awaited visit would be the signal for a big family reunion and celebration.

'But sad to say, when he did finally come it was to find a family fraught and fragmented. His two boys in Los Angeles had been drawn into the "Beverley Hills set" where they sold their souls to the secular society that had seduced them. They'd gone through several marriages and their present partners were threatening to leave them. His daughter had suffered from "burn-out", which had led to depression and the break-up of her family too. The poor father who had come to celebrate with the family he'd brought into the world had to spend what was left of his retirement trying to breathe back into them the love he had originally showered on them. Although Caroline responded, the two sons were closed to what their father had to give them. They refused to listen, and shut him out of their lives. Though his death certificate said he had died of a heart attack, it was more a case of a broken heart. I was deeply moved when Caroline told me this sad story herself. It reminded me of another story and of another family to which I belong.

'Christ's coming into this world "in the fullness of time" was originally intended to be a celebration, but this would sadly have to be postponed indefinitely, until humankind could be rescued from what had been its undoing. Now Christ had a new role, never originally intended. He had to explain to everyone what had happened to them. Then he had to inspire them to turn back to the only love that would restore them. Only this would enable them to be reintegrated into God's original plan and enjoy the experience of the fullness of love for which they have been created.'

Peter paused just long enough for me to ask him another question.

'I can see that, as a Franciscan, Scotus was inspired by St Francis and that the revelation on La Verna was the starting point for his theology of love, but did he really find what I can only describe as God's plan "A" and plan "B" in the writings of St Francis?'

Peter smiled at the way I had expressed myself.

'Yes, I'm absolutely sure he did,' he said. 'You see, for a start it would have been impossible for Scotus to have conceived the essence of his theology before he joined the Order at the age of fifteen, so it would be no exaggeration to suggest that it was first glimpsed through his study of the man in whose footsteps he had committed himself to follow. There is an old proverb that says that a dwarf could see further than a giant if he would only climb onto his shoulders. Scotus would not have been too proud to acknowledge that he was the dwarf and that Francis was the giant. Despite his unique theological vision, that vision would have been impossible without the vision of the man on whose shoulders he had chosen to climb. It would be impossible to pinpoint precisely when Francis had completed his profound spiritual vision, but what we know would have been known to Scotus long before he began to develop his systematic theology at Oxford.

'Long before the revelation on La Verna, Francis would have known, through mystical prayer as well as through his reading of the scriptures, that God was not just love but that he was "loving" – and loving all the time. He clearly knew, as he wrote in his *Office of the Passion*, that "before time began our most holy Father sent his beloved Son from on high and he was born of the blessed and holy Virgin Mary". He further knew from his favorite theologian St John that God's love had conceived us all in his Son, the Word, before time began, as he says explicitly in his *Letter to all the Faithful*. When speaking of the life and death of Jesus, he refers to him as, " He through whom all things were created". Further to this, he writes in his *Admonitions* that God actually chose to design our body and soul in the image and likeness of his Son. "Try to realize the dignity that God has conferred on you. He created and formed your body in the image of his beloved son and your soul in his likeness" (Admonition 5).

'Francis finally came to realize, then, that God's initial plan was to create the world and everything in it in the Word, and that this plan was made before time began. Furthermore, human beings would be created in his Son's image and likeness once again before his plan was implemented in space and time. This meant that human beings would be capable of being drawn up into the life of the Three-in-One to experience the ecstatic love that endlessly binds them together. All this was God's plan from the beginning, before the "Fall" and what later came to be called "original sin". Of course Francis was not a theologian like Scotus, so he did not explicitly distinguish between what you called God's plan "A", which was to create us to enjoy eternal happiness before the Fall, and his plan "B" to redeem us to enjoy eternal happiness after the Fall, but the two plans are there to be seen quite clearly in his writings. It was left to Scotus, the "Subtle Doctor", to make the distinction that became the foundation of his systematic theology of love, but that theology could not have been conceived without the vision of his spiritual father. In short, what you call God's plan "A" and plan "B", which are explicitly defined in the systematic theology of Scotus, are quite clearly to be found in the writings of Francis.'

'I've never heard any of this before,' said Bobbie. 'It's all new to me, but my diploma in theology was completed under the directions of the Dominicans so I suppose that would explain why they taught the Thomistic theology of redemption based on the teaching of St Anselm. I must say, I much prefer the approach of Duns Scotus. I found that the other approach seemed to make God out to be something of an ogre – as you said – who demanded the price of his Son's death as a ransom to get us all back onto the straight and narrow. But is there any evidence that the Church knows about or accepts how Scotus explains things?'

'No, not really,' said Peter. 'The Church might lean towards one system of theology rather than another for purely pragmatic reasons, but it doesn't say one is right and another is wrong, unless the theory damages or destroys an article of faith. However, it used the theology of St Thomas Aquinas to help explain its teaching at the Council of Trent and afterwards; that's why we've all been brought up on what's called the "Legal Theory of Redemption" first outlined by St Anselm and, as you rightly say, accepted by St Thomas. In other words, an infinite sin incurs an infinite debt that can only be paid off by an infinite redeemer. As I stressed before, this is only a theological explanation – and you can roll it up and throw it in the bin if you don't find it helpful. Can you imagine trying to explain the Christian faith to a modern open-minded searcher by explaining to them how the God of love is supposed to have chosen to redeem humankind with Anselm's little horror story? However, to get back to the question, I suppose you could argue that the Church favored Scotus when it declared the dogma of the Immaculate Conception in 1854.'

'How do you mean?' I asked.

'Well,' said Peter, 'Scotus argued that the very moment God freely decided that the Word would be made flesh, that very decision included a human mother – how else would he be made flesh? As Scotus put it, "If God wills an end, he must will the means." This was obviously before creation had taken place in space and time, so his mother would have been conceived perfect in every way as the mother of the Word to be made flesh; if you like, she would be "immaculate". She would be totally free from the sin contracted later by human sin. When sin did eventually stain humankind, God made sure that the human mother of his human son remained exactly as he had originally conceived her; otherwise his plan would be in jeopardy. It was inconceivable for a woman warped by sin and selfishness to give birth to and bring up a perfect man destined to be the King, as Christ claimed to be before Pilate.

'It was for these reasons, amongst others, that at the beginning of the fourteenth century Scotus was the greatest champion of the Immaculate Conception. Furthermore, he was in the minority, sometimes a minority of one, as he defended this doctrine against all comers, most particularly against the Thomists. Now Scotus wasn't anti-Thomas Aquinas; in fact there's no evidence that he ever read his works, except through the writings of others. Inevitably the Thomists, who held what's come to be called the "Legal Theory of Redemption", argued that all the descendants of Adam were infected by his sin and that included Mary. Many bitter battles were fought over this doctrine until it was finally defined *de fide* by the Church in 1854.'

I must say that as an Anglican I'd never really thought too much about the Immaculate Conception and, when I did, it was only to write it off as Catholic 'piety going over the top' again, as it always seemed to do when it came to Mary. However, I simply had to admit that in the context of all Peter had said about Scotus it did at least make a certain logical sense. It made me resolve to be a bit more respectful in future about articles of Catholic faith that I didn't understand. It also made me make a resolution to make a personal study of John Duns Scotus. I liked what he said and what he stood for, and after all he was a Franciscan like me and his works were inspired by the man I wanted to follow more than any other.

When I told Peter that in future I intended to study Scotus seriously, he said I sounded like Teilhard de Chardin. Apparently, the moment he heard about Scotus' teaching his immediate response was, *'Voilà! La théologie de l'avenir!'* ('There it is – the theology of the future!') Peter said that if there was more time he would like to introduce us to some of Chardin's ideas, because they not only resonated with those of Scotus but also added to them and even enhanced them. He told us that there was one thing Chardin did say that was relevant to what he had been speaking about and it was this: 'Love differentiates.' In other words, love makes things different.

Peter explained further:

'The prayer inspired by St Francis ends with these words: "It is in giving that we receive." In other words, when we try to love

God, in the very act of loving we receive his love in return; this love enables us to grow into our true selves and, in becoming our true selves, we all become different. As Scotus taught, love is the principle of individuation. There's an old saying: "People are the same the world over." And it's true – self-centered people are the same the world over. They're like a handful of different seeds. Even an expert horticulturist would find it difficult to distinguish one from another because they all tend to look the same; they all seem to be turned in on themselves. But put them in good soil, water them and make sure that they get plenty of sunlight and see what happens. Then, when they bloom, they will all become totally different, each manifesting God's beauty in many totally different ways.

'If human love can do this for common seeds, what can God's love do when it is allowed to enter into human beings? It will enable them to grow into their true selves. Then, as they become their true selves, they will gradually become more and more different from the crowd from whom they were hardly distinguishable before. Francis was a case in point: he was just "one of the boys" before his conversion, but the more he allowed the love of God to change him, the more he became what love made of him – his true self, which was miles away from the drinking pals he'd left behind. That's why all the saints were totally different. Compare Francis of Assisi with Thomas Aquinas, or St Teresa of Avila with St Joan of Arc, or St Ignatius of Loyola with St Benedict – love differentiates. Even the early companions of Francis – Leo, Angelo, Rufino, Masseo, Giles etc. – were, thanks to the love of God, all completely different. I have no doubt that most of them would have been canonized shortly after their deaths, but unfortunately it would have been seen as supporting one faction of the Order at the expense of another. What was more important at the time was supporting the unity of the whole Order, rather than stating publicly what those who knew them knew only too well.

'Well,' said Peter, 'that's about all that I have to say, except perhaps this. Chardin's famous little phrase helps to give us a further glimpse into the very nature of the Trinity – "love differentiates". As we have seen, the more Francis was enabled by love to draw closer and closer to God, the more he became aware that God's love is not just twofold. For the love that continually revolves between the Father and the Son is not just a blind impersonal force, but a person too in "his" own right. Furthermore, Francis realizes that the more that love enters into him, the more he becomes himself, not just here on earth but hereafter. The invitation to share in the love unlimited that binds the Three-in-One together to eternity means that his journey never ends. It is not just one continual ecstasy but "epecstasy", as St Gregory of Nyssa described it.

'When God's Secret Plan is brought to completion, all who have chosen to accept the love Jesus came to share will be bonded together into a vast community as a family, journeying on into Love Unlimited. In the beginning God's glory was only in himself and for himself, but when his Mysterion has been brought to fruition there will be an extra dimension to that glory. It would be not only invidious but also metaphysically unacceptable to suggest that the fulfillment of God's plan could add anything substantially to his essential glory. But one can't help feeling that there must be some accidental contentment for God, as there is for anyone when their plans are brought to completion, especially after many setbacks. I know it's pure anthropomorphism, but is it going too far to speculate that, in some way, there must be in God something of the contentment that you see in grandparents? I mean the contentment that they feel when they gaze with pride on the family for which they have been responsible and see each member successfully striving towards their fulfillment. But these are mysteries that cannot ultimately be penetrated by human words or metaphors of the mind's making; only the heart can go where they can never follow.

'When the heart first flickers, even before it bursts into flame, the desire for union has already been awoken. When love demands to know more and more about the person who is loved, the mind is marshaled into action. Although it isn't possible to love someone without knowing them, knowledge alone is not enough. Knowledge can collect all things knowable about someone and order that knowledge in the mind; it can gather them like pieces of a jigsaw to form an accurate picture of them, but it can go no further. Only the heart can reach out through love to bring about the desire for union that was there from the beginning. That's why St Bonaventure said that Francis was able to go where no mere theologian could go and understand with the heart what can never be understood by the mind alone. It was as he was being united with Christ on La Verna that he received the revelation of the Primacy of Love, but he received much more. Other secrets were learned through love, secrets that he swore he would never tell anyone; they were either too personal or too profound. Even if he could put them into words, they could never be understood by minds blinkered by knowledge alone.

'I've said all that I can say for now but, if you want to come to know the mysteries of love learned by Francis, you can only do so with the heart, not the mind. Go now into solitude as he did and go regularly to let the Spirit in. Only he can do in you what was done in Francis. Then, as St Bonaventure promised, you will be given the wings of a dove to fly high and "rise above yourself and above all creation to find yourself within the shaft of light that flashes out from the divine and mysterious darkness". It is here that you will be able to penetrate the mystery of love and experience something of the ecstatic bliss for which God made us from the beginning.'

After Peter had finished speaking, nobody said a word. We all went into the church and nobody moved until the bell rang for supper.

Chapter 12

The Primacy of Love in Practice

Early next morning we all went our separate ways. But just after breakfast Emelia gave me the notes which Peter had prepared for her. Then with Peter and Bobbie she set off for Fonte Columbo in the Rieti Valley. It was sometimes called the Holy Valley because Francis had loved it so much and had spent so much time in the hermitages that he founded there. They arrived to find David well and refreshed, and keen to spend another three days in solitude. First, however, he showed them the cave where Francis had written his rule with the help of Brother Leo and the room where the surgeon had cauterized his eyes with a red-hot iron. After this Peter took Emelia and Bobbie to Greccio for their three days of solitude and then drove back to Fonte Columbo for his visit with his brother.

Ellena and I set out for Lo Speco di Narni, using side roads and making a detour to visit the beautiful little town of Todi where the famous Third Order poet and mystic Jacopone da Todi was born. I could only liken my journey to Narni to that made by Francis from La Verna to Assisi after he had received the revelation of the Primacy of Love. I too felt as if I were enfolded in an ecstasy of love. But thankfully for both of us, I remained fully conscious! Nor would I have had it any other way – I didn't want to miss a moment of the exciting, exhilarating experience of feeling Ellena's arms holding me tight around the waist. I discovered that the faster I rode, the tighter she held me so, throwing all caution to the wind, I drove flat out all the way.

Although Peter had told us about Sant'Urbano, as the hermitage was officially called, we were still bowled over by its beauty. It had only three sides to its cloisters; the fourth consisted only of a low wall, beneath which a precipice plunged vertically down into the valley below. The view was stupendous. Padre Guardiano, who welcomed us, pointed out the road to Narni that Francis would have used when he first came to pray here in 1213. He spoke perfect English, having worked for over thirty years in Chicago – or perhaps I should say rather *fluent* English. He said he had come back only when his superiors promised to send him to Lo Speco di Narni, as it was affectionately called. Francis, he explained, came to pray in the caves behind the present hermitage, which had been built by St Bernadine of Siena almost 200 years after his death. He also showed us *Lo Speco*, the irregular fissure or crack in the mountainside behind the hermitage where Francis went to pray with others who followed his example, including St Anthony of Padua. After we had been shown the iron bed used by Francis and the piece of wood that he used as a pillow, we were taken to our quarters. I was given a room in the little hermitage while Ellena had to make do with a huge barn of a building used by visitors on pilgrimage.

The mountain behind the hermitage was so high that the cloister saw little of the sun after midday so even on a summer's day it could get quite cool in the evening. Late in the afternoon we sat for over an hour gazing down at the valley below, and we said very little. Then when I couldn't contain myself any longer I told Ellena exactly what had happened to me when we had first met, though I was terrified that I was making a fool of myself. I became more and more terrified when she said nothing but continued to gaze down at the valley below. Then, when I was about to apologize for making a fool of myself and for embarrassing her, she smiled wistfully and said quietly that exactly the same thing had happened to her when she first met me. I was absolutely overjoyed. In other circumstances I would have drawn her to me and kissed her, but she seemed to be in another world from which she didn't want to be disturbed and anyway the little cloisters were overlooked by the cells of half a dozen friars or more. We needed to talk but, as it wouldn't have been appropriate to invite her into my room or for me to invite myself into hers, I invited her to walk with me instead. We walked along the mountainside behind the hermitage, saying very little until we sat on a seat near the little church dedicated to St Clare.

It was here that we opened our hearts to each other. She laughed when I told her how jealous I had been when Fr Joseph had led her out of St Mary of the Angels and how I had been seething in the hands of the green-eyed monster till she returned. But she looked genuinely concerned and wanted to examine my lip when I told her what I had had to do to prevent me showing my feelings on the journey back to Montefalco. It had taken me fifteen years to find her after I had decided to marry again and search for my ideal wife. It had taken her only fifteen days to find her 'ideal husband' after she had made her decision.

Ellena was then, as she always would be, far more practical than me and so it was she who made the plan for the next three days. She said we would never have an opportunity like this again so we shouldn't just fritter the time away. The plan was that we should spend the mornings together, going over the notes that I had taken at Peter's talks, so that I could explain them to her and answer her questions. In the afternoons we would go walking in the mountains and then spend the evenings alone and in prayer in the tiny oratory. We made our pact and we kept to it. Ellena was a demanding student; she wanted me to explain in detail not only everything that Peter had said in his talks but all that he had ever said to me in the years since we had first met. She was a brilliant exponent of the Socratic method. What I mean is that she always asked the right questions. Her keen mind was always able to see the weaknesses in any theory or argument, not because she was over-critical but because she had such a sharp brain and wanted to uncover the truth.

She was particularly interested in how Peter had explained to me several years before, what he had called "Physical

Redemption", as the first Christian community had understood it.

'The first Christians,' I began, 'were predominantly of Jewish extraction and the way they understood the physical world around them enabled them to understand the meaning of the life, death, resurrection and ascension of Jesus in a unique way that still has implications for us today. Their primary under-standing of redemption was firstly formed by the belief that they had in the way God had created the world around them, and secondly in their belief in a universal truth. Their understanding of the physical structure of the world was, however, wrong. But the universal truth, namely that love is communicated by touch, was right. Nevertheless by putting these two concepts together, considerable light can be thrown on the essence of any authentic spirituality that claims to be Christian.

'In Old Testament times human beings believed they lived in a world with three "floors". On the first floor, upheld by pillars to stop the earth from falling into the waters below, men and women lived out their lives until death, after which they were sent down to the ground floor to live in the shadowy world of Sheol. What we would call the sky they called the "firmament". God was seated on a throne above it, using it as his "footstool". The firmament was visualized as something solid, rather like a transparent cooking pot that enabled God to observe how human beings were behaving. The firmament was supported on either side by the "eternal hills" and had flaps strategically placed, enabling God to send down rain and snow, wind and thunderbolts – and angels too, when their services were called for. Although the sun, like the moon and the stars, shone as it arched its way across the firmament, the ground floor and the first floor had been plunged into spiritual darkness. These were now the places where the demons ruled, ever since the first man and woman had rejected God. So in future, men and women would no longer "walk and talk" with God "in the cool of the evening", as they had done in the first paradise.

'When Jesus was born onto the first floor, his physical presence radiated the love that shone out of him, bringing light where darkness had prevailed before. First, dumb creation was redeemed by his presence and then, to whoever accepted him, he communicated the same love that animated him. This love, like all human love, was communicated through touch, by a kiss, an embrace, by the washing of feet – all common practices in the world into which he was born. The New Testament pictured Christ, the very moment after his death on the cross, descending into Sheol on the ground floor to redeem those who had died before him with the fullness of love that he had just received. It was believed that all who had died before Christ's coming would have to wait for his redemptive action. The same demons that were put to flight as he descended through the nether regions to release the "captives" were put to flight for a second time, as he ascended through the air above, leading them back to his Father. Now that Christ was seated at God's right hand, he and his Father could both send the Holy Spirit through the corridor made through the realm of the demons at his ascension. This enabled the love that the apostles had already received to be surcharged on the first Pentecost Day with the Pleroma that he had received on the first Easter Day. Now they, in their turn, literally handed on what they had received from Jesus to all who freely chose to receive it. That's why all the sacraments involved the laying-on of hands, so that what Christ had handed on to the apostles could be handed on generation after generation all the way down to us.

'So it's absolutely true to say that the love that Jesus experienced after his resurrection is handed on to us today through the hands of the priest who baptized us and through the hands of the bishop who confirmed us. The measure in which that love possesses us is limited only by our capacity to receive it. That's why Francis relentlessly exhorted his followers to seek out time for solitude, so that the repentance practiced there would open them to receive what cannot be received without it. These physical touches, which happen only twice through the priest and through the bishop, can be received every day through the touch of Christ himself in the sacred mysteries. For Francis this was the most profound mystery of all:

> He shows himself to us in this sacred bread as he once appeared to his apostles in real flesh. With their own eyes they saw only flesh, but they believed that he was God, because they contemplated him with the eyes of the spirit. We too with our own eyes see only bread and wine, but we must see further and firmly believe that this is his most holy Body and Blood living and true. In this way our Lord remains continually with his followers, as he promised, "Behold I am with you always even to the end of the world."
> (Admonition 1)

'The common belief of the first Christians in a universe with three floors was of course totally erroneous, but it is worth understanding for the insight which it can give us into the essential meaning of Physical Redemption, which cannot be discarded. It is the physical presence of Christ, bursting with uncreated life and energy, which brought and still brings to this world the love that impelled God to create it in the first place. It is this love and this love alone that, as was revealed to Francis on La Verna, unites us to God. It is not through suffering, as he, like many before him, had wrongly believed. And the idea that suffering somehow appeases an angry God is quite frankly pagan.'

Ellena had listened in total silence to all that I had had to say, but suddenly she interrupted me.

'I'm afraid I'm a little confused,' she said. 'What you've said is really wonderful – I can see that – but I can't help thinking that generations of Catholics, and Protestants too, have all been brought up with the belief that we have been redeemed by Christ's death on the cross. I used to love reading the Chronicles of Narnia as a child, but from what you've said it seems they've added to my confusion if they didn't cause in the first place.'

'You're absolutely right,' I said. 'These beliefs are still commonplace to Christians of almost every denomination. Even the most eminent theologians and writers hold, defend and popularize this archaic explanation of Christian redemption to this day. The Chronicles of Narnia are a case in point. In *The Lion, the Witch and the Wardrobe*, for instance, C.S. Lewis presents it in fairytale form to explain and popularize it for children and to predispose them to accept a meaning of the central teaching of Christianity that is semi-pagan. The success of his books and the popularity of the subsequent film versions of the story are therefore regrettable, because they continue to perpetuate primitive ideas about sacrifice and ritual appeasement that are not part of the essential Christian message. The perpetual winter into which Narnia is frozen cannot thaw, and the human victim of the White Witch cannot be redeemed, except by the death of "Christ in simile" – the Lion King, Aslan. He submits himself to be slain on a pagan altar made of stone, so that the shedding of his blood can save human victims from similar fates. This is not the sort of religious teaching to be taught in the twenty-first century – not that it should have been taught in any century for that matter.

'Human beings can be redeemed only by love or they can't be redeemed at all. This is not just a religious truth but a truth that is at the heart and soul of the human predicament. It is the theme of almost every story, every book and every film that tries to portray the power of human love. Now the most powerful form of energy that was originally responsible for the creation of the world entered into the world as human love in the person of Jesus Christ. The Gospel is the story of how this otherworldly love gradually penetrated every part of him, until it reached out through him to others, to transform their lives as it had transformed his. It was not his bloody sacrifice on the cross that was necessary to complete this work – it actually curtailed it. Indeed his death was premature and the result of the evil that ruled those who wanted to destroy him. If his message was not as clear, as complete, or as contained and consolidated as he would have liked, this was not God's fault but man's. Perhaps the scandal of so much Christian disunity might have been avoided if Christ's untimely death hadn't curtailed the time he needed to complete his work and prepare his followers for the future without him. If you read the account of the Last Supper that Christ shared with his disciples you will see for yourself how he was trying to cram in as much as possible of his most profound and mystical teaching, because his untimely death prevented him detailing it at length throughout the rest of his life.'

'So is it totally wrong in every way to say that we are redeemed by Christ's death on the cross?' asked Ellena.

'Yes and no,' I answered. 'Let's go back to Scotus. He insisted that God's plan to extend his glory into matter and form, into space and time, in the Word, was not conceived as a rescue plan to redeem fallen human beings. It was conceived before the Fall and was in no way dependent on it.'

'Yes, I follow that,' she said.

'Good. Well, just as Christ wasn't originally coming to redeem fallen human beings, he also wasn't originally coming to suffer and die to redeem them. The plan was that he was coming to draw all into the ecstatic life and love that he shared with God and the Holy Spirit. The fact that a couple of miserable human beings had fallen from grace couldn't possibly make God change his plan. Sadly this meant that the stage was set for the greatest tragedy the world has ever known. When goodness itself was made flesh to call a self-seeking and self-serving human race back to the peace and happiness for which it had originally been created, evil was chosen in its place and goodness was battered to death.

'If you want to understand how such a thing could happen, just imagine someone today who is consumed with goodness like Christ, who simply wants to tell the truth to make the world a better place. Imagine too that he or she is not only able to see what the world needs to make it a better place but to see what is actually making it a worse place, and to see with absolute clarity the motives of those responsible for making it such. Now imagine further that this same person uses all his considerable powers of communication to speak his mind loud and clear in Beijing, Baghdad or Tehran – or London, Rome or Washington for that matter. The more successful he is in proclaiming the truth and "outing" evil, the greater number of people there will be who will want to shut him up by whatever means it takes. If the "great and the good" find that he has rumbled their hypocrisy and exposed them with deadly accuracy, they will not only want to kill him – they will want to "crucify" him too. Such a person would be liquidated long before they ever came near high office where their honest-to-god goodness could be harnessed for the common good.

'This is what happened to Christ. It hardly took three years of his plain speaking to convince the religious and political leaders in Jerusalem that "one man must die for the sake of the people". Long before T.S. Eliot, Christ knew well enough that "man cannot bear too much reality"; that's why he knew and forecast so correctly the inevitable end, not only for himself but for those who would try to follow him. So when you look at a crucifix you are not looking at what the goodness of God has done; you are looking at what the evil in man has done to goodness. You see, the simple truth is not a dainty dish to set before the most dangerous animal on earth, particularly if he or she has political or religious pretensions. By choice, human beings prefer ambrosia to eat and nectar to drink; they have little stomach for humble pie. If you serve it regularly enough and in large enough portions, it can make them cross, very cross; and when they are very cross, they can crucify.

'Christ wasn't crucified because of the will of God but because of the will of man. It was God's will that Christ should do what he had come to do, come what may, but it was not his will, nor could it every have been decreed from all eternity, that his Son should suffer such an ignominious death. God cannot order murder by contract killers, no matter how high the motives might be.

'Now let me be clear about this so that there can be no misunderstanding. The revelation that Francis received, just before he received the stigmata, was as true in his day as it is true every day. That means in Christ's day too. In short, it is through Christ's love burning within, as it burned in Francis, that a person is united to the Father. That means that it is not through suffering – Christ's or anybody else's – that human beings are redeemed, despite the fact that millions of Christians have wrongly been led to believe otherwise.

'Nevertheless, as Peter explained, when a person feels God's love burning within them and they see what that love has done for them in the present and what it promises to do for them in the future, they feel impelled to do something about it. They want to express their gratitude with all their might and with all their strength. That's why they feel convinced that sacrifice is the best possible way that they can demonstrate the love that they feel; it seems it cannot be expressed in any other way. So, just as you can say that the suffering that Francis endured at the end of his life was the most perfect expression of his love of God, so too the suffering that Christ endured at the end of his life was the most perfect expression of his love of God and of those for whom he chose to die. In that sense, you can say he redeemed us by his death on the cross, in that it was the most perfect expression of the love that can alone unite us to God. However, it was not the physical pain and sufferings that brought about union with God, but the love that drove Christ to choose to submit to it. Physical pain and sufferings are in themselves evils that cannot of themselves unite a person to God. Love, and love alone, can bring about the sublime union of all creation. That was God's Secret Plan from the beginning, the Mysterion that can be brought to completion only by those who choose to receive the mystical love that was unleashed on the first Easter Day.

'It might seem that I'm trying to split hairs, but the distinction has an enormous effect on Christian spirituality. Two railway lines at Crewe junction may seem so close as to be all but indistinguishable, but if you take the wrong one you could end up in Inverness instead of Penzance. If you believe suffering is the only way to union with God then you end up with a medieval spirituality that is not only strewn with doom and gloom but with a whole misery of pious practices that are a million miles away from the teachings of the Gospels. If you believe that love is the only way to union with God then you end up with a biblical spirituality that is built around seeking the only love that can bring about that profound union. You do not therefore start by looking for penances to mortify your body, but for space and time for prayer, where you can open yourself to receive the same love that united Jesus to his Father. That's why, when I asked Peter to tell me what asceticism I should embrace, he introduced me to the asceticism of the heart. "Don't give up anything you like or enjoy," he insisted, "except if it prevents you from giving quality space and time for daily prayer."

'If you do that, come what may, you will eventually receive the love that will make you want to throw away all the so-called pleasures and pastimes that you once thought you couldn't do without, just as a miner throws away the dross when he has found true gold. The asceticism of the heart also prevents you from wasting what little energy you have, trying to inflate self-satisfaction with feats of physical asceticism. They will all ultimately fail to get you anywhere, other than to the apathy that always prevails when human weakness eventually forces you to abandon them. If a person insists that they do want to play their part in the spiritual journey, they will find more than enough challenges when they have to face the enemy within. The selfish little beast within, which has been nourished by self-love, will try everything to stop a love other than his own from entering in. That's why the struggle that ensues is called the "Dark Night of the Soul", and it isn't for the faint-hearted. It will provide more than enough scope for those who want to prove themselves and it will prove that they can do nothing without the love that they seek.'

'Thank you,' said Ellena. 'You've made sense of what has been confusing me for years. But tell me, just as a matter of interest, can what you call Physical Redemption be found in the scriptures – is it mentioned as such in the Gospels?'

'Once again I have to say yes and no. Yes, it is described in what are called the "synoptic" Gospels – Matthew, Mark and Luke – but it is not described in the same way in John. You see, the synoptic Gospels were primarily directed to the first Christian communities, who were deeply influenced by the cosmology that was accepted by the traditional Judaism in which they were all brought up. However, St John wrote his Gospel much later in Asia Minor for cosmopolitan Christians. They were influenced as much, if not more, by Greek thought than Jewish thought. So in a sense, in writing for them, John was writing for us. That's one of the reasons why Francis was influenced more by John than by any of the other Evangelists.

'Let me give you a few examples to show you what I mean. Firstly, with regards to Physical Redemption, when John is writing about the climax of Christ's life on earth, he writes about what he calls his "glorification", not about his resurrection, then he describes his descent into hell, followed by his ascension and the sending of the Holy Spirit. The reason why John does this is because, after years of meditating on these events under the influence of the Holy Spirit, he had come to see and understand that it was at the precise moment of Christ's death that all he had come to achieve was brought to completion – in that indivisible moment in time. The moment he dies, he is victorious over the powers of evil that have been pitted against him. The moment he dies is the moment when he ascends into heaven and the moment when he is united with his Father. Then, together with his Father, he sends the Holy Spirit to do in all his followers what has already been done in him. That's why John so emphasized the key moment in his narrative when this fact is symbolized by what happens when Christ's side is pierced with a lance: "One of the soldiers stabbed his side with a lance and at once there was a flow of blood and water. This is vouched for by an eyewitness whose evidence is to be trusted" (John 19:34–35).

'The flowing of blood symbolizes Christ's death; the flowing of water symbolizes the outpouring of Love Unlimited that "proceeds from the Father and the Son" to bring about the Mysterion, God's Secret Plan, in and through all who choose to receive it. The Gospels of Matthew, Mark and Luke tell the same story but in a different way, because they are writing most especially for Jewish Christians who share with them an understanding of cosmology that is not universally accepted by the Gentile world for whom John is writing. In their narrative, therefore, they show that Christ was crucified and died on the first floor of their "treble-decker" universe, bringing salvation to all on earth. But then he has to be shown descending into Sheol to bring salvation to those who died before him, whilst routing the demons who rule there on the way. Then they show him ascending into heaven forty days later, taking those he has released from Sheol with him, once again whilst routing the demons who rule in the air above. Finally, once Christ is seated at God's right hand, the Holy Spirit is sent, to be seen on the first Pentecost Day empowering the apostles to lay hands on all who would repent, so that Christ can live on, continuing his work on earth through them.

'In writing for a non-Jewish readership, then, John is writing in a special way for us. He isn't interested in explaining the Christian message in the context of a Jewish cosmology nor is he particularly interested in telling about events that once happened a generation or more before, in what was for his readers a foreign country with an alien culture. This is why, although he tells the same or similar events to those told in the synoptic Gospels, he tells them in a new way that will have more significance for those for whom he is writing. Let me give you a few examples to show you what I mean. When he tells the story about the blind man receiving sight, he is not so much interested in what happened sixty or so years before; he is interested in telling his readers what is happening now. He wants to show that Christ will give spiritual sight here and now to enable those who believe in him to see the truth. When he tells the story of the feeding of the 5,000, once again he is not so much interested in what happened by the Lake of Galilee more than a generation earlier as he is in what is happening now. He is telling his readers that Christ, who is alive now, is the bread of life and that all who receive him will receive something of the eternal life in this life, which will be received in its fullness in the next. That's why John, unlike the other Evangelists, does not use the word "miracles" but rather "signs" when referring to these events – precisely because he is more interested in showing the significance that they have for his readers in the present rather than in trying to astound them with what happened in the past.

'Finally, and more specifically to the point that I'm trying to make, when he tells the story of what happened at the Last Supper he is not primarily concerned with describing the farewell dinner that Christ shared with his disciples, but with the profound significance of that sacred meal and with the sublime mystical theology taught at that meal, which is as relevant for his own readership, years later, as it was for the apostles who were the first to hear it. It was at that sacred meal that Christ spoke about the Primacy of Love more clearly and more completely than at any other time. Notice, he didn't say, In a short time I will be leaving you to be scourged, crowned with thorns and crucified on Calvary, and if you want to be united with me you must do likewise. What he said was, If you love me you will do what I have taught you to do and then I will send my Spirit who will unite you with me, and then in, with and through me you will be united with the Father. This won't take place high up above the sky, but in the inner recesses of your own inner being where we will make our home within you and reveal ourselves to you. (See John chapter 14.)

'This is what Francis did; he was totally faithful to everything Jesus said and did, so that he was open and ready to receive the promises made by Jesus at the Last Supper. So, true to his word, Jesus revealed himself to Francis on La Verna, and what he revealed to him was the Primacy of Love, which had already been the essence of all he had done without his fully realizing it. Up to that moment he had not seen this truth with the clarity that was given to him moments before he received the stigmata. It might well have been the starting point for Scotus' theology of love, but it was in fact the theology of St John first – it was from him that Francis had first learned it. This theology had long since been forgotten, except in the writings of a few people who were never able to proclaim it to the many as Francis did, and as the spirituality that he inspired still does.'

When we met on the final morning of our stay at Lo Speco di Narni, Ellena was more excited than I had ever seen her before with all that she had read and all that she had heard and all the ideas that had come to her in prayer. The night before, she had read the notes Peter had prepared for Emelia and it had filled her with the practical wisdom that I was always to admire in her.

'Do you know,' she said, 'it struck me last night that all that has been said and written about the Primacy of Love, and the continual outpouring of that love, is just hot air if we do nothing to receive it! What Peter said to her, makes total sense to me. Self-centered people, who are full of themselves, simply cannot be open to receive love, whether they live in the religious life or the married life. I find the way he explains the psychological dynamics that underline all forms of prayer totally compelling. It explained perfectly how prayer is the place where repentance is learned and repeatedly practiced to allow love in. Then that love can begin to purge us of the selfishness that prevents the fullness of love from bringing Christ to birth again in us.

'When Françoise was speaking to me about married life, she said that marriage differs from all the other sacraments in that it is the married couple themselves who are the ministers, not a priest or a bishop. She explained that they give to each other the love that has been generated within them. Which of course is a wonderful thought, until you wonder what happens when the honeymoon phase fades away and one or the other of them finds they have nothing to give. It has convinced me of something that I should have learned from my mother years ago (but daughters are very slow learners when it comes to learning from their mothers!). Although she had six children my mother would always spend time each day in prayer, and enjoy a couple of hours in solitude on Sunday if we would let her. She would never let a year go by without making a retreat; in fact that's how you first met her, if I remember.'

Although Ellena and I made no secret of our love for each other, I never proposed to her, nor she to me for that matter. I realized that it had just been assumed when on that last morning in Narni she simply added, 'When we get married, come what may, we must find time for prayer each day – whether it's together or apart – and we must try to get away at least once a year for a retreat like Mum. After all, we know plenty of places to go to now.'

I don't want to give the impression that she was bossy or

determined to wear the trousers because that simply wouldn't be true, but as I have said, she was and is far more practical than me, and she is always far quicker than me in reducing theoretical ideas into practice. By the time we had arrived back in England she had already worked out that Chingford would be the best place to live in London. It would be ideal for both of us. It was only twenty-five minutes by train from London where I would be starting my new job in September and it would enable her to implement an idea that she had discussed at length with Françoise. Everybody entering into religious life has to go through a novitiate, where they are taught the spirituality that will sustain them. What Ellena wanted to do was to speak to David about setting up a novitiate for married life at Walsingham House. It would enable young adults to learn about the Primacy of Love, either in evening classes and summer schools or in residential courses that students could follow in their gap year. They would be able to learn how to receive the love in their own personal lives, enabling them to be less selfish in their married life. Then that love would overflow onto their children.

I thought it was a wonderful idea because in those three short days I had experienced for myself what she wanted to achieve. Every night we would leave the little oratory together. Then, before we parted, we not only kissed each other good night but also embraced each other with a long silent hug that seemed to get longer every night. On the last night it seemed to go on forever. The hugs seemed to add another dimension to our prayer. The love that we had both received separately, as we had tried to practice selflessness, each in our own way, found an immediate outlet. I will always treasure what we received from each other in those sublime moments – moments that I will never forget, though there were many more of them to come. We didn't want to leave Lo Speco di Narni, but we knew that we would have to go, because there was a new life waiting for both of us. We knew that we would return (and we did) to renew the love that we had first experienced there and to introduce it to the children for whom we both longed more than anything.

Epilogue

When we had all gathered together for the last time at Montefalco, Ellena told everyone our news. It was evident, however, that only Peter thought we were doing the right thing. The others thought three days was too short a time to come to such a momentous decision. We didn't get married until the following June, and thanks to Fr Joseph the Nuptial Mass took place in St Mary of the Angels. Although everybody else was able to make it to Assisi, Peter couldn't.

We spent the first two weeks of our honeymoon at Casa al Gallo, which we had all to ourselves as Emelia and Michael were visiting their son in Grenoble. The final week was spent on the island of Barra so that we could see Peter. We both cajoled him into letting us publish a selection of his letters to several of his correspondents, which are brimming over with profound spiritual wisdom, and we hope you will find them helpful when we can find a publisher. We began our married life at Chingford in North London, not far from Walsingham House. It was, as Ellena had promised, ideal for my new job and for Epping Forest, which was on our doorstep, not to mention Stansted Airport with a direct flight to Perugia.

BOOKS

O is a symbol of the world, of oneness and unity. In different cultures it also means the "eye," symbolizing knowledge and insight. We aim to publish books that are accessible, constructive and that challenge accepted opinion, both that of academia and the "moral majority."

Our books are available in all good English language bookstores worldwide. If you don't see the book on the shelves ask the bookstore to order it for you, quoting the ISBN number and title. Alternatively you can order online (all major online retail sites carry our titles) or contact the distributor in the relevant country, listed on the copyright page.

See our website www.o-books.net for a full list of over 500 titles, growing by 100 a year.

And tune in to myspiritradio.com for our book review radio show, hosted by June-Elleni Laine, where you can listen to the authors discussing their books.

MySpiritRadio